Other Books by Simon

Other books by Simon Fairfax

Sir James de Grispere series
A Knight and a Spy 1410
A Knight and a Spy 1411
A Knight and a Spy 1412
A Knight and a Spy 1413

Financial Thriller series
A Deadly Deal
A Deal Too Far
A Deal with The Devil
A Deal on Ice

Copyright © 2022 by Simon Fairfax
The moral right of Simon Fairfax to be identified as the author of this work has been asserted in accordance with the Copyright, Design and Patents Act 1988.
All rights reserved. No part of this publication may be reproduced, stored in a retrieval system, or transmitted, in any form or by any means, electronic, mechanical, photocopying, recording or otherwise, without the prior permission of the copyright.
Published by Corinium Associates Ltd.
While some of the events and characters are based upon historical events and figures, this novel is a work of fiction. The names, characters and incidents portrayed in it are the work of the author's imagination. Any resemblance to actual persons, living or dead, events or localities is entirely coincidental.
A CIP catalogue of this book is available from the British Library
Copyright Front cover images:
More Visual Ltd
Copyright © 2019 Simon Fairfax. All rights reserved.
ISBN: 978-1-7391470-0-6
simonfairfaxauthor@gmail.com
www.simonfairfax.com

A Knight and a Spy 1413

Simon Fairfax

Map of Paris

Parisian Defences in 15th Century

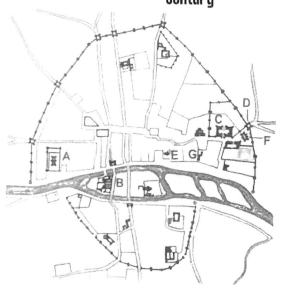

A – Louvre
B – Île de la Cité
C – Hôtel des Tournelles
D – Eastern gate
E – l'Hôtel-de-Ville
F – Bastille
G – l'Hôtel Saint-Pol

Map of London

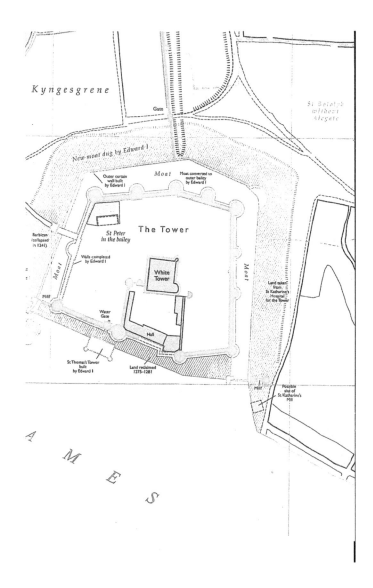

Part One
Scotland

Chapter One

Westminster Abbey, January

The huge, vaulted ceilings of the abbey rang to the hauntingly beautiful pitched voices echoing around the vast chamber. The choir's voices rose in tempo and their cadence soared to the very top of the heavenly rafters, inhabiting a space from which God himself seemed to oversee the service. Incense hung in the air with its acrid, sweet scent, and the pale grey smoke formed drifts around the pews, enveloping all in the pageant of the moment.

Despite the blissful ambience of the sublime voices washing over the congregation, there was an eschatological feeling in the air. The great and the good, among them many senior lords and leading members of the clergy, listened to the final words of Archbishop Arundel as he finished High Mass. When the voices of the choir fell silent, his words echoed around the cavernous chamber: "May we all keep in our prayers and thoughts His Majesty King Henry Fourth, whose health is in dire need of our spiritual support. May

God have him in his keeping and praise be that he makes a full recovery to grace us with his presence and rule us for many years to come."

Two pews back in a separate area of a raised dais a voice whispered in a penetrating rasp to those within ear shot: "What the old fool means is that he's dying." Henry Beaufort, Bishop of Winchester, was just eight years younger than his half-brother, the king. There had been many times over the years when they had fallen foul of each other, and in recent years Beaufort had been plotting to supplant the ruler with his eldest son, who even now was mere feet away on the other raised dais reserved for full blooded royalty. His plans were now coming to fruition – not by his own making, but by that of his God, who had struck down King Henry with a terrible disease that had been fought most valiantly by the failing monarch.

To Beaufort's left was the Earl of Arundel, nephew of the Archbishop of Canterbury leading the service. "Amen to that," Arundel said. "As soon as we have the young prince at the helm, we can move forward to conquer France."

There were nods from those within earshot, all of whom were sympathetic to the cause of a new and stronger England. One such, was Sir Thomas Chaworth, a northern knight who had participated in the Nottingham plot to usurp the king and put Prince Henry upon the throne two years earlier. He had barely escaped with his life for his treason, yet now he was pardoned and prospered, as had all those engaged with the plotting. Now a Member of Parliament for Derbyshire, he enjoyed a newfound power and had been elevated through the support of such men as Henry Beaufort and his coterie of powerful nobles who planned not only to rule England but also to control the reins of the prince, soon to be the fifth Henry.

Yet like many such men, Chaworth had a secret, and was bound by beliefs that he would never utter abroad. In this of all ecclesiastical domains, he knew he must hold fast and pray for the right moment to act. His parliamentary privilege would not save him and nor would his relations with the bishop if his timing was amiss. He was in his mid-thirties and having enjoyed a prosperous life so far, wished to remain in such circumstances and gain more wealth and privilege. "My lord bishop, you have the right of it," he said. "All I hear from Eltham Palace is news of a dwindling spirit and a failing body. The one that has formerly upheld the other is now ceding the task as untenable."

Bishop Beaufort looked sideways at Chaworth. "We shall speak more of this in private. Come to my chambers later and sup with me."

The service finished with all the pomp and ceremony appropriate to the occasion. On the adjacent dais Prince Henry's long frame remained folded and motionless, his head bowed in prayer as he leant against the rail before him, his hands clasped in supplication. Those around him, apart from his personal servant and esquire, left the prince where he was.

Sir Richard Whittington looked on with something approaching pity etched upon his generous features. His long, hooked nose stood proud, dominating his intelligent face. He tugged at his ear in a manner so well known to his familiars that bespoke a depth of thought that eluded most men. All were cloaked against the bitter cold of this pernicious January that seemed to send its icy fingers lancing through any gap in clothing. Whittington pondered upon waiting for the prince to finish his prayers, but recent experience had shown how dedicated he was to a new piety, brought on no doubt by the realisation of his father's imminent demise.

As if by a sign unbidden, he caught the almost imperceptible shake of the squire's head, who knew from long suffering duty that his master would not be rising soon. With that, Whittington acknowledged the warning with a nod of his head and moved to leave the hallowed ground. He had not missed the conclave of nobles and clergy presided over by Bishop Beaufort in his own court of conquest. And with sharp eyes that missed little, he noted the confident bearing of Sir Thomas Chaworth – an old adversary, and one whom he knew bore watching.

 —

Palais de la Cité, **Paris**

The beautiful, towered fortress lay on the Île de la Cité in the middle of the Seine. The gleaming towers that guarded the walls were capped with grey slate that reflected a frosted glaze in the light of a weak, wintry sun. The river itself had frozen over and was supporting the weight of skaters and stallholders who were plying their trade in the excitement of the frozen river. The citizens of Paris were grateful in other ways, for the freezing of the water and the cold conditions had all but extinguished the usual noisome odours, leaving only the press of humanity to assoil the senses.

Inside the palace, the assembly of *Le Etats Generaux de Langue,* like the congregation at Westminster Abbey, was comprised of senior clergy along with nobles and commoners. Yet this time the composition of the gathering was balanced differently, demonstrating a power in the city that was like no other in France. For these eminent citizens possessed the ability to govern the actions and control certain powers of the very king in whose name the assembly served. The power vested in the *Etats* had been invoked by the monarch to aid him in matters of counsel or fiscal endeavour. Yet all who knew the machinations of French politics realised that it was little more than a demand for help, and in return favour, praise and advancement were the currency of the day.

On this occasion, while the assembly had been raised in King Charles' name, it had been done at the instigation of the power behind the throne – the Duke of Burgundy. Since the defeat of the French army to the south and with the Armagnac faction licking its wounds after falling upon the mercy of Paris and the court, the duke had sought to capitalise upon the change in power. To this end he had pleaded with the king to call the assembly and begin the preparation of an ordinance that would have far reaching consequences for Paris and for France itself, indeed much greater than those intended by its signatories.

The commoners attending were deliberately granted

both presence and a say in the governance of the body, so it seemed appropriate that the order should bear the name of one of Paris's leading citizens, one Simon Lecoustellier. He was a butcher, and one of the leaders of the Parisian guild, who was known more familiarly under the sobriquet of Simon Caboche.

Seated away from the commoners in the centre of the beautiful round keep was John, Duke of Burgundy, and at his side was his proctor, Sir Galliard de Durfort. The duke was as ever beautifully turned out and had made a deliberate attempt to outshine all those around him. The ermine lining of his cloak was a comfort in the vast and draughty hall of the keep, and the gold chain at his throat glinted in the candlelight thrown from many sconces on the walls.

"You have excelled yourself, Sir Galliard, for the balance of power has shifted upon this assembly. We have more representation here from the university and commoners, and from low level clergy brought from the shires who have little interest in the politics of Paris. With such a presence we shall, I foretell, easily sway the outcome of the ordinance, and it shall prove our most powerful weapon against the Armagnac cause."

"Thank you, Your Grace. It cost more silver than I was wont to offer, yet should the result outweigh the payment, why then we shall find the scales balanced in our favour. Yet I still foresee an impediment to your grace's plans. To wit, the king seems to have regained his senses once more, and sallies forth to preside over the assembly with the support of the dauphin and the queen. Think you that they will still fall to our side when the moment is nigh?"

The duke looked sharply at de Durfort, seemingly annoyed that he should question the plot that Burgundy had so carefully implemented. But the frown soon passed, and with it any lingering self-doubt. "Like all else, it is balanced upon the timing of our actions. By this assembly we shall set in place the ordinance, locked in with many others all for his majesty's signature in due course. They will be implemented when the moment is propitious.

"We must continue our negotiations with England as the power in that land waxes and wanes, and we shall step in and control both the direction of the new king and the consequences of his actions. From what I am told, it cannot be long now for a new heir to the throne to emerge – one who is sympathetic to our cause and will aid us in our bid to control the throne of France."

"Think you the new King Henry will be as strong as his father?" de Galliard probed.

"Oh, he is martial enough, or was. Now I hear he seeks refuge in prayer, piety and a yearning for a united England. Let it be so. For with his mind thus focused, we can unite and fortify France and regain those disputed territories to the south, bringing them under French rule. The army there is under the leadership of Prince Henry's brother, and with that charge lies dissent and division which I shall do my best to widen. Beaufort is ambitious and will bend whichever way the wind of power blows to suit his own ends. With England thus divided and weakened, we shall prevail. And with Dauphin Louis on our side, we shall overcome all obstacles, however sane the king may be. He is weak and we will flourish."

The duke's last words were uttered with his fist clenched. They were lost in the hubbub of talk that buzzed around the vaulted ceiling and the many pillars that echoed back all the words spoken, producing a morass of noise that made it difficult to decipher almost anything that was being said. The milling crowds were the best place in which to hide a secret, as the Duke of Burgundy well knew.

Chapter Two

Westminster Palace, February

Whittington's chambers were, as ever, well buffered against the chill of the air outside. Whittington disliked being cold, and now only ever ventured out of the city to his family holdings in Gloucestershire. When the weather was clement, he was almost guaranteed a safe and dry passage. He warmed his hands before the fire that blazed in the hearth, mustering his thoughts as he prepared for the briefing that he was about to share with the seated figure before him.

Whittington's guest did not care whether it was warm or cold, for he had known the deprivations of a soldier in some of the coldest parts of the country in the Scottish Borders, and only the year before had braved the Alps to deliver gold to one of the two popes currently causing mayhem within the Catholic Church and all the kingdoms that lay under its auspices.

The young man was well clothed and had just divested himself of a beautiful red cloak fashioned by his father that now hung upon a peg behind him. The cloak was practical too, proofed against rain and snugly lined to insulate its wearer from the cold. The man's dark red hair was still bleached a little with streaks of gold from the suns of Italy and southern France. A scar had healed upon his cheek, standing proud and white against his tanned skin. The green eyes were flecked with hazel. They were observant and showed a wary concentration.

Sir James de Grispere had changed since Whittington had first brought him to his employ three long years ago. He had matured, hardened and maybe showed a more callous disregard for life, what with the battles he had survived and the life he had lived as a spy. In that life he had faced odds in ways that were more onerous than open battle, living with the knowledge that at any moment, trapped in an enemy camp or stronghold, he could be denounced, and his life made forfeit in any number of agonising ways. Yet Whittington knew he would survive. His sort always did; there was a supple steel within such men that would bend and not break. His intelligence was as much his friend and weapon as his ability with arms – which in itself was considerable, by all accounts. Whittington hoped so, for as his Godfather, he had a vested interest in the young man before him and would rue the day that he caused his untimely death.

"James, thank you for attending me upon this freezing day. There are matters which occupy me greatly and I have need of aid. I believe that you may well be able to surmise the nature of these matters."

Jamie's eyes crinkled slightly with a hint of a smile: "'Tis unlike you to hide your words as if they were frightened children to be concealed beneath a woman's skirts, Sir Richard. You wish to speak of the death of a king and the accession of a prince, I presume," he said.

Whittington snorted: "Just so, just so, yet do not breathe such words outside this chamber for we must all deny the evidence of our very eyes. Yet we know the moment is nigh upon us when a new ruler will oversee our realm.

"Do you realise that we are seeing history in the making? For since the death of King John in the year of our Lord 1216, nearly two hundred years past, this will only be the fourth English king to die of natural causes in his bed. Even then they say King Lackland was poisoned by one of the monks in the abbey. Yet no matter, for it is the present with which we are bound to deal. Young Prince Henry will inherit a kingdom and not have to fight for it as his father did. There will be a natural primogeniture to the throne, but for all that, I fear it will be a path that is not without peril."

"How so?" Jamie asked.

"I saw these days past the coterie of Bishop Beaufort at Mass, and from his demeanour I could discern much. Your past nemesis, Sir Thomas Chaworth, was in his group and I would not trust his loyalty as much as I would trust a lamb to evade the wolf. I fear that once the prince becomes king, the status of Beaufort and his like will rise. And with their ascent, so too will their influence increase upon the new king, mayhap forcing him to dance to their tune or be usurped. There is much trouble in this realm that remains as yet unsettled, not least fiscal, and only war will satisfy those who would seek to benefit and unify the country. There is no softer option. Yet war costs a great deal of gold and silver, and who will proffer such sums? And more important, whom do we fight?"

"Why the French, as ever, I would assume," Jamie offered, puzzled at this last question.

"Indeed. But a unified France? For if that be the case with Armagnacs and Burgundians following one king in one cause, then by the rood we would be severely disadvantaged, whatever the lords of Beaufort, Warwick and Arundel may say. This I fear more than anything."

"The Armagnacs, or some of their faction, fought with us in France, while the whoreson Burgundy stayed his hand and watched to see who would win, using Scots as his fodder. They have retreated to Paris, and are forgiven it seems for ceding sovereignty of French lands and recognising the kings of England as the rightful rulers of France," Jamie said. Then he paused as the realisation of what he had just said hit home. "Ah, I see it! You fear that with the Armagnacs back in Paris having broken their treaty with us, and the king brought under Burgundy's yoke, they could be persuaded to fight with Burgundy. Prince Thomas' army would not withstand the might of such a host, I fear."

"Just so, you have the right of it. Those are indeed my worst fears. Add to this potent mix the sway that Burgundy holds upon the Lowlands, ruling as he does all of Flanders. If the seas be mastered – which they would be with ease, for England has no navy of which to speak – then our income is severed both at home and abroad. How then will the king pay the dues of war?

"But to my greater concern I hear from my spies that the King of France has rallied and is currently of sane mind, having called a vast assembly of The Estates General. I hear there were secret discussions to which I am not yet privy, yet they disturb me still. This is Burgundy's doing, and he seeks the highest estate. His arrogance demands the throne of France – or at least control of it through that mewling mawmet the dauphin, who is under his thrall. And all this time England is stagnating, awash with plot and counter-plot and with no legalities or government settled. We are a rudderless ship on a high sea with no wind to fill our sails, and a ship in such a position is prone to all manner of piracy." Whittington finished eloquently.

"How may I aid you, Sir Richard? I am idle and without purpose now, save practicing my skills and mayhap marry soon, please God."

"My boy, I have left my senses at the court, and do most humbly beg your pardon. I must congratulate you, for I have heard that your nuptials will soon be blessed. You persuaded the old goat who is soon to be your father-in-law that you were acceptable to his estate, I assume?"

Jamie smiled at this riposte, for it was well known how irascible Sir Andrew Bloor, Baron Macclesfield, was, and how he protected the status of his daughter, Lady Alice. "Aye, I have stormed that castle and taken the keep, but it was not an easy campaign. We have made our peace despite his private view that I am still a secret Lollard after my covert campaign against the traitor, Glyndower."

"Even with the prince's knighting of you and his public acknowledgement that you acted at his bequest?"

Jamie nodded.

"Then have a care. For I hear that Lollardy is raising its

head again, and those who foment its evil teachings are deeply seated in all manner of positions. I have even heard some muttering amongst those in my guild who have sympathy with Lollard teachings and wish to seduce others to their side. Were this to increase, it would greatly divide the realm and cause untold chaos."

"What?" Jamie exclaimed. "I had heard nothing to this degree. Who is behind such malfeasance?"

"None other than Lord Cobham, Sir John Oldcastle."

"The prince's friend? Why he fought valiantly with Earl Warwick and others in Paris against the Armagnacs and is a close consort and companion to the prince himself, and many besides the prince would call him friend, or so we all thought."

"All you say is true. Yet a man's heart and his conscience will oft drive him from the righteous path."

"Dost thou think it will come to aught?"

"I know not. Yet am concerned, and it grieves me greatly to see the tendrils of such perfidy extend so deeply into the foundation of society, taking not merely commoners or malaperts, but guild members, knights and others of station and import.

"To add to my concern, another head of the hydra has been raised."

Jamie raised an inquiring eyebrow.

"The call to arms behind the old King Richard Second has been raised and claims have been made that he is alive and residing in Scotland, with many flocking to his banner according to one..." Whittington looked down to study a parchment that lay upon his desk. "...John Whitelock, who has been proclaiming in churches, and even in the abbey, that the second Richard is not dead, but escaped Pontefract Castle to side with the Scots, raising an army under a counterfeit banner."

"By the good Lord, and there are those who give credence to such rumours? We all know that the king died there, may the Devil keep his rotten soul, for many Londoners – including my father – suffered under his governance, and he was far from the misunderstood saint that many proclaim him to be. Who is the imposter skulking north of the border? Let him show his face here in England and we shall show him how we deal with such knaves."

"Well said and bravo, yet there are many it seems who would give him credence, and this strain of thought is becoming dangerous in its alliance with the Lollards. Both factions would engage Satan himself if it suited their own ignominious ends.

"I should like you to travel north, for at this juncture I know little more than you and the Borders will be rife with rumour and intelligence. You have many connexions there, including Sir Robert, who would I durst say be right pleased to see you once again."

"When would you have me leave? For my nuptials are due in a sennight and God forgive me but I could not endure the breaking of that date."

"No, Jamie, there is no immediate urgency and no requirement for the impetuosity of youth. If you could leave by the end of the month after you are wed and with the weather in your favour that would do well enough."

"As you wish, Sir Richard. I shall see if Mark will accompany me. For he has no wrestling, and with the court so quiet, he risks being hen-pecked to death, I do believe." Jamie smiled at the thought of his giant friend being bested by two women.

"And of your other companion? Do you have any news of your Italian friend? I hear that you left him in Florence wedded to the Alberti niece?"

Jamie caught himself before he spoke. There was something in Whittington's manner that he had learned to interpret as a sign that the statesman knew more than he was letting on, and was guarding his words to see what more he could learn.

"Cristoforo? No, nary a word. Jeanette was the last of us in his company. It is strange, yet with the winter closing passes, it is unlikely that letters would have reached me. I'faith I miss the rogue, for he is good company, and a better ally than any man could wish for. Why, do you have news?" Jamie asked.

"No, he has not corresponded with me. There is no reason for him to do so. I was merely curious, knowing how close the bond of friendship was between the two of you. And from your report we have much to thank him for." With that evasive answer, Sir Richard signalled that the meeting was over. "Travel when you may, yet favour me with your presence ere you depart."

With that, Jamie rose and slung his cloak about his shoulders in preparation for the cold outside the chamber, feeling somehow that he had been bested in the game of mental chess at which Whittington excelled.

Chapter Three

Abbé Saint-Sauveur-Le-Vicomte, **Cotentin, France**

The grey stone walls of the abbey made an impregnable fortress that dominated the surrounding area. Since 1346 it had been a stronghold, first to King Edward Third and then to his successors. Its walls and turrets were stoutly built and dissuaded any forces from attacking the fortified abbey that was set in the heartlands of a disputed France.

The small group of four travellers standing before the walls had heard the stories of the landing months earlier at Cotentin and the English victory over the mixed Burgundian and Scots forces that had been arrayed against them. It was, they had heard, largely due to the intervention of an English knight who had warned them of the planned ambush.

When Cristoforo Corio first heard that the knight's name was Sir James de Grispere, he had offered his companions a wry smile. Prayers were said in the honour of this valiant English knight, who along with the English forces led by Prince Thomas, had cut a swathe through the lands of

France only to leave the English forces ere Christmastide. It was through this cruel twist of fate that Cristoforo had missed his dear friend and companion at arms by only a few weeks, and now found himself standing outside the town, preparing to enter the abbey, praying for deliverance against the one thing he feared above all else – the open waters of the English Channel. Although bitterly cold, the air was relatively still and promised a smooth, if freezing crossing. Yet Cristoforo was still terrified.

"Come now, my love, surely you fear priests less than monsters lurking in the water's depths?" The words from the beautiful woman at his side were silky smooth, yet loaded with a deliberate barb. Alessandria's face was framed by her fur-lined hood, her extraordinary almond eyes gilded with tears brought on by the extreme cold. Yet they danced merrily as she teased her new husband.

Her maid, Francesca, smiled indulgently at Cristoforo while the groom tried to remain impassive to the women's frivolities. He had shared the boat journey across the Mediterranean the previous December with them, leaving his companion on the dockside in Genoa to take care of the horses that they left behind. Cristoforo's discomfort during the voyage had been obvious to all.

Cristoforo shook his head in disgust, his long black curls dancing. "Bah, *Dio mio*, let us get inside the abbey and may God have mercy upon my soul for this terrible undertaking. I think that I should rather turn and face the *assassini di Firenze* than the waters of the English Channel."

With that he strode forward and banged hard upon the double doors of the abbey, stamping his feet against the cold.

It was not long before he heard bolts being drawn and one of the huge doors opened inwards, swinging silently on oiled hinges.

A Benedictine monk appeared, dressed in the characteristic black habit of their order. He was of middle years and smiled a welcome. "Good day, my son, may we be of aid to you?" he asked.

Cristoforo bowed to him in deference to his status. "Father, we beg shelter for the night and wish to attend Mass and confession e'er it please you."

"Of course, my son, pray enter." Then he halted squinting into the cold, a slight frown upon his face. "The young lady without, is she your wife?"

"She is indeed, Father, is this permitted?"

"All is well, for we have special quarters where we house ladies who seek shelter for the night – yet they must be wedded or accompanied with others of their gender. I see she has a maid to attend her, and we shall accommodate them together." With that the monk opened the doors wide and the party entered along with their horses and mules. With the animals taken care of, the monk continued his gentle interrogation. "Have you travelled far?"

"Our journey began in Italy, but we have lately lodged at Bordeaux with the English forces there. Needs must that we return to England, where my wife has family. We shall seek passage upon a ship bound for England as soon as we are able."

"It sounds a most interesting story, and one which I am sure the abbot would like to hear. Would you break bread with us this evening? I shall place you at his side that you may enlighten him as to your news."

The monk showed them all to their lodgings and offered to fetch a prior upon learning of Cristoforo's need for confession. Later, during the short summary of his many sins – including the killing of the assassins in Bologna and the murder of a member of the *Parte Guelfa* and one of the Albizzi in Florence – the prior let out a small gasp as he struggled to reconcile the brief view he had glimpsed of the smiling Italian with the murderous acts that had just been recounted to him through the grille of the confessional. He allowed Cristoforo to continue to unburden himself until he had offered up all his sins for absolution. The prior gave him his penance and told him that he should avoid bloodshed in the future except in matters related purely to defence of his own body and those of his wife and family.

Cristoforo thanked him, feeling his burden lighter for the absolution and knowing that he could now make the sea passage to England with a clear conscience.

As Cristoforo left the confessional, the prior watched him go, walking happily out of the chapel, seemingly with not a care in the world. He shook his head at the tales he had just heard and despite the sacristy of the confessional, he knew that he had to speak with the abbot as a matter of utmost urgency.

Later that evening the four newcomers dined at the high table, with Cristoforo seated at the abbot's right hand as promised. He found the clergyman good company and worldly in his knowledge and view of matters beyond the confines of the abbey. "My lord abbot, if I may be so bold, you seem very well informed in all matters concerning the world outside these walls."

"Thank you, my son. I do, as part of my duties, travel far on occasion, and have but recently returned from a meeting of the *Etats Generaux de Langue* in Paris. I am not sure if you are aware, but the assembly is called from time to time by the king when he is in need of spiritual guidance and..." Here the abbot hesitated, permitting himself a wintry smile. "...financial aid, as the Mother Church is ever munificent in such matters."

Cristoforo was as cynical as any other Italian as to how manipulative the Church could be, and having grown up in Florence, a hotbed of corruption, he knew only too well how easily the piety of that august body could be bent and twisted to the avaricious ends of its leaders. "It was most generous of their lordships to grant you presence there."

The abbot snorted gently: "I see that you are as cynical as am I as to their motives. Let me explain; it is one of the rules that lower orders should be present to prevent the great and the good supplanting the wishes and needs of the common man. It is normal that many far flung *apostoli* are asked to attend to balance the proceedings away from the central needs of Paris." The sharp mind of the abbot changed tack. "But tell me of your own travails, Signor Corio. My brothers tell me that you have come far to find yourself sheltered here."

"I come in the footsteps of a former travelling companion, one whom your order tells me is well known here. Sir James de Grispere is a faithful English knight, and I am proud to call him friend. The friar who opened your doors to me spoke of his actions here, and his bravery comes as no surprise..." Cristoforo's words trailed off as he realised the abbot was giving him a shrewd and appraising look.

There was a moment of silence at the table before the abbot leaned forward and whispered: "Perhaps you would join me in my chamber later for Armagnac and further discourse?"

Cristoforo was a little thrown by the request, yet readily acceded and found himself sometime later alone with the abbot in his private rooms.

"We cannot tarry long, my son, and I thank you for attending me privately. There is much I would impart to you that may aid both my country and your new-found home. Yet I demand that you swear upon the cross that you shall tell no one of our meeting and all that I shall impart to you, save Sir James himself and those in England whom he deems should receive this knowledge."

Cristoforo pulled up the crucifix that lay on a chain at his neck, kissed the cross and said: "I swear on the blood of Jesus Christ our saviour and the blessed Holy Mother that I shall do as you bid me, so help me God."

The abbot nodded: "Just so. I have here a letter that must be delivered directly into the hands of its recipient, yet you must know the contents. The Canon Jean Eusoris of Notre Dame cathedral is an informer for the English crown and serves it faithfully at great peril to his own fate. Were he caught, I dread to think what tortures might be brought to bear upon him.

"As I mentioned at supper, I attended the *Etats Generaux* but I was not privy to its innermost workings, and

I know that further amendments were made in the days that followed the assembly. Yet the gist was there for all to see. A rising is planned in the king's name, to bring down the Armagnacs and supplant the king with the House of Burgundy in all but name."

"*Dio mio!* Is such a thing possible?"

"Aye, you may question and wonder, yet it is, and it could be accomplished with remarkable ease. For there are many in Paris who bear grutch against the lordlings, most particularly those of Armagnac birth who many claim betrayed the crown with treason. But what they do not see and cannot foretell is what would happen if there were an even more corrupt power behind the throne, pulling all the strings of a puppet king and those of the young dauphin. Anarchy would rule and all power would be in the palm of Duke John of Burgundy's hand."

Cristoforo stood and paced the floor, rubbing his chin between finger and thumb as he considered all he knew of the power struggle within France and what such a rising would mean for the English crown. He was no newcomer to the darker side of politics, having seen power and avarice for himself as the Albizzi and Medici schemed and fought for the command of Florence and the papacy. Yet here it was happening to a whole country, and the results for the English crown would be catastrophic. "When is this uprising planned to take place?" he asked the abbot. "Will there be time to warn those in England afore all is lost?"

"Ah, there's the rub. We know not a date, but suspect it will be in the spring when the land has thawed and the mud has dried, and the campaigning season is once more upon us.

Canon Jean and the monasteries are closely watched, and Paris is all secrecy and rumour. Even the pigeons are routinely brought down in case they carry missives to England, and all roads to Calais are barred with barriers and traps. No man may pass with ease, and all are searched. It is said that every second man is a spy in the duke's employ. The canon managed to pass this to me within the confessional at prayers, and I but a lowly abbot of a far-flung parish much overlooked. Perhaps this was the canon's purpose – yet beware, for there are spies abroad in every port that could furnish travel to England's shores, in especial here. For English sympathies at Cotentin are well known, and with the English army camped at Bordeaux, we are a natural target for censure.

"Now go, and guard this missive with your life. I, or my confederates will be in contact again as soon as we are informed of new movements. Remember and have a care, for all are looked upon with suspicion by Burgundy's spies and what you carry would be a death sentence to you, should it be found."

"Why then should I destroy the missive itself and carry the tidings you have imparted to me in my head?"

"'Tis a good thought, but nay. The letter carries the seal of Canon Jean of Paris, and those in power in England will believe the truth of its contents more readily if they can vouchsafe the origin of such shocking news."

Cristoforo nodded his acquiescence, and taking the missive from the abbot he opened the frogging on his doublet and slid the document into a hidden pocket within. He bade the abbot goodnight and walked back along the corridor of the abbey to his own lodgings within the building. He knew that he was watched from behind a pillar, but chose to ignore the spy. It would avail him little to challenge the man, and he may even have been there to protect his master, the abbot. Yet now Cristoforo was wary and on his mettle. With a secret smile upon his lips, he doubted that he would be able uphold his recent vow of abstinence from killing for long.

Upon reaching the safety of his own chamber, he pulled out the parchment to discover that it was addressed to none other than Sir Richard Whittington.

Chapter Four

The party of Italians made an early start, despite the protestations of Alessandria, who liked to lie abed and was reluctant to venture forth into the icy wind that blew from the direction of the coast some seventeen leagues to the northwest. She and her maid wrapped themselves against the chill in fur lined cloaks as the horses set their heads down against the wind.

Cristoforo was lost in thought, considering the identity of the letter's recipient. Whittington! He prayed that Jamie was safely returned to England and could aid him in this matter. After a long day and a short halt at a tavern for a repast and to rest and feed the horses, they made the port town of Cherbourg de Cotentin before the gates were closed for the night. It had been a long day, but Cristoforo was grateful for the frost as the roads stayed hard. The ruts had been worn down by many travellers over the winter, but when the thaw came, he knew it would turn into a quagmire of thick, squelching, hoof sucking mud. He bespoke lodgings for the party at one of the better inns in the town and went off to seek information on the time of the following day's tides.

"My heart, I needs must seek travel for tomorrow and will return shortly," he told Alessandria. "Take care whilst I am gone and answer the door to no one save me. The abbot warned of new spies, and we still have a price upon our heads from Burgundy. If any knew what I carry, why half the town would sell their souls for the price our lives would fetch."

"Take Gino with you," she commanded.

"No," he replied vehemently. "I leave my groom here as your guard. I work better alone, more so when I only have my own wits upon which to rely." He kissed her passionately and held her to him for a moment, then stepped to the casement and peered down to the cobbled passageway a few feet below. It was an easy enough drop of some ten feet, and no one would see him leave. He tested the cord attached to the frame, lowered himself over and dropped five feet to the cobbles. He landed lightly and silently, and blowing a kiss to his wife above, he padded off into the darkness, following the directions given to him by the landlord.

Upon reaching the quayside, Cristoforo found a tavern and sought out the masters of any ships that would be making the crossing to England on the morrow. It would expose his position, but it could not be helped. There was little secrecy in port towns, and all knew the times of tides and passage.

He entered the tap room with a draught of cold air, and

the occupants of the small room looked up to see who had come in. They saw a lithe young man, well dressed and foreign by his vestments, with tanned skin and shining dark hair. No weapon seemed in evidence save a knife at his belt. This was noted, for often a well-dressed merchant or traveller would be girded with a sword. The man appeared to present no threat, and most of the men in the room resumed their conversations or their drinking. He closed the double doors behind him and allowed his eyes time to adjust to the light of the tallow candles that threw a yellow glow across the company gathered within, using the moment wisely to sum up all who were present. He made his way to the rough wooden bar, ordering a drink and asking the landlord for information on ship's captains.

Cristoforo soon discovered that it would be late morning upon the following day before the tide would be in their favour, and he booked passage for his group, telling the captain he would arrive just before noon. It would be slow sailing, the ship's master told him, as they would have to tack against the breeze and new rules had been proclaimed by the crown, forbidding any merchant ships carrying wares from crossing the channel unless accompanied by at least two war cogs as escort. Two such vessels had recently sailed down from Calais and would be ready the next day to guard their voyage back to the safety of England. The threat of piracy from France and from independent raiders from further south was strong, and England had become an island fortress, isolated against all who would steal her trade.

Cristoforo finished his goblet of hot, spiced red wine,

bade the master goodnight and made to leave. He allowed himself to stumble slightly and caught the table's edge as though to steady himself against a befuddled head. "Strong Bordeaux wine and little to eat is a poor diet for a traveller," he apologised to the master.

Two men overheard the comment and looked at each other in the dark corner of the candlelit tap room. His apparent clumsiness allowed Cristoforo to take another quick glance around the room, and he spotted the men with ease. Pulling his cloak around him and replacing his padded hat, Cristoforo set the feather at a jaunty angle, showing himself as a slightly inebriated popinjay as he left the tavern and took the street back to the inn.

The streets were almost deserted and the breeze had dropped, leaving the freezing air to carry wisps of sea mist in from the quay. He heard swift footsteps parallel to his current position and noticed that someone had overtaken him. He sensed the two men who had been in the tavern close the distance from the rear.

Three of them, he thought. A grin crossed his face that had little to do with humour as he loosened his cloak slightly and flexed the fingers of both hands. The odds held no fear for him.

There was a call from behind as the two men closed the distance between them. "Ho, there, sir, we would have words. We are of the Watch. What is your purpose in being abroad at this hour?"

Cristoforo turned around, a seemingly startled look upon his face. He noted as he did so that his escape to the front was cut off by a further man with a lantern who effectively blocked his path.

The runner, he thought. *So be it.*

"Messieurs?" Cristoforo answered in a deliberately overstated Italian accent.

"We should like to speak with you, monsieur, on matters of formality within the town. What is your mission to be abroad at this hour and where do you stay?" they demanded.

To anyone else these may have seemed legitimate demands, but Cristoforo knew full well that they were not men of the Watch, and he was wary. He allowed his voice to show apprehension as he answered them: "I am merely a sely traveller bound for England. I seek passage upon a ship for me and my family upon the morrow. I return now to my lodgings at the inn of the *Cinq Tuns*."

"That will not suffice. You must accompany us to respond to further questions, for we have orders to detain all those who travel to England. I needs must inspect your papers of travel." An air of menace came into the leader's voice. He was a burly fellow who stood taller than his companion, and a hand reaching for the hilt of his sword beneath his cloak emphasised his demand. Cristoforo permitted himself a glance behind. The third man had closed his distance to six feet. The leader continued. "You will accompany us to our quarters of office."

"As you wish, monsieur. I have no need of trouble and for certes this is all a misunderstanding." Cristoforo shrugged nonchalantly in the lamplight, his bearing calm and relaxed, showing deference to his interrogators, who knew that they had him cornered and would rob him if he was legitimate by way of a heavy fine. "My papers are here within my cloak." He made to rotate his cloak around and unleashed the clasp chain, fingers clumsy in his haste. The cloak fell free, and he bent swiftly to catch it in a seemingly reflex gesture before it touched the dirty ground.

The leader smiled, shaking his head at the nervousness of their prey. They did not smile for long. Cristoforo let the cloak fall, both hands stopping at his boot tops in a swooping movement as he rose into a defensive crouch. A pair of blades flickered in the lamplight, and thrown underarm they flew to the necks of the two men before him. They gurgled and grasped impotently at their throats as their life blood sprayed out across the icy cobbles, struggling for breath through severed windpipes, unable to cry for help.

Cristoforo span around to face the third assailant, pulling a falchion from its scabbard between his shoulders, ready to face the lamp holder. The man ran at Cristoforo, the pole holding the lamp aimed as a crude spear. It was a simple move to bat the pole aside, and following on with a blocking movement, Cristoforo drove the hilt of the falchion upwards to smash into the teeth of the incoming man, who was unable to halt his momentum. Such was the force of the blow that it cut up into the roof of his mouth, leaving him bloody and mewling as he staggered for balance. Cristoforo wanted him alive and conscious, at least for now. There had been little noise other than their conversation, no voices had been raised in anger, and there was nothing to disturb those who were barred and warm in their houses.

Grabbing the lamp man by the hair he dragged him down a side alley, filled with old barrels and rubbish. "Now talk or lose your tongue. For whom do you work?" Cristoforo rasped, bringing the point of the falchion up under the man's chin.

His eyes wide with fear and surprise, the man mumbled a reply through mashed lips and broken teeth.

"Again!"

"We...we work as agents for the Duke of Burgundy and are under his protection. You had better beware his vengeance and spare me my life," he spluttered, his voice barely audible.

"Why here? Why me?"

"We are to stop all those seeking passage to England... all those that travel abroad. Looking for spies and traitors to France."

"There is more. I see it in your eyes. Speak or lose your tongue."

"I... we were told by a messenger early this morning from the abbey to watch for an Italian bearing a message. Please mercy, my tongue."

"Bah. Your tongue? I will not take your tongue." The man relaxed and dropped his hands. "Just your life." With which Cristofero stabbed the point of his falchion into his throat. The last assailant was dead within seconds. *Now*, he thought, *what to do with the bodies? They must be hidden ere we depart on the morrow.*

The lamp was still aflame, and he used it to search the alleys. He heard the sound of running water, and following it to a back alley he saw what amounted to an open sewer that would no doubt lead to the sea, as was common in many French ports. It was deep sided and stank of every imaginable form of human waste. All the houses and businesses seemed to back onto it, with cuttings leading off the street. The stream of rushing water seemed in the grey light to enter a conduit running for many feet under bridges and roads, perfect for his needs. He spent the next few minutes hefting the bodies towards the sewer and dropping them into the current, which he noticed with satisfaction carried them swiftly away. He hoped that they would not be noticed or missed until after they had sailed. Already rats and other vermin were licking and rooting around, disposing of the blood of the fallen men.

Cristoforo looked up at a sky that was deep with cloud. By morning snow may fall, and he prayed that it would. He made his way back to the inn, entered the back alley and found the cord still there, too far out of reach for any normal assailant to make use of. Crouching for a moment, he leapt up, using the wall to propel himself higher until his fist closed around the very lowest part of the cord. He pulled himself up to scale the wall, arriving at the open casement above.

He was greeted by a vision of his wife holding a dagger, standing close to the opening ready to defend herself if it was not Cristoforo who appeared. "*Dio Mio*, you are hurt!" she cried, seeing the dark red splashes and stains upon his doublet and rushing forward to his embrace.

"Fear not, my love. This blood belongs to someone else. You think three Frenchmen could best me in the dark?" he joked, with a flash of white teeth making light of the matter.

She shook her head.

"Yet now, I have another problem."

"*Cosa?*"

"I swore not to kill again at my confessional, and I fear the Lord may punish me. I do so hope that the crossing on the morrow is calm."

Chapter Five

21st February, Westminster, London

The royal barge transported King Henry across the River Thames from Lambeth Palace, and his servants and courtiers saw the weakness that assailed their sovereign. They knew he would never use the royal ships anchored downriver waiting to be fitted out at his command that had been commissioned to take him to the Holy Land. A horse litter waited at the quayside, and patient servants gently helped their king from the barge to the litter. Archbishop Arundel shook his head, distressed to see his lifelong friend so disabled and discomposed.

The litter took the king to the Royal Chambers within the Palace, and he rested there before eating a light supper and attending a private Mass held in his name. Rumours of his weakness were spreading through the Palace, and it was not long before Bishop Beaufort called upon Archbishop Arundel in his private chambers.

"How does my brother the king?" he asked piously. "I am sorely distressed to hear rumours of his sudden decay."

Archbishop Arundel's face hardened, not fooled by Beaufort's disingenuous concern for the king. "Why do you ask? So that you may hurry him to his grave with your prayers?"

"Why, Your Grace, I know not what you mean and am sorely burdened to my very soul that you should think so poorly of me. I merely sought to inquire how his majesty rails against the terrible adversity that has been sent against him. My thoughts and prayers are with his gracious majesty, as ever."

"Then let God be your judge, for he alone will know your true thoughts and the spirit of your heart, for I cannot fathom it, and from what depths I do plunder, I see only darkness and the gaping hole of hell that beckons," Arundel retorted.

Beaufort was angered beyond his usual façade of banal piety. "Then you, my lord archbishop, should look to your God for help also, as for certes his majesty will not last forever and when the prince ascends the throne you may find yourself at the pointed end of the sword, not holding its pommel!" With that he swept out, muttering under his breath, his face red and suffused with rage.

For days the court held its collective breath, with no one daring to ask directly after the king's health, lest it be seen as an urge to hurry the process of his demise. No papers were signed, no rules or laws of government enacted, and the court lay in a moratorium of paralysis.

Archbishop Arundel called a select number of council

members to effect, holding an unofficial meeting in an effort to continue the act of government as the king lay dying. To his private chambers came the lord chief justice, Lord Chamberlain and Lord Grey, together with others who had served the king with unfailing loyalty, including Sir Richard Whittington.

"I worry, my lords, for it is now proved that one John Lay, a chaplain of our own church, is suspected of heresy as he celebrated Mass in the presence of Sir John Oldcastle in a private chapel. I have asked that he produce upon cross-examination certificates of his ordination, and proof of his right to celebrate Mass. But what gives me greater cause for concern, is not the act but the manner by which such heresy should have been performed so openly and with a known heretic present, one whose alliances are so close to the very prince who shall soon be king.

"Lord Cobham, Sir John Oldcastle, dost support and encourage the heresies of John Lay abroad with proof of them in Hereford, London and Rochester. If this continues to ferment and grow, why it will divide us all, not just the clergy, and such vile practices can only lead to civil war." Arundel finished, his voice strident and vexed.

"And so the wolves do congregate, waiting, sensing that the moment is nigh to pounce ere a new leader is chosen. What with this and rumours of Richard Second risen from the dead, reincarnated by the Scots, what else may be thrown at our poor troubled realm so acephalous and pregnable?" Whittington considered.

"Please God, nothing more comes to threaten us at this juncture. Do your words presage some untold fear, Sir

Richard?" the Lord Chancellor, Sir William Gascoigne, asked.

"None that I may yet bring to bear without burden of proof. I merely hear rumours of a revolt in France that may be a precursor to acts that could define that country's very unity. Should this occur, we needs must face a united France and all would be lost." Whittington shook his head gently, unsure of how to proceed. "All we can do is watch and wait and prepare ourselves for the worst. You, my lord archbishop, must be ever wary and proceed to persecute this new religion where'er you may find it. For the power of the throne." Here he chose his words very carefully. "Whomsoever it may be, shall need your counsel and guidance through the ecclesiastical maze in due course."

"Amen to that, Sir Richard," Arundel enjoined.

The others looked worried and concerned at Whittington's suspicions, yet the statesman would not be drawn further on the matter or on other subjects, which were conducted with such business as they were able to conclude, given the restrictions placed upon their power at that time.

 —

Berwick Castle, Berwick-on-Tweed

The trip for Jamie and Mark had been ever more arduous as they travelled further north. The weather had worsened into one of the coldest winters either could remember.

Jamie was glad not to have taken Lady Alice, now his wife, any further on from Macclesfield, where they had wed in a beautiful winter ceremony at Macclesfield Castle, her family home. She had finally relented, realising that he would be travelling as a soldier and would not have time to play the role of doting husband. Even now, just two weeks after leaving her, he pined for their warm bed and the charms that she brought to it. She had been virtuous before their marriage, and he praised God that all had changed following the nuptials. Someone must have coached her – mayhap her mother or her sloe-eyed lady in waiting borrowed from Alessandria seemingly so long ago. It mattered not, for the result was above his expectations, and she had surprised him with a pent up passion and little reserve, which disappeared completely with his impending departure.

Jamie and Mark were made welcome upon their arrival and Jamie sought out old friends with whom he had trained whilst under Sir Robert de Umfraville's charge. He found that many now were knighted by Prince John, as he had been by his brother, Prince Henry. It was especially good to see Sir Geraint Hampton, a squire from an old family of landowners with manors in Hertfordshire. He was the same age as Jamie, and both had fought on many border raids with Sir Robert. They now sat with others in a tavern within Berwick the day after Jamie and Mark had arrived in the north.

"Is there any more knowledge of the pretender that the

Scots claim to be Richard second reincarnated?" Jamie asked of his erstwhile companion in arms.

The dark-featured man seated before him grimaced and shrugged. "Nary a little. He is kept from all prying eyes save those of the court in Edinburgh, and I would not wish to venture there without an army at my back. Rumours spread by those that have supposedly seen the man are that he is in the image of the dead king. Yet these are servants, and some who were sent to spy did not return." Sir Geraint raised an eyebrow. "The strongest rumours that are cast abroad are that this pretender was found serving in a kitchen in the Western Isles, if you can believe such janglery. Though whether he was cast there by sorcery or not, is unexplained. The old King, Robert Third, was said to have received him from the clan Donald of the Isles after being recognised by his fool, who had served at the English court and was a suspected spy. Now I prithee, who is the fool here?"

"Well," Jamie responded, "with the death of Robert and his son held hostage by King Henry, the old rogue and charlatan the Duke of Albany took charge. Doth he fashion himself as Lord protector and ruler of Scotland whilst his nephew would lie rotting in an English gaol through lack of funds, all of which have been sequestered by his uncle awaiting his majesty's pleasure? Bah! The man is an opportunist and a usurper. For there is the rub. The whoreson Albany would use any means at his disposal to turn England upon itself and weaken its defences and break the Treaty of Bourges. Consider how little the Scots hold such pledges sacrosanct. They fought with the Burgundians at Cotentin just last year, breaking just such a pledge, their word is as thin as that of the Armagnacs. Treaty breakers all," he spat.

"Yet I hear that you were covered in glory and captured Douglas' whelp of the Lord Wigton," Sir Geraint said.

"I did, with the help of Mark here." He nodded at his giant friend. "Mark was with me on that day and fought valiantly at my side. 'Twas a good day's work and my purse is ever the heavier for the encounter."

"Well, have due care, for he curses your name I've heard, and tells all that he was bested by trickery."

"Ha! The only trickery employed was by the knave himself, who broke the good faith of the treaty pledged by his father, the Earl of Douglas then sought a duplicitous bedfellow in Burgundy. The dissembling bastard still skulks north of the border, breaking his word of honour in lieu of the hostages held in his name, who live only by the grace of his majesty," Jamie said disparagingly.

"And of his majesty, what news?" Sir Geraint lowered his voice. "For we hear he ails most badly, lingering unto death, with the Grim Reaper hovering at his shoulder."

"I have not heard now for two weeks, yet the news was not good afore we departed London." Jamie absentmindedly stroked Forest's ears as the wolfhound sat by his side at the table. "His majesty fades quickly if rumours are to be believed, and God help us when that void is filled, for the filling shall not be as smooth as some would believe. Prince Hal is young and a fine man, yet I fear that he will be sorely tested ere his reign be out."

"May God have him in his keeping," Geraint said, crossing himself. "For we needs must have a stable realm."

"Amen to that," Jamie and Mark intoned. They continued their conversation and tried to piece together as much information as they could gather of the mysterious pretender, seeking any scrap of rumour that would aid them.

Later that evening Mark and Jamie went to attend an audience with Prince John, Duke of Bedford, brother to Prince Henry and third in line to the throne. They strode through the inner bailey of Berwick Castle leading to the magnificent square walled keep that towered above the surrounding buildings and dominated the landscape. The castle itself was perched atop a craggy mound overlooking the River Tweed, and stood as a beacon of hope and strength, keeping the Scots at bay under the strong right arm of the prince and his garrison.

Yet both men now saw how ragged and unkept were parts of the curtain walling that followed the contours of the undulating landscape, and how rundown they looked. Little repair work had been done due to lack of funds from parliament and the exchequer. Building works were in evidence, no doubt supplied by the new release of funds but Prince John, keeper of the castle and marshal of the Scottish marches, was forever petitioning for more funds and had over the previous two years received just four thousand pounds for maintenance and strengthening. It was a precarious situation, but one that was aided by Sir Robert de Umfraville, who raided north from Innerleithen.

Once within the keep they were shown up a flight of steep steps by the captain of the guard and ushered into the prince's private chamber. Someone had managed to get rosemary to grow in these frozen wastes, for Jamie and Mark instantly recognised the scented herb from their time in Italy. It permeated the warmer air of the chamber. Fresh rushes had been laid upon the floor and one of the prince's favourite hounds rose as they entered, curious but satisfied that they posed no threat.

Before them, in front of an immense stone hearth that radiated heat, stood the prince. Although as tall as his brother, he was not as handsome, his build squarer and his strong shoulders developed by long use of arms. His face was round with a small straight nose and slightly slanted eyes. Women apparently found him very attractive, or so the rumours around the court had it. He was dressed well in a heavy houppelande of rich tapestry, embroidered with floral patterns and leaves of magenta interspersed with blue stars. The lining was of a rich vermillion wool, much needed in the northern wastelands to repel the freezing winds.

Sir Robert looked the same as always – bluff, hearty and martial. He was tall and strong, an excellent soldier and one of the best fighters Jamie had ever seen. He had taught Jamie all that he could, and had been an excellent teacher. It had been here on the Borders that Jamie had gained all his experience of fierce battles, raids and deadly infighting in the alleys and backstreets.

Jamie and Mark bowed before their prince, and Jamie smiled at Sir Robert, who acknowledged him with a broad grin.

"Your Royal Highness, Sir Robert." Jamie greeted them formally.

"Sir James, we thank you for attending upon us at this late hour. For the tide is with us and we have found a boat to take you to the northern shores. The captain is from the Low Countries, and this will work well with your story. He is a merchant and has cloth for sale, so the likelihood of suspicion will be slight. You speak the Flemish tongue, we believe, and it would not be beyond the ken of such a man to have a strong Cornishman as a labourer or servant." The prince finished. His manner and mode of speech were very much of the court and his words demanded instant acceptance and obedience. When he gave an order, he expected it to be done as of right immediately, with no dalliance or recourse.

"As Your Grace pleases. Where do we meet with the boat?"

"It is docked now below the castle on the Tweed. The master awaits your audience at the quayside shelter. There is little time to delay, for the tide will run before the hour of Compline. Have you all that you need?"

"Yes, Your Grace. I shall leave my hound and our horses here for our return. It would not be seemly for merchants to be so well mounted, and Forest may well be an incumbrance. We shall of course be armed, yet not so as to draw attention."

"Just so. Now bring us back all that you may pertaining to this traitor who calls himself our uncle. They will no doubt have him well guarded, yet all the talk and all manner of janglery is of this man who is to be foisted upon us as a false king, whilst our father lies terribly assailed by illness. The timing is poor, and is no coincidence for all that. It comes alongside talk of Lollardy and a rebellion within England no doubt aided by the Scots."

Sir Robert frowned. "Jamie, remember lad, 'tis not the aim to take the castle and defeat all the Scots by yourself! Do you hear? Intelligence is what we need, not your head on a spike."

"Aye, Sir Robert. Yet should the moment arise to take the traitor, why I foreswear that would be a bonny cope, would it not?" Jamie replied, grinning broadly as he did so.

"No lad, name and intelligence only. For if he were taken it would be used as a clarion call to arms, with banners raised in the traitor's name as a martyr to whatever cause they deem best. I'faith if you should come away with your skin intact I should deem it a miracle, for it is to the Devil's nest that you travel. I warned you many moons ago of the court and Whittington's schemes, and now I see he sends you to where many would fear to tread."

"I know of the consequences and shall fortify myself against such actions," Jamie responded, nodding in acquiescence to Sir Robert, who did not believe a word of his former charge.

"Very well. There is more intelligence that may help your quest," the prince continued, and Jamie was suddenly very alert, as anything that helped him avoid being hanged as a spy or at best remain captive would be welcome. "There are friars there who hail from France, a peace contingent. If you can connect with them, they may yet aid you."

"I should be grateful for any help I can receive, sire, yet my mind begs the question as to why they would render such a service to the English crown," Jamie asked cynically.

The prince smiled a wintry smile: "For one simple reason. Though they be French, they serve in Notre Dame cathedral on an episcopal visit. They may be servants of God, but they have another master here upon earth in the ranks of the Armagnacs, to wit Charles, Duke of Orleans." At which the prince raised an eyebrow as he could see the young knight take stock of all the implications now put before him.

"By the rood, Isabella of Valois, daughter to the king of France and the former queen of England who went on to marry the duke after Richard's death and produced an heir for Charles afore she died in childbirth," Jamie said. "By God's legs, I see all now, for if this be a true king and not a pretender then it means that Isabella was bigamous, which will have terrible consequences for Duke Charles. By God, what a web of deceit. Why, it would affect everything from the French alliance to that of Scotland."

"Ah, the scales are lifted from thine eyes and you see how important this is to all our countries," the prince opined.

"I do, my lord prince, yes, certes I do," Jamie confirmed, realising now just what was at stake and the terrible weight that had settled upon his shoulders.

"Very well." The prince stole a glance at Sir Robert. "Our father had his cousin Richard openly displayed in St Paul's cathedral afore being buried with full state at King's Langley priory. Yet if there be any doubt in your mind that by some sorcery this truly be the former king, our uncle, you must kill him upon our behest, for the good of our kingdom. Is that understood?"

Jamie's eyes widened at the pronouncement and order. He would be guilty of regicide! Only men of history killed kings. He stumbled the next words as though in a trance. "As you command, my lord prince."

"Then I wish you Godspeed, and may the Lord have you

in his keeping. May you find the answers we seek and mayhap settle this matter for ever."

Jamie and Mark bowed. "By your leave, sire," Jamie said and the pair stepped backwards three paces and moved back to the door of the chamber.

As they left the chamber, Mark turned to his friend: "Did I hear aright? We are to kill a man if he be a king? Jamie, if that be so then the court is a murky place where a man's soul can be sold to the Devil mostly cheaply," Mark opined with a sigh.

"Aye, you have the right of it, and this sits no more easily on my shoulders than yours. Mayhap we shall ne'er be given the choice. Whittington has lured us into a pretty coil this time and no mistake. I wonder if he foresaw such an occurrence?" Jamie muttered.

Mark looked askance at his friend and shook his head. He liked not the politics of the court, and by his own admission was not adept at navigating the perils of the subterfuge meted out there.

"Come then," Jamie said. "Let us gather our gear and go down to the meet the ship and see what manner of man we are to accompany on this difficult journey."

Chapter Six

Jamie and Mark returned to their quarters, where Jamie took a fond farewell of Forest, leaving her with trusted servants. Crouching to his dog, Jamie rubbed her head affectionately, noting the emergence of a few grey hairs in the tufts of fur around her muzzle. Then carrying their war bags they made their way down the winding stone steps to the quayside on the estuary of the River Tweed.

They saw anchored there a large cog in the Flemish style that swung gently up and down upon the current, looking deceptively large and cumbersome in the failing light. There was a man at arms on guard cloaked against the cold, though only a misguided fool would venture forth on a night like this, Jamie thought. From the railing of the vessel a weather-beaten face looked down, darkened by sun and wind and weather and barely discernible in the gloom.

The man called down in Flemish, as if to test what he had been told: "Are you my two passengers for Scotland?" His rough voice floated down to them on the breeze.

It was always welcoming to hear the tongue of his fatherland spoken again, and Jamie fell straight back into the language. "That we are. I am Sir James de Grispere and this is my companion, Mark of Cornwall."

"If he be a Cornishman, he is even further from home and even colder than am I," the voice floated back.

As Jamie translated Mark mumbled. "Amen to that, for I've never known such cold!"

Laughing at Mark's discomfort, the two men boarded the cog, crossing the short, railed gangplank to secure a footing upon the deck.

"Are you bound for Edinburgh?"

"Aye, that I am," Jamie replied smiling at how easily he slipped into the vernacular of the north when he had been back but days. He was a mongrel, he acknowledged privately, but none the worse for all that, for it gave him the ability to pass hither and thither in whatever guise he chose.

Another figure appeared, emerging from the forward cabin under the fo'c'sle. His rich clothing defined his profession – a merchant by his dress of soft wool cotehardie, and cloaked in a manner not dissimilar to Jamie's own spectacular raiment. He was of middle years, soft around the girth showing his prosperity, and his jowls hung padded about his jaw. The eyes were shrewd and summed Jamie up in a heartbeat. "Ah, messieurs, you arrive. It is provident for we must away upon the favourable tide if we wish to see landfall by morning. I am Herr Laurence Dietmar, merchant bent upon trade with the Scots."

Jamie introduced himself in Flemish, at which the

merchant scowled, peering at him in concentration. "You are of Flanders?"

"My father was of the country, and I was born there myself. Now I reside in England, though my mother was of the Scottish race." Herr Dietmar nodded as though confirming that this was a perfect mix. He did not know the exact nature of Jamie's mission to Scotland, only that it would require subterfuge and stealth. Jamie continued: "My father is of the guild of merchants in cloth and wool, and I travelled with him as a lad, learning the trade at his side. I shall fall right easily into the mould again, fear not."

"Very well. That is good to hear, for I would not wish to cross the Scots or be cast as a spy in their eyes, though many of my fellow members ply that very trade, passing information as they may, for we live in uncertain times, with many rumours travelling abroad. Come, stow your gear forward and see something of the wares that I have brought for sale."

Jamie nodded and beckoned Mark to follow. They entered the forward hold under the fo'c'sle, where Dietmar removed some of the waterproof bindings, showing the quality of cloth he carried as samples. In the lamplight Jamie marvelled at the shine of silk that caught his eye.

"Tartaryn? Why by the good Lord this be rare – and too good for the Scots, I'm bound," Jamie exclaimed as he ran his fingers over the expensive silk brocade.

The merchant smiled wryly. "So, you know your cloth. I sell it to any man that pays my price, and the Scots will pay good silver, for they wish to be well spoken of and match the grandeur of the French court, though that they'll never do, of course."

Jamie and Dietmar caught their balance as Mark stood stock still, smiling for the first time. He was born to the sea, and as the cog cast off drifting into the outward current, he naturally adapted his stance to the change in balance.

"Does the captain know these waters well?" Mark asked. "For they are dangerous, I've heard, with many a foul rock to wreck a ship."

"Fear not," Dietmar assured him, reverting to the English tongue. "Many's the time I've sailed these waters with Pieter, and I forswear he knows them well."

"Then I shall go back onto the deck and see how we fare." With that Mark left the other two to give further discussion to cloth and trade, as Jamie knew his father always liked to hear news of his homeland and how matters were in Flanders.

The seas were choppy with an easterly breeze that blew sleet and bitter cold with it, driving the ship onwards as it hugged the land that they could see dark against the ambient light. Eleven hours after they left Berwick, the huge craggy mass of granite that was Edinburgh Castle loomed up out of the dawn, as they sailed up the river Forth. The rocky escarpment upon which the fortress was built glistened, covered in a frosting of hard packed snow and ice. It looked as impregnable as ever to Jamie's eyes, and he would not wish to mount a campaign against it in the winter. It had been conquered, he knew, by King Edward Third in 1334, but it always fell back to the Scots. King Henry had been the last English king to besiege it, but was forced to withdraw to deal with Glyndower. Now it was supposedly held in good faith against the hostage of the uncrowned Scottish King James I, lodged now in London after being hunted down by the same Lord Douglas who sided with the French and whose son Jamie had defeated at Cotentin the previous year. He shivered involuntarily, not against the cold, but more against history and the fact that the circumstances did not augur well.

"Cold?" Mark asked.

"Aye, and for more than the weather. The Scots give me great cause for thought. I durst trust them as much as they each other, as a sparrow would an eyasmusket. For if they cannot respect their own king, his brothers murdered to gain the crown with the trail of blood to Albany's hand, then I fear our lives' worth are the poorer for it."

Mark leant on his quarterstaff, moving easily with the rise and fall of the ship.

"I say Amen to that, and either I have spent too long in yours and Cristo's company and see shadows where there are none or I discern a true foreboding of this fiat upon which we embark."

Jamie nodded in understanding, then in an effort to lighten the mood offered: "I wonder how does our Italian companion, for I do miss him."

"As do I," Mark affirmed. "No doubt he is tucked up somewhere warm and snug with the lovely contessa, awaiting the bright sun of Italy to reappear and warm his back, revealing himself as a bright butterfly, for what did they call it...? Ah, yes, *prima verde.* I miss their lovely language, and though I caught but a few words 'twas easy upon the ear.

And much about the country was easy upon the eye, too, truth be told. Yet I wonder if we should see our friend again should we not venture once more to the land of sun and brightness, for that is how I remember the place in my mind."

"I do feel of the same mind, and long to feel the sun upon my face again, in particular when faced with the oppression of the cold and this bleak landscape afore us. But come, let us not be maudlin, for we have much to achieve."

At which they felt the cog change direction, fighting the current and crossing to the southern bank beneath the great castle fortress and the walled city of Edinburgh.

Chapter Seven

Cotentin, France

The day had begun well for the party of Italians. No hue and cry had been raised concerning the death of the duke's men, and the party stood waiting to board the cog upon the rising tide. Cristoforo crossed himself and squeezed his wife's hand tighter before setting foot upon the gangplank as it rose and fell with the swell of the waves. It became no easier for him to board a ship no matter how many times he was compelled to do so, and only the fear of discovery and *bella figura* at not wanting to appear a coward in front of the groom and Francesca prevailed.

Alessandria bit back a smile at her husband and encouraged him with a squeeze of her own hand, watching as he marched boldly onto the waiting ship with only the tension in his jaw to show his fear, muttering Hail Marys as he went.

The ship cast off a few minutes later and they all looked back, wondering when they would next set foot on mainland France and follow the road back to Italy.

As they set forth into the open waters of the English Channel they saw some half a league back men rush to the quayside gesticulating as though beckoning them to return. However, neither the two war cogs nor the captain of The *Rose of Kent* showed any sign of heeding the request, and Cristoforo turned to Alessandria with a wry smile and a raised eyebrow. "Mayhap they have found the duke's men at last. 'Twas fortunate that they did not discover them sooner." He was gratefully aware he had come away unscathed once again, and now all that remained was to deliver the missive to Whittington and see his two friends once more.

Later that that day, after a calm if freezing crossing, the cog docked at Southampton, sailing up the Solent on the strong south easterly breeze. Standing once again on solid ground, Cristoforo breathed a sigh of relief, smelling the clearly identifiable odours of a different land, at once familiar yet foreign. He noted not for the first time how different each country was, especially one that was separated by a comparatively small division of water.

The gulls cawed and screeched; the smell of seaweed was much more prevalent here and the freezing temperatures weakened the all-pervading stench of raw sewage. The coarser accents of the English tongue again felt familiar, different as they were to the tongue of his native land or even France, the words unique to this island that he would now once more call home.

"Come, Gino, let us find horses and a carriage," he commanded, watching with amusement as his groom and Alessandria's maid stood aghast at this strange land, so alien to Italy and even to France, which Cristoforo had ever perceived as a half-way house between the two countries in terms of manners and language. "Fear not," he added in Italian, "they will not eat you, at least not until Lent has passed."

With a carriage and horses secured, they proceeded north towards London and on the fourth day, they set sight of the great city, walled and obdurate against all who might wish to conquer and change her.

Approaching from the south bank of the Thames, they crossed the bridge, and both of the young Italians were amazed at the breadth of the connection and the dwellings and shops that lined the sides of the span.

"It all seems alien now," Cristoforo intoned, "yet I am persuaded that you will come to enjoy it, Francesca, for it is cleaner than all other cities and the shops are something to behold. And Gino, the women here, they do so love Italians," he added with a wink, which earned him a fierce cutting look from Alessandria and a tap of her quirt against his arm from inside the carriage.

Undeterred Cristoforo laughed out loud. "Except for an old married man such as myself, who of course is wrapped in the *catene di amore* and only has eyes for a certain beautiful contessa."

"Fie on you, peacock, for you strut and preen as ever you did afore we were married." She raised her chin imperiously and strove to ignore her laughing husband.

They crossed the mighty bridge that led them onto Bruggestrate, which widened out into Garscherch Street. They turned left into Langburnestrate, making for the house of Alessandria's uncle. Memories assailed Alessandria and Cristoforo: the familiar street where they had begun their journey to leave London nearly a year earlier, before they were man and wife.

Francesca looked nervously out of the carriage, finding it all so alien. At last they came to the front of Alessandria's uncle's imposing house. It was set back from the street front, the walls cast upon stone foundations raised up from the street level and an impressive portico cantilevered out above the solid door.

Cristoforo slid from his horse and knocked loudly upon the oak portal.

Noise of a catch being freed came from within and the door swung open to show Signor Alberti's steward, who blinked in amazement at the sight before him and broke into Italian in his joy, welcoming the party, beckoning them to enter and calling within for grooms to take care of the belongings and horses.

Gino stayed with the horses and Francesca stepped down from the carriage, heartened by the sound of her mother tongue spoken so freely again for all to hear.

Then a figure appeared, wealthy by his dress and urbane in manner, having an air of confidence and authority borne of right. "What garboil is this that darkens my door...?" Then the man's manner changed from haughty and aloof as the sight of his niece melted his heart. "*Dio mio!* You have arrived. By the good Lord and all the Saints, you are returned. Come here, child," he commanded affectionately, "and embrace your old uncle."

Alessandria ran forward to greet her uncle and was crushed within his embrace. He was the last of her male line to remain alive, and she babbled at him in rapid Italian, the words pouring forth.

Finally he managed to take advantage of a brief pause and pushed her back, hearing the news of his brother-in-law. "*Aspetta*, Rafaello is dead?" he exclaimed.

"*Si*, he was murdered by the *assassini*." She started to explain the whole story to her uncle, who pulled her gently inside, urging Cristoforo and Francesca to follow.

"Now *di mi tutti*," he encouraged.

The story fell from Alessandria's lips, although she broke down in sobs as she told him the details of her father's death. With wine ordered, and seated at a table in front of a raging fire, she finally finished recounting all to her uncle, who turned to Cristoforo.

"May I thank you, Cristoforo, for salvaging our honour and revenging us against the *bastardi* Albizzi and the *Parte Guelfa*."

Cristoforo acknowledged with a slight nod of his head. "Signor, it was my devoir to take revenge and they died badly, both the assassins and the Albizzi *stronzi* that caused the murder."

Francesca was introduced and food was brought while the party refreshed themselves. Replete and not looking forward to leaving the warm confines of the house, Cristoforo finally begged to be excused.

"My love, I must visit Sir Richard and then Jamie and Marco. For they all must know of our return."

✕✶✕ —

Cristoforo was shown into Whittington's quarters within the palace, and found the room was exactly as he had remembered it. It was the warmest place in England in the winter, he recalled, warm to the point of stuffiness, yet Cristoforo welcomed it.

"I bid you good morrow, Sir Richard," Cristoforo offered as he came forward.

"My good Signor Corio, 'tis good to see you safely back upon our shores," he greeted. "Come, warm yourself by the fire, for the chill of the winter is most uncivil this year, or I am ageing badly.

"We of the court are most grateful to you for aiding the payment to the Pope, for James gave good reports of your deeds and you were most well thought of by both prince and king."

"I merely did my devoir, Sir Richard. But if I may, sir, you seem less than surprised to see me returned thus."

"Rumours in court are ever rife. I did hear something to the effect that your return was imminent and of course rejoiced at the news. And now here you stand, and bring intelligence with you, I am bound."

Cristoforo was a little nonplussed but knew better than to try to interrogate the spymaster further. It would be an exercise in futility.

"As you please, Sir Richard. I have a missive here that I was given specific instructions to pass it directly to your hand."

"And where did you acquire this document?"

"From the Monseigneur – the abbot – of Saint-Sauveur-le-Vicomte, near Cotentin. He in turn received the information from Canon Jean Eusoris of Notre Dame. He–"

"What? By the rood, show me this parchment," Whittington ordered. "Do you know its contents?" he asked, as Cristoforo took the sealed missive from the secret pocket in his cloak.

"I do, my lord. The document pertains to an uprising secured by the Duke of Burgundy that was agreed with King Charles at the assembly of *Les Etats Generaux de Langue*. The abbot was most insistent that I place this in your hands as he felt that the revolt, such was the word he used, would begin in the spring of this year. An insurgence that would remove all power from the Armagnacs and place the ruling of France in the hands of Burgundy, with the dauphin as his mawmet." Cristoforo's memory was excellent, and he had been trained to always write down very little that might prove incriminating to him. He related all he remembered.

Whittington blanched, turning pale. "It is worse than I had imagined," he muttered. Taking the scroll, he broke the seal and read the contents twice before raising his eyes. He did not say anything, but turned away to pace his chambers, his mind in turmoil. Finally, he turned to the Italian who waited in silence, ever patient in such matters. "You have, as ever, done England great service by placing this information into my hands. I now needs must consider what measures are to be taken to damn this most treacherous plan to failure. For if unity be achieved and all of France fall under one banner united against England, we are lost. Particularly at this most pernicious moment when the future of the realm is in balance," he said, as much to himself as to Cristoforo.

"I see your predicament, Sir Richard. I prithee, if there is aught I can do in the service of the realm, you need but ask," Cristoforo offered.

"Aye, and well said, signor. I may yet call upon your services and those of your companions, who are even now aiding the crown in another matter on our northern borders." Whittington explained all to Cristoforo of Jamie and Mark's current mission. At length, he finished. "Where do you dwell, now that you returned to London?"

"At this moment, at Signor Alberti's house, and word may be left there or at the residence of Thomas de Grispere."

"Very well. And I do give you my eternal thanks for delivering this to me, for much hinges upon the matters contained within these words."

"As you wish, Sir Richard. Now by your leave, I shall bid you good morrow, for I must visit Master Thomas and his family."

"Yes, yes of course. I shall send word to you shortly."

Cristoforo mused to himself as he left, navigating the maze of corridors, passages and towers of the Palace of Westminster, lost in thought. He reflected that Jamie was ever caught in the coils of intrigue, entangled by Whittington and his scheming. *May Mary Mother of God look down upon my friends wherever they may be*, he silently prayed.

Chapter Eight

Edinburgh

They found themselves among a host of smaller boats and seagoing craft, all crowding the wharfs and quays at the foot of the town. The river harbour was a mass of frantic activity, fishing boats leaving as other craft arrived, and a cacophony of shouts, cries and orders given hither and thither. Their landing was given little notice by the men-at-arms who stood guard at the quayside. The harsher accents of the Scots sounded loud upon Mark's ears compared to his own soft Cornish burr. To Jamie they were all so familiar, and he slipped easily back into the accent of his early time in the Borders.

With the ship docked and the ropes tied off, the unloading of the cargo began. Jamie oversaw the process as Herr Dietmar went to pay the kaiage at the harbour master's office.

The wooden garrets moved back and forth, rope cages

swinging with the momentum like pendulums, restrained only by the guiding ropes of the steves. The cargoes were lowered into the waiting waggons as the horses stamped impatiently in the cold, their hoary breath billowing forth like that of dragons of myth, their winter coats long and shaggy, ready to be shed as soon as the spring thaw arrived.

"Durst the sun ever shine upon these shores, Jamie? I do fear I'll ne'er be warm again," Mark asked.

"Fear not, with a wee dram inside you, you'll live to wrestle another day," Jamie retorted, smiling at his giant friend, who seemed to long for the warm Italian climate that had characterised their previous year's journey.

"Work is what I need, whether by virtue of loading or to have a bout or two. I wonder, do they wrestle up here?"

"Aye, they do, but not to the Cornish rules. We'll settle in at some lodgings and then we can find some time to practice," he assured Mark.

Like all knights, Jamie's training had involved different martial arts, including War Wrestling both in and out of armour. Many was the time when the battlefield became a melee of scrappy fights, with footing or swords lost and daggers seeking weak points in armour following a throw or lock. Such skills had saved his life on many an occasion. He was not in the same class as Mark, but could hold his own well enough and enjoyed the physical aspect of the art.

With the kaiage paid and the waggons moving slowly up the gently sloping icy road towards the gates of the walled town above them, Jamie, Mark, Dietmar and his servants followed on foot, walking the short distance from the quayside to the main gate of the fortified city. They saw that it was set out in a huge quadrangle with crisscrossed streets in the Roman fashion that were almost perpendicular to each other. Everything was dominated by the huge crag of rock that supported the castle above them.

At Dietmar's direction, they made for an inn where the landlord welcomed the merchant as a regular customer. With the cloth stored away securely in a nearby warehouse, Jamie and Mark were shown to a private room for their stay in the city.

"On the morrow," Dietmar directed, "we shall be granted an audience within the castle, where various lords will wish to see my cloth, including Lord Albany and his clan. I shall call upon you early on the morrow to break your fast, and thence we shall go forth to the castle, so be ready, messieurs." With that Dietmar bade them good day and bustled off on other errands to which he needed to attend.

Jamie and Mark set to practising wrestling holds and throws, which occupied them for two hours until Mark felt replenished by the exercise. Jamie then fetched two wooden swords from his war bag. They were shorter than the real sword at his side, but would do for exercise, and with daggers blunted with a special sheath of stiff leather and steel rims, they set forth upon another hour's practice. Mark still preferred his quarterstaff or poleaxe, at which he had become extremely proficient. Being immensely strong, he could wield it as most men would wield a sword.

"Now we practice with you as though in armour," Jamie said, to give Mark the advantage, "and you should assume that I'm only with gambeson or doublet, no more. This means I must choose my targets with especial care, while you have carte blanche to strike where you will."

Mark smiled, enjoying the prospect all the more, for subtle sword play was not his forte. "So be it," he agreed.

There followed an interesting by-play of counter-strikes and grapples, a closing of distance on Jamie's part as he sought ways through Mark's defence at close quarters, where in a real encounter he would need to find the holes and gaps in his opponent's armour while avoiding being stabbed or slashed.

Jamie often took the upper guard, seemingly leaving his lower half undefended.

Mark leapt in, at which Jamie's sword came down to parry or block. Jamie then pivoted in closer where a dagger could piece the gaps in protection at the armpits where the gorget overlapped the breastplate, always seeking and probing. The wrestling had helped Jamie to choose his opportunities, and he put this to good use, grasping for the head or neck where Mark relied upon his weapons alone.

After an hour or so they put up their weapons and stood back, panting with exertion.

"'Tis good practice, for if there be conflict of arms here, we shall be unarmoured and likely those around will at least be in maille, if not full harness," Jamie said.

Mark nodded in agreement, more unsure than ever of their latest mission.

They washed off the sweat of the exercise, dressed and then went out into the main tap room of the inn and to seek food, for Mark was, as ever, hungry.

The main room of the tavern was crowded, and a mixed

selection of customers populated the bar. Most of them seemed, by their dress and snippets of conversation, to be foreigners to Edinburgh, and there were as many that wore the sash, proudly displaying their clan of origin. As Lent was still upon them, roasted fish and pottage were on offer. The salmon was fresh from the sea and seasoned well with herbs and salt. The ale they drank was dark and strong, revising old memories for Jamie. They avoided eye contact with everyone, seeking insouciance to all, and even Mark's great height and build were not as noticeable here as one or two hefty highlanders were approaching his physical state. They had one more tankard of ale and left early, ready for what the next day would bring.

The morning found them in the company of Herr Dietmar, following the main road up to the castle before them. The city sprawled below them on the lower ground, and once the inner walls were passed, the land was open with fields and crops planted to almost half the area. This would, Jamie surmised, feed the citizens and the garrison in times of siege, and the animals as well, that even now grazed on the yellowed winter blades, waiting for warmer weather to encourage new shoots to sprout upwards.

They pushed on up Castle Hill, and halfway up the incline which became progressively steeper, they found their way once more bisected by another curtain wall with a fortified gatehouse and portcullis. Their passes and wares were checked by the guard, and once within, they saw that the true Edinburgh landscape of harsh granite now prevailed. The climb became steeper still and the hired mules huffed with every step, seeking secure purchase upon the cobbles.

The main stores of cloth had been left behind and they carried just samples on the backs of the two mules.

Jamie and Mark strode easily up the hill, and between breaths, Mark asked: "Why do you take so little? Would it be better not to have to return again?"

Dietmar smiled wryly: "I know the Scots of old. They are a cautelous breed, and I am wary of taking all my stock to such a gathering, afeared that my payment would be severely delayed or never seen, with nought but promises to pay as dues," he opined.

"Aye, farmers be like that in Cornwall," Mark agreed, his burr contrasting with Dietmar's Flemish accent. Mark was curious. "How old be this Earl of Albany, for I have heard he is past his allotted three score years and ten?"

"Aye that he is, and guards his age well. He is at least of seventy years and three, I believe. Yet what he lacks in physic he stores in his mind, for he is evil and rules all within his court with a rod of iron. So have a care and trust no one," Dietmar warned.

Jamie smiled at the discourse. He would not trust the Scots either, but then he reasoned that there were few that he would trust these days. Times had given him a deep distrust of his fellow man and their motives. From the court to the French turning on themselves and the rebellions and revolts against the English King, to the Italians and how they fought with Papal backing to assassinate rivals, little of man's treachery surprised him in this world.

They made the end of the long winding road that led to the outer gate of the castle at last, and passed through to the Outer Ward through Portcullis Gate to the Middle Ward, where Jamie looked up with a soldier's eye, seeing the ramparts and curtain walling that linked all.

Finally, they entered the castle's heart, and set on a flat crag of rock lay the Inner Ward. Passing up the Long Steps, they found the forbidding David's Tower standing before them, linked by another stretch of curtain walling to the Constable's Tower that was but thirty years old, Sir Robert had told him. The harsh granite had barely begun to weather in that time, and still looked raw and jagged in the pale sunlight, silvered by frost and snow to a high sparkle, seeming to challenge anyone to try and assail it.

When he saw the magnitude of the fortifications, Jamie knew that there would be little chance of smuggling the counterfeit king out alive and he prayed that the pretender was just that – a false usurper with no credibility or claim to the crown. Could he flee from here alive after killing a king? He mentally shrugged. It could be done, but not by retreat through the castle. There were too many barriers and sheer faces of rock to overcome. He shivered at the prospect and wished Cristoforo were here, for he would find a way, he felt sure.

Jamie estimated the height of the tower to be some hundred feet. To the west was an open gallery through which steps led down to a long building with a pitched roof that he could only assume was the Main Hall. If the pretender was here, he would no doubt be housed in the tower.

The mules were unpacked, and they were escorted up to what Jamie surmised was the Main Hall. He paused before entering the smoky atmosphere, for out here on a crisp morning with the air clear and bright, he could see for miles across the beautiful Scottish land, rich with winter colours of purple and sage. It was a magnificent view, and one he would not forget in a hurry.

Mark came up behind him and aired his thoughts. "Why, 'tis one of the most beautiful scapes I have ever seen, different to Cornwall or Italy, but with its own rugged beauty." He sighed, enthralled at the stunning panoply of land, people and water before him.

They were hurried inside and found that despite the high roof, the air was filled with smoke from fires that burned at regular intervals in iron braziers. Scottish nobles and ladies walked about the hall, intermingling and gossiping, aided by servants who brought food and wine at their behest. Jamie spied a group of friars to one side of the raised dais at the end of the hall, and guessed that they would be the friars from Paris with whom he must make contact. Harpists were playing lilting music and the court was a dance of colour. Bright reds, russets and greens fought battles with the tartans of the clans.

Many of the ladies wore sashes over their gowns and houppelandes, the sarsenet linings extending a little way from long open sleeves to clash with the colours of the plaid. The crespins here, as in France, whose fashions they copied, were closer to that court than to England, and were teased into long horns and draped with netting, silk and jewels. It was an elegant scene and a rich tapestry of shade and colour. Some older matrons wore draped turbans in their tartan against the cold.

All turned as Herr Dietmar was announced and walked

forward with aplomb, knowing that he had a captive audience.

Jamie came forward with Mark, both carrying bundles of cloth, Jamie with his load upon his shoulder, hiding his face as best he could. On the journey north he had grown a beard, thick now and roughly trimmed, aiding his change in appearance. He knew not what enemies might be lurking, and did not wish to be recognised.

They made obeisance before the aged Earl of Albany, who looked frail yet still commanded all before him, fierce in his dotage. His once dark locks and beard were now grey and wispy, but the dark eyes were ever alert and strong, glimmering with a malign intelligence. Those eyes missed nothing.

To his side stood the Provost Marshall of Edinburgh, George de Lawedre, himself a man in his dotage, of some sixty years Jamie surmised. He beckoned Dietmar forward to where two tables had been cleared, and the ladies began to crowd around. The bait had been set and with this, Jamie slipped sideways to allow Dietmar, Mark and his remaining servant to orchestrate the unwrapping and displaying of the cloth.

He caught the eye of the leading friar of the Order of Notre Dame and addressed him quietly. In the mele of voices and crowds around the cloth laid out for inspection, the men held back, leaving wives and the unwed ladies to inspect the goods.

Mark stood back once the cloth was arranged and was noticed by one of the lairds.

"Yon's a fine figure of a man, Archie." He pointed to Mark, nudging Archibald, 4th Earl of Douglas.

"Aye, I wonder if he'll wrestle, for we've a champion wi'us to better any man here, I'm bound. If we could gain the bet to lure Dunbar and take his merks, it would please me well. Tis a shame that my son be not here yet, for he too loves to wrestle." Douglas showed his teeth, looking to his old enemy George Dunbar, the 10th Earl of March, who had recently been accepted back into the ranks of the Scots after siding with King Henry. They were bitter rivals, and March had defeated Douglas on a number of occasions and was now becoming more powerful and a bigger thorn in his side where the politics of the Scottish court were concerned.

"Mayhap we can trade his pride for the contents of his purse," the laird, Turnbull offered. "I'll see if I cannae stir the pot. But let us first see if yon man's game or no."

With that he moved forward to draw beside Mark and engage him in conversation. After an amicable start he ventured further. "So, from Cornwall are ye? They say that they have bonny wrestlers from that land. Would ye be one, by your build?"

Mark sensed a trap of sorts, but he was willing to take whatever bait was cast. He would not shirk from any challenge in that regard and would be happy to pit his skill against all and any. "Aye, that we do, an' I likes to wrestle when I gets the chance," he answered disingenuously, giving nothing away, smiling genially as he played the role of country bumpkin.

"Then 'tis fortunate, for we have our man here and both the duke and mayhap a visitor of the blood royal who would like the entertainment, I'm bound. If ye're no afeart, o'course. What say ye?"

"I be game enough. We leave in two days' time, so mayhap on the morrow?" Mark countered.

"We have a bargain, Cornishman. I will bring our man to wrestle with you afore supper on the morrow's eve."

Chapter Nine

"What did you learn, Jamie? Were the friars as set against the pretender as we have been led to believe?" Mark asked, once they were safely back at the inn for the evening.

"They would seem so to be – yet we have hit good fortune, for the pretender who normally resides at Stirling Castle away from all, is to be brought before an audience of the friars here at Edinburgh. Of greater import is that he, the false Richard, lives by virtue of a stipend provided by the royal court and approved by the Council of Scotland. If this be true, why it brings credence to his claim. For why should they do this if he be false? 'Tis much to offer in the name of subterfuge alone," Jamie said thoughtfully.

"Aye, 'tis true, and there is more, for this royal visit, whatever it may be, is to offer all manner of entertainments, including wrestling. I have been invited to attend, as I understand that the pretender is most partial."

"What? How came you by this?"

Mark explained all, telling Jamie of the proposition by the Lord Turnbull and of the king's visit.

Jamie listened attentively, frowning as he did so. "This bodes well to pair with the friars' story. Yet it worries me still, though it may offer me the chance to speak with or attend some form of private audience with the pretender Richard, which is what the friar will try to achieve. It could do well to aid our cause, Mark, yet have a care. I know your skill, but the rules here are lax at best and absent at worst. They are beasts with little respect for how they may win, and will do so at any cost. I have seen damage done from such matches abroad that would put to shent a bloody field of battle," he averred.

Mark put a giant hand upon his friend's shoulder. "Be not afeared, Jamie. I have had my share of brawls and know which way be up in such matters."

"Aye, maybe, but I feel that there is more at stake, especially with the false Richard here to witness all – and on one of the rare occasions that he is at liberty to meet with those outside the court. Now, with this new intelligence, I must seek out Herr Dietmar and make new plans. For mayhap needs must we shall make a swift departure from these shores, and I would know the time of the tide on the morrow and thereafter."

With that, Jamie left Mark to order supper and made his way the short distance to the warehouse where the cloth was being stored. He knew that he would find the Flemish merchant there taking inventory of orders and preparing his stock for his return to the castle.

Working by shielded lamps, Jamie found the merchant was indeed sorting the goods.

"Ah, Sir James. Is all well, for you look perplexed?"

"I have much news to impart and would ask your forbearance."

"Prithee, set to and tell me all," Dietmar responded affably.

Jamie told his new ally all that he and Mark had discovered, both of the plans to move the pretender for interrogation by the friars and of the planned wrestling match. At this last, and on hearing Jamie's intention to find and interrogate the pretender, which he had not been party to before, Dietmar became agitated.

"But what if you are caught or disclosed? What of me and my trade? I will be seen as a co-conspirator. Should I be caught up in this coil, my ability to return and trade will be forfeit, if not my life!"

Jamie's voice hardened: "You knew full well what you were to be embroiled in when you took the prince's silver. You did not then bark or balk at this venture, and rightly accepted your wages of loyalty to the English crown. Well, now the payment is due in kind, and you will serve me well or trade with Scotland will be the least of your worries.

"And I forewarn you, should aught be said of this to the provost marshal or others and I am undone, there are those who will hunt you down and avenge me if I am betrayed." Jamie snarled, moving closer until both men were face to face.

Dietmar looked frightened and sought assistance from his burly servant, who made to intervene.

Jamie span, his dagger drawn in the close confines of the aisle to face the startled servant, who was surprised at the transformation of the man with whom he had travelled. Gone was the cheerful countenance of the traveller aboard ship. Before him was a killer, a man he saw who had killed before and would do so again without compunction.

"Scullion, I will kill you as soon as I would kill any who crosses me and the crown. So better now than later with you at my back to slide your dagger so. What say you, friend of foe?"

"Friend, sir, friend," the servant stuttered, putting up his hands in submission. Yet there was something in his eyes that Jamie did not like. The tendering was too easily won.

Jamie turned carefully back to Dietmar. "Mark him well, Herr Dietmar, for any transgression on his behalf will be visited upon you tenfold, do you understand?" Dietmar nodded, a sheen of sweat upon his forehead despite the cold. "'Tis well. Then I needs must tell you what I have planned."

Jamie left after a few minutes, watching his back well as he made his way to the tavern where they stayed. As he entered the room, he found Mark was ready with a sword in his hand, alert at the feeling of being in enemy territory.

"'Tis well that you are so prepared, for just now I was nearly set upon by Dietmar's servant." Jamie nodded.

"'T'would appear that we have no safe haven, and all whom we can rely upon are ourselves," Mark contended.

"Aye, 'twas ever thus upon a fiat from Whittington," Jamie offered, at which the two grinned, brothers in arms against adversity as ever. "Come, for I would call you blanchemain, and no other save Cristo would take that role, and he, nowhere to be found when needed." They laughed at the old refrain, and Jamie relayed all that had occurred.

"Tell me, how will you know for certes that this man be or not be the true king? Have you seen him close to?"

"Aye that I have, and not so many years back that I would not remember him. For many times he paraded in London, on horseback and I waved a hand more than once as he rode by, at no greater distance than you are to me now. His looks are distinctive. There is another matter particular to him in especial. He is very pious and would pray deeply, unlike the Prince Hal whom he knighted – whose gods are Venus and Mars it would seem, for all his courtly ways. They say this pretender is none of these things and is more jape-worthy than cleric. By this shall he be known, they say, so we shall see upon the morrow."

"So be it. Now let us to supper, for I fear that I do fade away with lack of nourishment," Mark complained, patting his stomach.

Jamie laughed, and the two men left in search of their repast.

Chapter Ten

It was late the following day when Jamie and Mark rose. They were not due at the castle until the mid-afternoon, so they spent the morning with Mark practising rolls, locks and throws, using Jamie as his partner.

When he learned that Mark was to wrestle that day, the landlord offered the services of his barrelman to aid him in his practice. He was a strong young fellow with sloping shoulders rounded with muscle from his trade, and he had often competed in local wrestling matches. Some of the techniques he employed were strange to Mark and would be called illegal in true Cornish wrestling, and he was grateful for the advice he received from the man.

"I know of what you speak, master Mark, yet here if ye go to the floor to throw your man, 'tis allowed if 'e be in control. Dinnae let 'im cross you." He demonstrated. "For if he gets his thumbs in your eyes, ye'll ne'er get back to beat him and ye'll never see proper again. I'm thinking it'll be the Laird Douglas' man, and a right bastard he is, too. He's blinded more than one man using his thumbs, so have a care."

Mark raised an eyebrow and took it all on board, aware that this could be one of the hardest bouts of his life, with little to recommend it save as a distraction for Jamie's endeavours.

They found themselves once again at the castle by late afternoon, this time with all the cloth loaded and transported. In one bundle of rougher yarn, lay Jamie's sword, secreted in the middle, for no long weapons were allowed within the court save those carried by guards and men-at-arms approved by the duke or the provost marshal. Mark carried his quarterstaff, and this was dismissed as being of little consequence by the guards, who little realised that he was more lethal with the wooden stave than with a sword.

They entered and set out their goods for the Flemish merchant as before, with Jamie keeping a wary eye upon Dietmar's belligerent servant in case he sought to betray him. Business was brisk and most of the cloth soon disappeared, with two bolts remaining – one containing Jamie's weapon, which had been deliberately held back against any possible sale for the weave.

Looking up at the raised dais, Jamie saw a figure seated at the Duke of Albany's side. He was flanked by two knights in full harness, their armour shining in the light of the candles and torches in what seemed an unnecessarily ostentatious display. The figure was mounted upon a carved chair, almost a throne, that matched the duke's own. He would, to Jamie's estimate, be of a similar age to the dead king Richard, who now would be in his fifth decade. The face was lined and framed by reddish hair fading to grey at the temples, and by his size, he would match the king's frame. Yet to Jamie's eyes he lacked the piety, depth of purpose and stern demeanour born of kingship by a man who is born and cast to rule. He quickly decided that the man was not regal. There was something almost intangible about him, difficult to define, but by that very contrast it seemed lacking here, and even at this distance Jamie could see that the man was an impostor.

As though at an unseen signal, the waves of courtiers and ladies moved away. Tables were cleared and a space was made in an open shape. Rough horsehair mats were brought forward to make a gladiatorial rectangle. It would still hurt if you were thrown hard upon them, Mark surmised, and watched carefully as the herald called the first bout.

Both wrestlers were clad in tartan plaid and rough leggings. They were, to Mark's eyes, much flimsier than the strong canvas he was used to wearing, and would not stand the full strain of pulling and tugging. The match began, and soon became a brutal bout, with one man thrown by the arm that dislocated at the shoulder to a popping sound that echoed around the hall. To his trained eye it was a nasty, deliberate move that was designed to incapacitate the man, and it gave Mark warning of what to expect.

The next bout was faster and more skilful, with two lithe fighters who kicked with the flats of their feet against shins, seeking to unbalance each other. Both men were good fighters, seeking balance and opportunity in a flash of speed. Then the taller of the two, swept with his left foot, catching the forward motion of his opponent and tugging at the same time. The man's knee twisted and he fell awkwardly, yet still tried to grab the legs of the opponent to fell him. It was a futile move, and the bout was declared in the taller wrestler's favour by the stickler of the match.

A chorus of cheers erupted from the royal dais, the supposed king calling in joy upon seeing the outcome, clapping his hands and almost jumping from his seat.

Jamie looked up in surprise, taken unawares. Surely these were not the actions of a king? A lull followed, and in that quiet moment Mark and Jamie felt a movement as a man appeared at their side, dressed in the clan tartan of March.

"Good evenin' to you, sirs," the man began. "I am the factor of my lord the Earl of March, who stands yonder. Our belief is that Mark of Cornwall will fight the champion of the cur Douglas, be that so?"

"I know not of any champion," Mark responded genially. "I was asked to wrestle their man for sport, and this I agreed to do."

The factor snorted in disgust. "As I thought. Yet there is money wagered upon the bout, aye, and more besides, for reputation and pride are the contenders here as much as merks. So beware, for the man will fight you to the death. He is dirty in his tricks, and watch your eyes when he goes for the grapple, d'ye ken?"

This was the second time Mark had been warned, and he nodded his appreciation. "I shall mind that, and I thank ye for it."

"You would be well to. Are you any good, man?" the factor asked candidly.

In his modesty, Mark was unsure of how to respond to such a direct question, so Jamie answered for him.

"He is the best I've seen," Jamie said.

"Very well, sir. I shall have a wee flutter upon your man." At this he left, merging with the expectant crowds as they waited for the final bout.

"Good luck to you, Mark, and watch and 'ware all that was advised. I've not seen this champion yet, but all I've heard bears out what you've been told."

"Do not worry. Look after your affairs and get back safely. I shall bustle master Dietmar down to the boat once I am done and ensure that we wait for you upon the tide. Fear not."

"Aye, I shall," Jamie assured him – and then stopped dead. For across the hall by the side of the Earl of Douglas was his son, Earl Wigton, whom Jamie had defeated and sold back for ransom to his father. He paled and turned his back upon the crowd. "Mark," he hissed, "by God's legs Wigton is here! Did he see you well upon the field at Cotentin?"

"Nary so, for I fought his fellow knights and killed them both. I barely saw him and was helmed at the time when you settled him for ransom."

"Then all is well, yet have a care. I shall watch your bout from the far end where the monks will meet with me and guide me after the feast. From there they will escort the usurper to the chapel for his reluctant prayers, I'm told. I shall beard him in his lair, and all will be confirmed." With that he squeezed Mark's arm and wished him a final good luck before hoisting the bolt of cloth that contained his sword upon his shoulder and moving off around the periphery of the court, heading for the western end of the hall, to the exit and steps that led to David's

Tower and the private royal quarters that included the chapel.

A friar awaited him there. Yet Jamie hesitated. He wanted to see how his friend fared. He had wanted to be there to help and encourage him, but it was not to be, for if he were recognised by Wigton, all would be lost.

Mark now moved forward, having first spoken with a reluctant Dietmar, who beckoned his servant to aid Mark. Cheering came from Earl Douglas' side of the matting and their man appeared. He was as tall as Mark, and wore a sleeveless jerkin made of thick plaid cloth that hung loosely upon his huge frame, which had already begun to thicken around his ample middle. His bare arms were covered with dark matted hair that disappeared over his massive sloping shoulders.

The face was round and brutish, with slanted eyes that hinted at malevolence set between a nose that had been broken many times. The high widow's peak in the man's long dark hair was accentuated by the rough ponytail bound by a leather thong. The jawline was long, and the man's chin was pronounced. There would be no give here, Mark noted. He was there to win at any cost, with no thought of what damage he may do to his opponent and with little sanctity for the rules, such as they may be in this dark and God-forsaken country.

Mark came forward and pulled off his boots to gain better footing. He slipped off his gambeson and linen shirt and pulled on a borrowed plaid jacket. The dark eyes watched him grudgingly, arms swaying with his gait. Then Mark noticed his hands, on which each thumb had a thick, dirty nail that had been filed to a sharpened point. They would be as lethal as the tips of daggers to his eyes. A strategy formed in Mark's head, and he knew how he must fight this man. For he was assured that it would be a fight, not a bout, whatever rules may be proposed by the stickler.

The two protagonists came forward onto the matting and nodded at each in mutual recognition, neither taking his eyes off his opponent.

The Laird of Douglas' man, Dougal by name, was aware that he faced an opponent worthy of his status as champion of his clan. Yet he was confident. This was his home territory, and he knew what fierce and terrible damage he could wreak upon his opponents.

The stickler called out: "Come cleanly with no clenched fists or kicks, do ye understand?"

Both men nodded. If those were the rules here, so be it, thought Mark. An alehouse ruckus by any other name.

The stickler called: "Wrestle!" and the bout began.

Both men rolled their shoulders in reflex action, feet apart to take their balance, each sizing the other up. Rarely had Dougal faced another of his height, yet while he was thickened of waist, Mark tapered to a slimmed middle, honed by exercise and contestant training with men at court and with arms of war.

Dougal sought to close the distance, slapping his feet hard on the matting as he did so, assured of his footing. He reached up quickly, seeking to grab Mark's plaid, and in doing so caught his cheek with a lethal thumb nail. The move seemed accidental, but as it struck home, Mark knew it had been deliberate. The slice into the cheek drew blood instantly, like a cut with a fine blade.

The crowd howled at the sight. As Mark hesitated, the brute was on him in an instant, closing the distance and locking two massive arms around his waist, lifting, grunting in effort as he sought to raise Mark off the floor for a throw.

His weight surprised the Scot. Mark's solid mass was greater than he thought, and in his surprise, Dougal stopped for a split second, and Mark brought his forehead down upon the bridge of his nose. A brutal animalistic cry came from the man, and his grip slackened enough for Mark to break the hold, blood dripping from his cut cheek. He was astounded at the strength he'd found in his opponent. The crowd of courtiers brayed encouragement, completely undeterred by the blood or by Mark's apparent foul in using the headbutt.

Dougal shook the blow off, relentless now and angry after the strike. Mark stepped back, encouraging him on, and each time he reached to grab the hands with the lethal thumbs, he slapped them with stinging energy.

Mark moved freely, taking his advantage, and each time a hand moved to grab him he swatted it away with a ringing slap, allowing no hold. This annoyed the crowd, who wanted a grapple, and they began to boo and hiss at Mark. But Mark wanted none of it, and continued to keep his man at bay. Then, seemingly by accident as Dougal forced an almost straight arm forward in an open-palmed slap of his own, Mark allowed it to penetrate his defences.

Dougal grinned – but not for long. Keeping his left arm down, Mark deflected the force of the blow, forcing his right arm over and under his opponent's, jerking up against his elbow joint in a standing arm lock. The arm popped, just short of breaking the joint, the tendons ripped and torn by the unnatural tension upon the joint. Dougal howled in pain and swung across with his left elbow into Mark's jaw.

Mark had enough time to half block the attack and step back. Dougal's elbow connected, but some of the force was absorbed by Mark's his right hand, although the blow still shook him, landing as it did with all Dougal's weight behind it. Both men stepped back, breathing heavily, wary now.

Dougal circled, shaking his arm in pain. The joint would be swelling and solidifying, Mark knew, as the tendons contracted and stiffened against the abuse. On any other man he would have snapped the arm and ended the contest then and there, but such was the brute strength of his opponent that he withstood the assault and continued, albeit weakened. Encouraged by Mark's lack of aggression, he moved to attack once more, seeking targets for his thumbs, disguising his grabs as holds as Mark's face bled down his cheek and onto his tunic.

Each time Mark moved he used his better agility, slapping Dougal's hands away or pulling his tunic back with his arms as he retreated. The court booed, and there were cries of "Fight man, fight! Dinnae run away."

Dougal grew angry, which was exactly what Mark wanted, and with increasing speed and assurance he stepped forward once, twice, each time quicker and less controlled in his movements.

Mark stepped forward at last, sweeping Dougal's leg as

he did so and catching the outflung arm which Dougal threw out in instinct to regain his balance or break his fall.

Mark kept hold of the forearm and twisted the already injured limb, wrenching the tendons and straining the muscles further. Stiffening at the unnatural pain and angle, Dougal wrenched his shoulder as he fell to the mat, dislocating it with an awful popping sound. He lay panting for a moment, his face creased in agony, then he pushed himself upright, cupping the damaged arm with his left hand at the elbow.

Mark stood ready and expectant, for he had seen others get up and continue in brawls, but never in a formal bout.

Dougal's face snarled in fury. "I'll blind you! You think I'm finished? I'll show ye..."

There were cries of alarm from the crowd, and calls for Dougal to yield, but Dougal ignored them, standing in his pain, swaying a little and straightening his arm to let it hang by his side.

"Don't be a fool, man. You be done," Mark called to him.

"Never!" The Scot surged forward and dropped despite the pain in his shoulder, trying to encircle Mark's legs and bring him down.

Mark knew that he could give no quarter and jumped up, avoiding his opponent's arms, and landed hard upon Dougal's good hand. Dropping to his knees, he smashed his forearm straight into Dougal's jaw, breaking it with the force of the blow. The man's eyes rolled in pain as he fell back unconscious.

The crowd was silent, then cheers rose from the Earl of

March's coterie. Black looks were cast from the Douglas clan as the stickler appealed to the Duke of Albany, who nodded his assent. At this, the stickler held up Mark's hand, signalling victory to the Cornishman. Mark smiled and dabbed the flow of blood that had continued to flow from the wound to his cheek.

Mark saw the Earl of March's factor approach: "'Twas well done, laddie. You'll take a wee dram with the earl now, for we've defeated Douglas again, so we have."

Chapter Eleven

As Mark was ushered into the jubilant circle of the March Clan, Jamie slipped out of the hall. He was relieved to see that his friend had emerged relatively unscathed from the encounter as he followed the friar across the stone walkway to the main door leading into David's Tower. With the cleric as his escort, the guard who admitted him barely gave him a second glance, so well did he fit with the circumstances there within the castle.

The door opened out onto an entrance hall, where servants bustled in and out of the rooms off the main staircase that divided the tower vertically, with a smaller winding stair off to the right.

The friar turned to Jamie: "These stairs offer access to each of the five upper levels and thence to the roof and battlements. On the third level, the chapel is to the right. I will guide you there, where you will await the arrival of the supposed King Richard. Our canon, with whom you spoke yesterday, accompanies him to the chapel, hears his confession within, then leaves him to his prayers – where we all know that naught is done in our Lord's name, and he merely sits drinking the wine of the sacrament until a suitable time to leave is found. That is the moment you will find it most propitious to interrogate him as to his bona fides."

"What of his guards? How many accompany him here?" Jamie asked, as they ascended the staircase to the chapel.

"There is usually a squire, a page and mayhap two men-at-arms."

"How are they armed? Are they in full harness?" Jamie needed to know the full facts, as it would impact upon how he dealt with the defences that would be raised against him.

The friar considered for a moment, not having given thought to such matters before. "Let me see, the men-at-arms are as you might imagine, with sword and helm, and with long arms similar to a spear. The squire or knight is fully armoured, I believe, as he is one of those who attend the usurper now at supper."

Jamie cursed. "By the rood, four men to take down and a king to silence without fear of garboil alerting all within? Why, 'tis a task in itself." He shook his head in disgust. "Where may I hide as I await the pretender?"

"Here." At this, the friar pulled back an arras to reveal a deep alcove with some shelves holding sacred objects. Set upon the floor was a high backed stool.

Jamie nodded agreement, and pulling his scabbarded sword free from the bolt of cloth, he belted it in place, feeling all the better for it. "Is there any rope here? A bell rope mayhap?" Jamie queried.

"Yes, why for certes, I am here able to assist to you. I shall return, fear not."

"Do not daddle, Father, for I would be prepared ere long. The odds here are against my purpose and all that I might arm myself with shall greatly aid my position."

The friar bustled out, and Jamie opened the small stained glass window and looked out over the scene to the east of the castle. There below were ramparts of the curtain walling, and to his surprise a small postern gate that would just accommodate a horse leading to a ramp that gave access to the castle via a cantilevered wooden drawbridge. This bridge, from what he could see, spanned a deep natural ravine, giving access to crofts and other buildings constructed upon a ridge of rock outside the city walls. It would, he assumed, be an overflow from the walled town, and in times of need, the crofters could run to the castle for shelter against any attacking army. But how could he obtain access to this means of escape? he mused, for the small opening afforded by the window of the chapel would not be large enough for him to squeeze through.

He looked again, and in the glow offered by torches, he saw guards parade to and fro along the ramparts in the fading light. They appeared bored and expected little trouble. So be it, for if he could gain legitimate access to the ramparts from the tower, he would look as if there was true purpose to his journey and they would let him out. It was his only hope for a swift exit from the castle.

The friar returned, carrying a length of rope that was striped and ribbed with colour. "Please ask me no questions of its provenance," he pleaded, crossing himself, "and may God forgive me in this work."

"Amen to that, Father. Now I shall secrete myself behind this arras and await the entrance of the pretender," Jamie said.

Two hours later, he had grown bored and had long since given up sitting on the stool. He had practised different moves and cuts with his sword. Eventually he heard footsteps upon the stone outside the chapel along with the sound of faint voices. Retreating behind the tapestry, he waited his chance.

The English accent of the pretender echoed around the small chapel. "You may leave, Sir Hector, for we shall abide here with the canon and our page."

"As you wish, sire, I shall be without the door should you have need of me," the knight offered, as Jamie looked through a small hole he had opened in the tapestry, through which he could spy upon the proceedings within the chapel. He was relieved to see only the remaining knight, the page and the priest, no other men-at-arms. The knight moved out with a clanking of armour, leaving just the canon, page and the pretender Richard as he shut the chapel door behind him. Jamie breathed a sigh of relief.

The monotony of the prayers floated to him, and then the tone changed: "Sire, my lord king. I beg you now that your confession be heard. Before God, is there any weight upon your soul that you would wish to dispense? Perhaps pertaining to your right as heir to the English throne?"

Jamie held his breath; would he now hear all and a

confession to the knavery that had been played upon them by the Scots? It was not to be.

"How dare you address us so? We are of the blood royal, and no ecclesiastical debate shall be heard to disparage our position. This interview is at an end. Leave us, for we have no wish to partake of discourse upon such matters." The supposed king's voice rose as he spoke those last words.

The canon took a deep breath, clearly containing his temper. He bowed three times and left. "As Your Majesty pleases, by your leave," he said, with a subtle emphasis on the royal title.

The cleric was clearly incensed, yet could gain no further ground. He left the room and the knight on duty outside the door was briefly waved back by the pretender, giving him a short bow.

"Fetch us the communion wine," he told the page. "For we had it filled specially to fortify us in this tedious time afore we are allowed to return to the hall," the pretender ordered.

The page turned back to the altar. Jamie pushed back the heavy arras from the alcove that was hiding him, took two steps forward and brought the heavy stool down upon his head, dropping him unconscious to the floor with no knowledge of his attacker.

The pretender turned upon hearing the blow, and as he did so, Jamie span around, pressing the sword tip to his face less than an inch below the man's left eye. He raised a finger to his lips and hissed, "Silence, or your life is forfeit!"

The figure before him recoiled in horror. "You... you would kill a king?"

"You are no more king than I, coxcomb. You aver the questions of a friar, leaning upon your status like a cripple upon his staff. I serve good King Henry Fourth, and do not recognise any pretender. Now, call the knight without, and no intemperate thoughts of raising the alarm, for your life will be forfeit at the first bell. Come to the door with me." Jamie lowered his sword and pressed his dagger into the pretender's back. Behind the door, with the false Richard in front of him, Jamie commanded, "Tell him your page has taken ill and beckon him forth."

The pretender pulled open the door beckoning the knight into the chapel. "Roland, our page has taken ill, would you look to him for us?" the pretender spoke, his voice quivering.

When he saw the prostate figure, the knight strode in, still with no weapon drawn. "Yes, sire," he said.

Once within, Jamie brought the hilt of his sword down upon the pretender's head and he fell unconscious. With that, Jamie closed and bolted the door. At the noise and motion, the knight turned just as he was squatting to inspect the page.

"What treachery is this?" he called, standing and drawing his sword. "Why you were at the feast supporting the merchant. What do you do here, scullion?" At which he pulled down the visor of his bascinet helmet and moved forward to engage with Jamie.

Jamie did not respond, but struck instead, slashing with his sword to see how the man responded. He knew that a man in full harness was virtually invulnerable to a sword slash, and that the heavier impact of a mace or battle-axe would be needed to dent or damage the wearer's armour. The point here would be his friend, that and close quarters, as he had practised with Mark in anticipation of this encounter. Yet it was hard to avoid the instinctive reaction to a slashing sword and the knight raised his sword to parry the blow with excellent speed. *So,* Jamie thought *you are not just a token knight to serve as guard.* He was all the more wary for it, and he was ready.

Sir Hector's sword sliced forward, striking at Jamie's head. It was a full blow with complete commitment and force behind it. Jamie took the blade of his sword in his gauntleted hand, forming a cross with the weapon taking the full force two-handed, then in response drove the pommel end forward, sliding along the opposing knight's blade and smashing into Sir Hector's visor. The blow was hard, driving his head back with the impact of a mace. He retreated one step, unbalanced, withdrew his blade with speed and attempted to slash at Jamie's unprotected legs.

Pushing the pointed end downwards, Jamie barely had time to parry the attack. Again he smashed the pommel into his opponent's visor. It was the weakest part of the helm and the Scottish knight had not had time to pin it shut. This time the visor slipped up as the Scot fell back. Jamie smashed again from close quarters, seeing blood spurt from a mouthful of broken teeth as he made to wrap his arm around the armoured neck of his opponent and throw him. The move was in part successful. The hold pulled the Scot forward and Jamie braced his right leg to throw him. He went with his opponent's momentum, rolling beneath the weighted armour and rising to one knee.

With his helmet filling with blood and breathing heavily the Scot pushed back the visor in order to see, opening his face to attack.

Jamie gave him no quarter, he made as if to charge in recklessly to press home his advantage, but at the last moment he reversed his sword, stopped driving pommel first, changing to a full slash at the Scot's exposed face.

The knight parried the blow with ease and used the time to regain his feet. He, too, now held the sword in two hands, seeking power and the advantage of armour over his opponent. Jamie's sword point flicked out directly to the breast plate, and thinking himself invulnerable there the Scot allowed it, driving forward to assail his unarmoured opponent.

Jamie dropped both his stance and his hand, changing the angle as the tip of his sword slid up, forcing itself hard under the gorget and mail to pierce through to the skin beneath. It missed the throat but struck through under the collar bone, bringing a stinging pain to the Scot, who withdrew flinching at the wound. Jamie twisted the point, stepping past the guard and grappling again, throwing his opponent and pulling free his sword tip. Jamie stamped down upon the knight's sword arm, trapping it, and stabbed him full through his mouth, severing the neck behind and killing him instantly. He leant upon his sword for a second, breathing heavily and sucking in air, before retrieving his weapon and wiping it clean. He sheathed his blade and went to the pretender, who was groaning as consciousness returned to him.

Drawing his dagger, he knelt by the semi-conscious

figure. "Now, goky, who are you really? Answer me, for I'd as soon put an end to this janglery and have done with you." He snarled at the prostrate figure.

"I, we are King Richard Second of–"

Jamie placed the dagger to his lips. "No more lies, or you'll never lie again. Who be ye, and whence did you come?"

"Mercy," the man cried.

"'Tis odd that all who would plead for clemency would be the least to grant it. Talk!"

"I am Thomas Warde of Trumpington in Cambridgeshire. I was fleeing my land accused of foul murder and escaped to the isles. Here I was taken for my likeness to the old king and harnessed to that purpose for the benefit of the Scots, who provide for me thus."

"Now that is a more likely tale, and is as much as I thought. Then, Master Warde, you shall escape with your tongue and be bound, not killed – Your Majesty!" Jamie finished sarcastically.

With that he took the bell rope the friar had brought him and bound the man, gagging him with a strip of altar cloth. With Warde secured, he carefully opened the door and saw only servants hurrying forth. He slipped out and onto the small spiral staircase that the canon had indicated earlier, and finding himself at the side of the entrance hall, he moved to the side door. No one challenged him, for he was within the tower and his presence had already been established, but once outside he breathed deeply, knowing it would not be long before all was discovered. He moved to the left, crossing to the ramparts and assuming his Scottish persona, mimicking easily the accents of his mother's land.

"A bonny night, sirs, is it no?" He addressed the guards at the postern gate.

"Aye, 'tis that and not one to be naish, for it fair chills the bones up on here."

"Ye have the right of it. Can you open yon gate for I've a fiat upon which to attend without the walls. Himself has called upon me tae leave ma' bed and the comely wench within its sheets that was warming it for me."

"Aye, 'tis always the way when called by those who should know better," the man-at-arms agreed. He unbolted the postern gate and bade Jamie follow him to the cantilevered drawbridge that was at this moment hoisted high. It swung down with an easy motion.

"Thank ye, sir. I wish you a bonny night." Jamie strode off, losing himself in the darkness before he turned right to skirt the town and head downhill to the quayside below. It would be close to midnight, he estimated, and the tide would be turning in their favour now. It would not be long before the hue and cry came from the castle as the pretender was missed. As Jamie passed down to the quayside, he looked up to see that more torches on the high crag had been lit. Trumpets blared. They had found the pretender and his dead knight, he speculated.

He hurried on in the darkness, coming now beneath the pooled light of the brands that illuminated the jetty running out to the cog that thankfully still awaited him.

A giant figure appeared at the gangway and called. "Ho, Jamie, come. We must away while the tide still runs for us."

Mark's voice floated towards him. But at his call, four figures emerged from a tethered fishing skip that was slapping gently against the jetty, tugging at its moorings.

"Hold fast! I'm captain of the Watch and we believe you've violated our peace." The man-at-arms growled.

Three men fanned out around him, each with a spear, and mailed in the torchlight. Jamie was not about to submit, and drew his sword in readiness. They would have little time, he knew, before the whole town was raised against them. He heard footsteps from the ship as Mark ran down, his quarterstaff in his hand.

Two of the spear holders turned to face the new threat and Jamie launched his attack. He gave no time for the leader to prepare, lunging with his sword as the man's spear came to guard. Jamie allowed the parry, then twisted and grabbed the end of the blade. Releasing the hilt of his sword, he swung overhand driving hilt-downwards in what was known as the murder stroke. The cross-guard arced overhead and came down upon the unprotected skull of the watch captain, who dropped dead instantly, blood spurting from the fatal wound. The second man came forward, lunging with the spear tip, using the advantage of length.

Jamie swung down, his sword still held by the blade. He parried the spear thrust, and stepping under the defences of the guard, he drew his dagger with a left handed grip and plunged downward with the point underhand. He drove for the neck, where the mail shirt stopped, and with no mailed coif or helm to protect him, the man was vulnerable to a close quarter attack, and Jamie's point drove home with such brutal force that it ended hilt deep in his chest.

In the meantime, Mark faced the two other spearmen. He always felt easier with the staff, being opposite in terms of stance to the sword. He held the staff to his left in the upper guard with that leg forward, ready and balanced. Like most yeomen, he had trained all his life with the staff and was lethal in its use. He smashed into the spear thrust, allowing the end of the staff to drop into low guard, and as the second member of the Watch attacked into the opening, he drove the end straight, bringing his right hand to his left armpit. The tip went straight to the guard's sternum, shattering his ribcage through the mail with the concussive force of the blow. The man could neither breathe nor speak, and his mouth opened and closed with the agony of his broken ribs.

Mark did not pause, pivoting instead to face his second attacker, taking a step back out of range into rutter guard, the staff seemingly useless behind him, his body twisted at the waist. The spearman lunged in, relying on the deadly steel tip of his weapon, and Mark responded with speed, spinning at the waist as both arms brought the staff around to deflect the tip, throwing it off the all-important centre line. Taking a step as he moved, Mark was now inside the man's guard, but the spearman was good. Aware of the counter move, he pivoted to the left, keeping his distance to use the spear's length to its full advantage. Mark changed tactics, thrusting hard on the overhand line, footwork aiding his balance as he extended his arms to bring the end of his quarterstaff down upon the guard's head, dropping him senseless to the ground.

"T'was well done, Mark," Jamie said. "Come, let us away afore more guards are roused against us."

Mark nodded and they left the dead and dying to their fate, running for the cog that was even now straining against the flowing tide, held fast by just one tie line. As soon as they ran aboard, the stern line was released, and the strong current carried the cog into the larger body of the Forth Estuary. Here there was little wind, and they would have to tack to gain the full benefit of the south-easterly, but for now the master let the tide do the work for them. They were lighter with all the cargo sold, carrying just a few bales of raw wool that Dietmar deemed of sufficient quality for him to take back with him.

"From whence did those watchmen come?" Jamie asked. "For certes I thought we had made our way clear. There was no time to muster from the castle, surely."

"On that subject you shall mayhap be not surprised to learn that Alyten, Dietmar's servant, is not aboard and seems to have disappeared," Mark replied.

"The treacherous whoreson!" Jamie spat. "I knew his heart be faint and his manner serpentine."

"Well, he be long gone. Now tell me what occurred with the pretender? For your gambeson is slashed and you appear the worse for it."

"So, too, do you, for your face bleeds prodigiously and the wound was not taken in the melee here."

The two companions in arms then told each other their stories.

"So the man was a pretender? Damn his eyes," Mark opined. "Pray tell me, why didst you not kill him?"

"Had I done so, the Scots would have had a likelier story – that a man had come and killed the true king, a traitor to the Scottish crown working under orders from the south and from London. With the pretender alive, the Scots may stick with their story, and we can at some point capture the man alive."

"Amen to that." Mark nodded his understanding.

"I shall not cross Dietmar until we land, upon which we needs must bustle to Berwick, report there to my Lord John and hasten thence to London," Jamie decided. "Where my Lord Whittington shall no doubt welcome our news, as will all of the council."

Part Two
France

Chapter Twelve

19th March, London

Jamie and Mark returned to London, cold, tired and hungry. The bitter winter seemed unwilling to release its chilling tentacles and the cold northerly winds still blasted the land. It made adhering to Lent and the lack of meat harder than usual.

Forest had waited at Berwick for her master's return and had trotted happily at his side on the return journey home, seemingly immune to the winter weather, being in the prime of her life and happy to chase anything that could be brought down by her strong jaws and rapid turn of speed. Though even she had become thinner, she brought down a deer one day, and Mark and Jamie made a secret camp within a knotted forest off the road and roasted the illicit meat, eating their fill, grateful to the wolfhound for their supper.

Bidding Mark farewell on the way into the centre of London, Jamie left him to return to his wife Emma and a well-earned rest. He made his way to St Laurence Lane in

Jewry and his father's house to collect some belongings and change before he arrived at his new home in Fletestrete that his father-in-law had bought for the couple as a dowry upon their marriage. He had wanted to see his father, Thomas, and warn him of all that was happening in the Guilds and tell him to be wary of Lollard influences. He led his mount, Richard, to the stable, unsaddled him and rubbed him down, refusing all help from the groom before making his way into the place he had once called home.

"Jamie! You are returned to us hale and well. This is a happy event," his sister exclaimed. "How were the barbarous northern borders?"

"Jeanette, 'tis good to see you, my sister!" Jamie moved forward to embrace her. "And as to the north, it was as ever taxing, cold and treacherous," he answered, not wanting to be drawn upon the events north of the border until his father and John were present. "By God's legs, I need a bath to ease my aching limbs. Can hot water be fetched? for I've barely been warm for days, since setting forth from Berwick."

His sister wrinkled her nose at the smell of horse, dog and the sweat of travel. She knew better than to pry until her brother had settled, being as close to him as any other. She called a servant to fetch hot water and arrange a bath for him and then a small smile played across her lips. "Yet I have a salve for you that may bring warmth to your breast in another manner." She looked at him coyly.

"How so? Be Lady Alice here?" His voice rose in expectation.

"Nay, yet another is who is dear to you." She continued the game of tease.

"Oh, come now, sister, for I am tired and pebble-hearted towards all save good wine and a hot bath. Prithee fence not, for I wouldst know your intelligence," he snapped.

Jeanette noticed that his demeanour was the result of fatigue, so capitulated to his demand and enjoyed the moment. "Enjoy the tonic, for I am sure it shall revive you: Cristoforo is returned!"

"What? By the Good Lord, that is indeed most excellent news! When did he arrive, and with Alessandria, I hope? Why is he here?" Jamie asked, heartened at the thought of his friend's return as his questions flowed forth.

"He has so much to tell, and there is grave news to attend to as well as good. Take your bath, I shall have wine brought. When you are refreshed, attend me in the solar where it is warm and snug against the cold. There I shall reveal all – and fear not, for Cristo and Alessandria are hale." With that she waved him away in a sisterly manner that he knew not to gainsay, and he went to attend to his ablutions. A while later, refreshed, clean and changed, Jamie emerged to be given all the particulars of Cristoforo's return.

"May the Devil visit the Albizzi and take all who are associated with them. My heart goes out to Alessandria, for she was most dear in her father's embrace and would have suffered terribly to bear witness to such a heinous act. Yet it cheers my heart to think of the vengeance Cristo wrought, for he would brook no mercy in that regard and for certes, all will be settled."

"I have no particulars in that regard, yet I am sure that you have the right of it," Jeanette answered.

"Where do they lodge now that they are returned?"

"At her uncle's house in Langburnestrate, yet they are soon to take a new dwelling close by."

Jamie learned that his father was at a guild meeting and John was out exercising the horses, at which he promised to return on the morrow with Alice. Now he only had thoughts for his new bride. With his belongings brought by a servant, he made for the house on Le Straunde that had become so familiar to him. His father-in-law would still be settled in the north at his estates, and he prayed that his new wife would be safely returned to London, where they could steal some precious moments alone with her family elsewhere.

He went around to the rear stables, leaving Richard there, and with Forest following closely at his heels, he bade the servant take his belongings inside. At that point he saw Nesta, Alice's maid. *It bodes well*, he thought to himself.

She smiled as he entered the house: "My lord, you are returned. I shall inform my lady, who is within." She bobbed a curtsey and withdrew with a rustle of skirts to find her mistress.

Jamie dismissed his father's man, and a household servant appeared with wine and sweetmeats. After what seemed a lifetime, his new bride descended the stairs, looking radiant in a houppelande spun of turquoise tartaryn, her hair unbound, a cloak of pure gold that shone in the light, and clever kohl accentuating the beguiling cornflower of her eyes. It was more than he could stand, and as they found themselves alone with no servants present, he rushed forward to greet her in a warm embrace. Their lips met in hunger, at which upon her urging, he swept her upwards to the bed chambers above. Bidding Forest to stay, the hound responded with a mournful look that was almost human, as her master took his bride to the upper chambers.

Hours later they dressed and descended to the lower floors, where they showed decorum in the presence of the servants. With reluctance, Jamie told Lady Alice that he had to attend Sir Richard Whittington, but would return as soon as he was able. Leaving Richard to his well-earned rest, and being much closer to the palace than his father's house, he strode out on foot to attend the statesman.

Although pleased to see him safely returned, Jamie found Whittington in a pensive state of mind, with much seeming to occupy him.

"James, the court is as ever in your debt. The celerity of your actions and report will be used well by the Council and the king. The pretender is just that, by the rood. I shall make enquiries of the circumstances surrounding master Thomas Warde of Trumpington and see what he is about. For the danger is still present, like a serpent that continually raises its vile head. For with this circumstance that links the Scots to Lollardy, we are besieged on all sides.

"To wit there is more news that I must impart of a most dangerous occurrence. Your Italian companion, Cristoforo, has returned and been most complete in his report, aiding our cause greatly in this regard. Yet there is much that would undo us. The rumours that have reached me have been confirmed by a missive passed by Cristoforo directly from

France. This missive assures me that there is now an order to raise a revolt, by any other name and rise up against the Armagnacs, taking with them in this tide the king's power and all that may resist the Burgundian cause."

Jamie frowned in horror at the thought. "A truly united front against whom all of France would rally. That would be terrible, and even my Lord Prince Thomas and Beaufort combined should not be able to withstand such a unified force – and at such a juncture, for I hear that his majesty does fail and looks to his time on earth," Jamie finished nervously.

"Aye, that he does, and dangerous will be the void that shall be left. For if his majesty foresaw the problems that he would inherit with the crown, the new king will find more of a clandestine nature, cloaked now and only to be revealed when 'twill be too late. Thus we needs must be ever vigilant on his behalf and spring those traps ere they are baited.

"I fear I shall be calling upon you once again ere long, James, so be ready with your sword and your wits, for I foresee that both shall be needed," Whittington proposed. "So terrible that his majesty should be laid so low. This great king, who in his prime was considered armipotent in battle, was feared throughout Europe and fought all comers to gain the crown, prevailing against plots of assassination, revolts and rebellions. He defeated all, and now he needs must face the enemies none may defeat: his own body and the will of God."

"Amen," Jamie said. With a few final words of warning from Sir Richard, he left the palace to find that dusk had fallen. He made his way back to his new home in Le

Straunde and as he walked from the palace, he noticed that the church bells had just struck Vespers.

Passing the guards as he exited, Jamie moved on some distance, and as he did so he had the feeling that he was followed. There were eyes upon him, he was certain. He felt the old familiar prickling at the base of his neck, the sense that all was not as it seemed. Yet despite using all his ploys he could not detect any soul who stood out.

He strode deliberately past his new home and turned north as the great road split with Aldewichestrate and the great church of St Clement Danes that had been commissioned when the Danes were conquered and now held King Harold's tomb stood before him. He moved to the church, still with the feeling of being watched. Here, he reasoned, more would become apparent. He slipped inside through the great oaken doors, and as he did so he saw one of the side doors close off to the southern riverside. Two figures moved into the church, yet in the gloom he could not discern their appearance. The door behind him opened again to permit entrance to a new party, a merchant and his wife by their dress, attended by a servant.

A few of the pews were half filled with worshippers, yet to Jamie's eyes no one seemed to show any special interest in him, although the feeling of being followed had not left him. Whoever followed him had ventured somewhere into the church. He sat watching as the choir of monks entered with the high clergy leading. The pew behind him was empty, he noticed, looking around and trying to appear as unobtrusive in his movements as possible. He looked back towards the front of the church again, his senses screaming at him that something was amiss. Should he stay, he mused, or seek the streets again? As he considered what to do, the chanting started and in the muted torchlight a blade glinted as an arm snaked around his neck. He went to move but knew he would be too late.

"*Amico mio*, you picked the wrong place to sit," came a mocking whisper in an instantly recognisable accent.

Jamie turned quickly to find a lithe figure dressed all in black, all but lost against the gloom that surrounded him. "Cristo!" he said, expelling a sigh of relief.

"Shh," Cristoforo whispered, "for you are followed not just by me." White teeth showed in the dark features. Their brief outburst drew glares from other supplicants who were seeking to pray as the service progressed. "Come, let us leave for there is much to discuss," Cristo urged. "You proceed first to the south doorway, and I shall follow and see if we can snare our prize."

Jamie agreed without demur, trusting his friend implicitly. Once outside he waited for Cristoforo to emerge. A few moments later he did so, shaking his head in disgust.

"I know not where he went. For certes he appeared to be cowled as a monk. Yet all who appeared there were in the sacristy, or leaving for the parade to the altar. I am sorry, *amico*." Cristoforo shrugged.

Jamie moved forward embracing him. "By the good Lord Cristo, I care not, for you are returned and there is much news to impart. We shall be wary of such followers, yet the feeling of being watched has left me and we should find a tavern to slake our thirst on this cold eve – or mayhap we could return to my new home, where you will be made most welcome."

"A tavern first, I think, then I would dearly wish to see your new bride and persuade her that she has made a terrible mistake and should have run away with me in your stead."

The two companions made their way to the White Horse Tavern, their old haunt in days gone by.

"All that is missing is Marco. How does he?" Cristo asked, as they entered the familiar surroundings.

"Why, let us summon him." Jamie decided on a whim and called for one of the servants, bribing him with some coin and directing him to fetch Mark from his new house that he shared with Emma, which was not too far distant.

Within half an hour Mark pushed open the doors and stood with his bulk blocking the light, seeking his two companions. Finding them, he marched over and enveloped Cristoforo in a bear hug that squeezed the breath out of him. It was a happy reunion for all three men, but before they could begin to catch up on all that had happened, Cristoforo noticed the weeping sore upon his friend's cheek.

"What happened? Did Emma catch you with some doxy?" Cristoforo mocked.

"No, 'Twas a wrestling match in Edinburgh, which I won, yet came off the loser with this token to bear, for it festers and will not heal."

Cristoforo inspected the wound more closely, drawing Mark into the lamp light. "Fear not, *amico*, I shall cleanse and heal it for you after we have talked and supped some ale."

Cristoforo launched into his tale of all that had

happened, with Jamie and Mark sad and amazed at how far the reach of the *Parte Guelfa* stretched.

"And Alessandria, she recovers and flourishes despite all?" Jamie asked.

"She does," Cristoforo answered. "There are black days, yet she consoles herself with the knowledge that those who caused the villainy lie cold in their graves." At which he smiled wolfishly with no hint of remorse at the killings that he had undertaken in the name of revenge.

"Amen to that," Mark opined. He remembered the count and all that he had stood for with respect and affection. As they supped their drinks and called for more, they caught up with each other's stories.

"So 'twas you brought the tidings to Whittington," Jamie said. "Upon which he has news that compounds that which you provided. It bodes not well and may be our undoing, for the old king lingers on in life, may the Lord God bless him. Yet the new king shall need to move with utmost celerity if he is to master this realm and prepare for the adversity that looms ahead. He appears divided on three fronts and another from within as Lollardy threatens."

"Is there much news in that regard?" Cristoforo asked.

"No," Jamie declared, "other than his majesty's death is imminent, and meanwhile all is paralysis where no laws or government are heard, and disparate groups of vultures wait to swoop upon the new prey."

Cristoforo considered all that he had heard, liking none of it. He seemed to have left one corrupt and uncertain realm for another.

"Now come, for we shall sup together this evening.

Prevail upon your wives to attend us at Le Straunde and there for a few hours we shall forget all that is abroad and celebrate being reunited once again in fellowship," Jamie offered. "For when matters are in such a state of change we shall stay constant in our companionship, and it pleases me to call you both blanchemain." At which they broke up, promising to return later for supper at Jamie's home.

Chapter Thirteen

20th March, Westminster Palace

The king woke that morning and demanded to be taken to the shrine of Edward the Confessor. This, Arundel knew, was of particular significance to him, as he had been both exiled and crowned on the feast day of the saint.

Two braziers were lit in the small chapel to ward off the chill.

"Leave me now to speak with my God," the king commanded the two servants, who had helped him to his knees before the shrine.

Two hours later his chamberlain arrived at the guarded door.

"How does His Majesty?" he demanded of the sergeant at arms.

"I know not, my lord de Vere."

"Open up, man, let me pass." Sir Richard de Vere strode into the chamber to see his king lying seemingly lifeless upon the steps of the altar. "Fetch a physician immediately. Hurry!" he cried to the guard.

Two hours later, the recumbent figure, who had been laid upon a cot, showed his return to life by the flicker of his eyes. He looked around the large chamber, seeing the blazing fire offering warmth to his dying body as the cot upon which he lay was placed before it. His eyes turned to the arched trusses above him and then to the stained glass window at the far end of the room. His eyes focused upon the chamberlain's face. A sigh emerged from his lips and his voice quavered as he asked: "Where are we?"

"Majesty, e'er it please you, thou art within the abbot's lodgings, in the Jerusalem Chamber."

The words struck home. Even in his pain, a small smile etched itself upon the king's lips. "Praise be to the Father of Heaven," he uttered, "for now we shall die in this chamber, according to the prophecy told of us, that we should die in Jerusalem."

His surgeon bustled in followed by Prince Henry, who had come to be at his father's side. With him was Henry's confessor, John Tille, and also a royal chaplain, Thomas Elmham, who was close to the king. Whispering prayers, his wife Queen Joan entered the chamber with Prince Humphrey and wept to see her husband so wracked with pain. She knelt by his side and clasped his hand, her tears falling upon their entwined fingers.

Archbishop Arundel enjoined the Bishops of Durham and York to offer prayers, along with Sir John Pelham, Sir Robert Waterton and Sir John Leventhorpe, Lancastrian knights who were present as they had been faithful to the king throughout his life.

The king enjoined Prince Henry to come closer. "My son, we have had discourse and dissention 'tween us, yet at this juncture we exhort you to respect and love your brother Thomas most especial, as you are both of so great stomach and courage."

"My father, Majesty, we would love and honour our brothers above all men so long as they remain true to us. Yet should they conspire or rebel against us, we assure you that we shall as soon execute justice upon any one of them as upon the worst and simplest person within your realm."

"My son, that is most equitable, and we are marvellously rejoiced of mind to hear this. Consider, my son, and behold thy father who once was strenuous in arms, but now is adorned only with bones and nerves. Our bodily strength is gone, but by the grace of God, a spiritual strength has come to us which even in our sickness that shall prove fatal renders our soul braver and more devoted than before. My son, pay faithfully your father's debts, that you may enjoy the blessing of the Most High, and may the God of our fathers, the God of Abraham, Isaac and Jacob, give thee his blessing, laden with all good things, that so may you live blessed for ever and ever, amen."

With these words the king gasped and strove for breath before uttering his final words to all present: "Now I hope to see God in the land of the living under His most gentle mercy. I await my death."

At these words Henry Fourth, King of England, sighed for one last time and gave up his life.

All around breathed deeply and wept at the sight of such a monumental moment in history being cast before them as their monarch, once one of the greatest knights in Europe, passed away just short of his forty-sixth birthday. They realised that a new era had begun – one in which the House of Lancaster would rise to hitherto unknown heights.

Two days later, Whittington summoned Jamie to his house rather than to the palace so that he would remain unobserved. "Now we are at our most vulnerable," he said. "For the heir apparent is as yet uncrowned and without true rights of anointment. We must be vigilant, for even as the king lay dying, a scullion whoreson named Richard Whytlock breached the abbey, claiming sanctuary and crying out that King Richard Second was alive and would re-take his throne. Already Prince Henry changes the council, sacking his brother Thomas as Captain of Calais and installing in his stead, the Earl of Warwick. Yet he sheds the skin of his youth and of a sudden becomes devout, spending much time in prayer – which is well, yet may be perceived as weakness when he should be grasping all before him. Time alone will have the reckoning."

"When is the coronation appointed?" Jamie asked.

"For the ninth day of April. 'Tis little over two sennights hence and needs must bring stability back to our realm.

Prince Thomas is here, and Prince John should be returned from the north shortly, and all the princes shall come together to preside over a united realm, please God."

"I hear that he has already made changes to the Household, with Sir Thomas Erpingham steward and Sir Henry Fitzhugh chamberlain."

"Indeed, and I fear for Arundel that whilst he shall remain archbishop, he will be relieved of his position as chancellor. 'Tis a position of much power, and I worry about the incumbent who shall fill that void, that they may serve their own ends and not the king."

Jamie was quick to see where the statesman was leading: "You fear Bishop Beaufort, do you not? For if he were to achieve those heights with his brother in charge of our armies in France as Admiral of the Fleet and Lord Lieutenant, why 't'would make for a most powerful alliance."

Whittington offered a wintry smile: "Just so, James, just so, for now your mind twists in line with the coils of the court, which are as serpentine in its meanderings as those it finds itself pitted against. With the advent of such appointments comes peril that must be overcome by a strong hand, and I pray that our new king is aware of the vipers he lets into the nest. The Beauforts are ever asotted of their own purpose, and that of the realm comes a poor second. Now that they are recognised as legitimate in law, they hold a strong route to the crown, and would seek to undermine all if their own ends are not met."

"How would you have me aid you in this circumstance?"

"As yet I know not, for I am to attend upon the prince this afternoon. I know that he wouldst press upon me with talk of finance, for without it the realm will be hamstrung. Yet there is more besides, and once I am apprised in greater detail, I will be better placed to ask of you what I may in the king's name."

Jamie agreed that he would be at the court's disposal and left Whittington to his appointment with the heir.

×✤× —

Whittington's interview with Prince Henry was drawing to a close. Much had been discussed, yet the main tenet of all decisions had pertained to finance and how to achieve funding for the realm. Whittington had agreed to loans and promised finance from the Guilds and other merchants. Yet it would only act as stopgap and more would be needed, the heir apparent knew only too well.

"Sir Richard, you serve us well and aid England in her time of need. For such alacrity we are most truly grateful, and you shall not be forgotten by us when we are crowned."

"Majesty, I am here to serve and deem it an honour to support you thus. Yet I would ask, do you turn now to the Church for further emoluments?"

The future king of England sighed, already feeling the true weight of the crown upon his head. "We fear that is a road we must tread, and sacrifices must be made and fences mended to bring accord to all."

"You speak of Sir John Oldcastle, I assume, and his break with the Church?"

"You are most prescient, sir, for we do. Archbishop Arundel is quite rightly mightily afeared of what is occurring in our kingdom. For 'tis not just the heresy of Lollardy; we fear that the rift grows deeper and may include many the length and breadth of the country, be it guilds and even churchmen who now flock to the banner of Oldcastle's cause, with him as their figurehead. To wit we must bring him onside, one whom we once called brother and would again if he can be brought to heel. We have dismissed him from our household knights and wouldst seek to continue so, for he will taint us by association. Yet in return for such reforms and assurances, the Church promises much in terms of coin and notes to wage forward the debts of the realm."

Sir Richard nodded sagely, letting his king speak freely.

The heir continued. "Once we are king and crowned, we shall seek to close this schism within our realm once and for all. We will deal with that and other matters that you have loyally brought before us. Not least of which is the matter of my late uncle, to wit the pretender who perpetuates lies of all manner in Scotland. We have plans in this regard and shall seek to redress the balance once we are fully empowered."

"Just so, Your Majesty, just so," Whittington agreed.

"Now we are offering cloth of scarlet to those who attend our coronation, this an extravagance given the pecuniary nature of finances, yet a statement must be made."

Again Whittington nodded in assent. The look of the thing would underscore reality and underscore the change of monarch. More details of cost were discussed before Sir Richard took his leave, satisfied in his own mind that all would be well with the new king if he could but retain his crown for long enough to flourish. He vowed to do all in his power to ensure that happened.

Chapter Fourteen

9th April, London

The day had started with a bitterly cold wind that whipped snow into the eyes of all who followed the procession. But despite the weather, the streets of London were thronged with loyal subjects, showing just how popular was the new king to be, and all who came out on coronation day to witness their new monarch, dressed themselves against the cold. There were all manner of lords, every lord's servant in their master's livery, all the burgesses and Lombard merchants of London, and every craft with their livery and device lined the route of the parade. Here was a man, who in their eyes, was primogeniture inheritor of the throne, succeeding from his father and from his grandfather, Edward Third.

Some called the snowstorm a bad omen, others said that it symbolised a pure new world of white that would cover all the sins of the previous two monarchs, whose reigns had been marred by controversy and discord. Here, all thought, a new age was beginning, heralding the golden years of the Lancastrian dynasty.

Riding down the last leg of his journey, the king entered Le Straunde, mounted on his favourite warhorse who pranced and jumped in the cheering crowds, requiring all the pressure of the monarch's long legs to keep him under control. The new King Henry was in full armour save for his helmet, showing that he had cut his hair in a most severe fashion tight around his head as if to signify that with such a radical display, his old ways would be discarded in favour of chaste and pious devotion to his subjects and his realm.

At length the procession arrived at the steps of Westminster Abbey, where guards of honour stood in two immobile lines on either side of the steps. All were clothed in royal livery of bright gules and azure quarters filled with fleur de lys designs with three lions passant in each segment. Heralds blew upon their trumpets, and the flags rattled against their poles as they flapped in the steely northern breeze.

It seemed that all of London's citizens had turned out to see the new king crowned, as thousands merged into a huge crowd around the abbey, cheering the king as he dismounted, handed his horse to a squire and raised a hand to acknowledge the crowd. He was accompanied by the bishops of the realm and close household knights, each garbed in a sumptuous red cloak made from the cloth that Henry had gifted. This group included Jamie, who as a household knight was there by right. The heir to the throne of England strode up on his long legs into the grand entrance of Westminster Abbey, and before him the doors were opened as the panoply of the ceremony began. He walked sedately down the main aisle to the awaiting Coronation Chair, which was now positioned to face the High Altar as tradition demanded.

Waiting for his arrival was Archbishop Arundel, arrayed in the formal gowns of his office, the huge mitre towering upon his head. As he came closer, the king saw the gold lions acting as feet guarding the Stone of Scone, made for his great, great, great grandfather, Edward Longshanks, to house the infamous stone that he had brought back from Scotland nearly a hundred and twenty years before. The beautiful gold filigree and gilt depicted birds, foliage and animals at the rear, while in front of King Henry Fifth was a picture of his ancestor in all his glory.

Henry moved to his throne, where a servant placed the purple gown of kingship trimmed with ermine around his shoulders, and the ceremony began. All who witnessed the event knew that history was being made that day, for an heir apparent was being crowned without rancour or dispute – or so it seemed, as some present knew that darker forces were well hidden, secreted behind benign smiles and obsequious praise. With the anointing ceremony over, using the oil of Thomas Becket that had supposedly been offered to him by a virgin in a miraculous vision, the procession of the new King Henry then moved forward to leave for the Great Hall of Westminster Palace and the celebration festivities.

Once the king was seated at the high table in the huge hall for the coronation banquet, silence was called so that more drama could unfold. The doors were flung back, and two men entered the hall: Baron Sir Thomas de Morely, Earl Marshall and elder statesman, together with the Lord High

Constable of England, none other than King Henry's own brother, Prince John, who was latterly returned from Berwick.

Behind them the sound of steel-shod hooves was heard as the King's Champion, Sir Thomas Dymok, rode up the steps to enter mounted on his warhorse, fully armoured, his horse caparisoned in his own coat of arms showing a lion rampant set against a cross divided shield of black and white decorated with fleur-de-lys. Before him went a squire and page, each bearing a sword and a dagger. The procession stopped before the king and a scroll was presented to his majesty.

Breaking the seal, the king declaimed in a deep, sonorous voice: "If there be any here, knight, squire or gentleman, who dispute our right to rule and govern England in the Lord's name, that would say that King Henry was not rightful king, he was there ready to fight with him in that quarrel before the King or where it should please him to appoint."

The declaration was carried and repeated by a herald in six places in the hall and in the town to the sound of a fanfare of trumpets. All fell silent before a loud cheer went upon from the king's own brother John: "To King Henry Fifth, may God bless him and keep him."

The sounds echoed around the great hall to cheers and shouts in response. The festivities continued well into the night, before the new king of England and his household retired to their respective bedchambers.

×✤× —

The following morning there were sore heads about the court after the evening's celebrations. Despite this, the new king summoned a meeting of the Council for all the clergy and lay members who had served his father. Before him in the council chamber were the most powerful men in the land, and the leading prelate stood before him, Archbishop of Canterbury, Thomas Arundel. Now an old man, he had served King Henry Fourth well and was known to have been a good friend to the previous monarch.

"My dear Archbishop," the king began, "we are most pleased to see you here this day and would offer our immense gratitude for all the service and devotion that you showed to our father. With this in mind, and considering your years of service, we would shed some of the weight of office and relinquish you of your burden of chancellery, so that you may continue to devote your time to running the Church and all matters ecclesiastical in our name and that of God Almighty."

There were catches of breath around the chamber and a few exchanges of looks amongst the gathering. It had been neatly done by the king, yet it severed many ties with his father's regime. Arundel had been the leading protagonist in denouncing and prosecuting his former close friend, Richard Courtenay, who had been brought to trial before his father and lost.

Archbishop Arundel had expected some such changes in the new council, but this surprised him, and he was barely able to school his features, catching his breath before bowing and replying: "As Your Majesty pleases. We shall continue to be a loyal and faithful servant, sire."

The ageing archbishop bowed a second time and retired, allowing the next courtier to appear before their new king. Others were dismissed as King Henry moved through the list presented by his clerks. The bitterest blows were saved for last, for now was the time for the approval of new royal positions, and with it came shocks and sourness.

Bishop Henry Beaufort was summoned.

"My lord bishop," the king said. "We would ask that you accept the rank of chancellor over our lands and court from this day forward, serving us in all matters pertaining to our council and finance."

Bishop Beaufort managed to suppress his smile, bowing deeply: *It is done!* he thought, *I ascend, and my old rival is defeated as I take his position.* "Your Majesty is most gracious, and I honourably accept this noble position of state bestowed upon me."

The king nodded. "Very good, let it be so recorded."

So the meeting progressed, with others promoted to the Council including the Earls of Warwick and Arundel (the archbishop's nephew) and Sir Henry Scrope, who had fallen from favour with his father. The new king was stamping his authority upon the court and surrounding himself with his favourites once again as he had with his own Council two years earlier.

The following day, as newly appointed chancellor, Bishop Beaufort held a private meeting in the bishop's palace south of the river. The man before him had chosen with care to stay relatively sober the night before in order to have his wits about him at this meeting.

"Sir Thomas, 'tis good of you to attend upon us at this early hour, yet I perceive that we are ever of the same mind."

At which Sir Thomas Chaworth nodded, interested and a little scared at what might be imparted to him.

"Now to matters at hand. The king is crowned, yet seems to regress from martial warlord to pious priest, his hair now cut short to match his ambition. I hear that he seeks to free the traitor Edmund Mortimer, knighting him and his traitorous brother Roger as Knights of Bath."

"Mortimer?" said Chaworth in surprise. "Does he not realise that he is the heir apparent to Richard Second, who even now is magically reincarnated north of the border?"

"Yet think on't. His plans suit him well for it dilutes the power of a pretender returned so miraculously from the grave. The Mortimers are indeed traitors and would as soon turn again to bite the hand that feeds them as a wolf cub seeming trained would turn upon its master. They cannot help themselves. Their ambition knows no bounds, and being of the blood royal, they think they should rule." Beaufort finished, his fists clenched in anger.

A little like the man before me, Lord Bishop, Chaworth mused, watching the anger grow in the king's uncle. Sensibly he kept his opinion unspoken, and continued in a different slant: "Your Grace, what needs there to be done in this regard?"

"Hah! Well should you ask. We needs must attend to France and capture the lands that do rightly belong to the realm of England. Yet if the king be pious, weak and lacking, then we must bring him to bear or find a means to rule England under another. To wit I should know all that the Lollards do. Oldcastle leads them, as I understand, and he is a friend to the new king and still not taken. So, too, did Richard Courtenay and others of Wycliffe's persuasion defend them, raising Oxford University against the will of the Church. Courtenay is also great friends with the king, and mayhap this can be turned to our advantage. Insinuate yourself, for you were married to Oldcastle's niece, were you not?"

Chaworth nodded and opened his mouth to speak, but Beaufort continued. "Then by God's grace you are perfectly placed to aid us and the realm. I wish you to take their confidence and become a Lollard in name. Your mission shall be to action and report to me all that happens within their cause – in especial all that pertains to the king, Richard Courtenay, and all others of the court who may be dragged into this vile nest of idolaters. By the Good Lord, I shall know them and use them to control the king, if not the crown itself, and through civil war, I shall regain my power and open a path to the throne."

Chaworth was taken aback. He knew that Beaufort had been behind the Nottingham plot when he and others had been caught and brought down, but the purpose of that plot had been to usurp the old King Henry and place Prince Henry upon the throne. Now it seemed that Beaufort's overweening ambition for himself and his brother knew no bounds, and any man who came between him and the crown was to be forfeit in this game of power.

"As Your Grace pleases. I have need to see Sir John at Cooling Castle on other matters."

"'Twill do well, and I hope that we may yet turn all to our advantage. Yet speak to no one else of this, even the lords of Warwick and Arundel. It must remain our secret, for we know not whom we shall trap in our net."

Sir Thomas Chaworth nodded and left the chamber, his mind in turmoil, desperate now to meet with Sir John and tell him all. Chaworth knew that Beaufort would pull his strings, and that as his supposed mawmet, he would do Beaufort's bidding, and right well. For Beaufort's bidding would undermine the crown and the cruel and corrupt religion that went with it.

I shall adhere to this fiat, whilst all the while being sanctioned by a bishop of the true Church, Chaworth thought. *So be it.*

Chapter Fifteen

15ᵗʰ April, Westminster

"I presume you heard the king announce that his uncle, Richard Second, shall be publicly re-buried in Westminster later this year?"

Sir William Stokes, financial spy to the king and Council, nodded. He'd heard the proclamations declared on the street corners by the town criers on his way from his offices in the Port of London to see Sir Richard Whittington. "Just so, and it is all the result of Sir James de Grispere's mission to Scotland. It was good work, and the king is ever grateful, for we can now decry the pretender by name – and he has also been denounced by the Armagnacs as false."

"I can imagine that it has enraged the Duke of Burgundy, who would like nothing better than to have a divided realm upon which to play different sides," Whittington opined. "To wit I would advise that on this day members of the duke's embassy have arrived to continue negotiations with King Henry – which include a proposed marriage to

Burgundy's own daughter, I'm bound, for such a troth would ever seal the bond that he already perceives is pledged.

"Yet I remain concerned, for even now rumours continue to bloom faster than the flowers of spring that an uprising is being planned in Paris against the Armagnacs with the authorised signature of King Charles and the General Assembly, all with Burgundy's hand behind it, I have no doubt. I await more news with much worry. Yet to alert them too soon would be as terrible a calamity as too late, for all think that the papers awaiting signature are for the diminution of powers to the Armagnacs and the granting of more power to the guilds in return for support of the king. Yet so much more is planned and schemed, and all I can do is wait upon the moment and send dispatches to warn of the cope when our news is sure."

"Then we shall await to hear from either the king or those close to him – or mayhap someone from the assembly itself," Sir William concluded.

A day later, the king's spy, Thomas Burton, rapped quietly upon the door of Whittington's town house. He was let in by Sir Richard's servant, who bade him wait in the snug, warmed well against the cold night air as were all of Whittington's chambers. He was not long in the waiting before footsteps sounded and the financier appeared. Whittington saw before him a man still cloaked against the cold, a man of unremarkable appearance, dressed as a clerk in dark colours with a silk doublet of good quality that was common for his rank.

The man's hair was short under the felt hat and a small, trimmed beard graced his chin. His build was not that of a knight or a man-at-arms, being slim yet supple in movement. The indifferent appearance was exactly what Burton aspired to. He was amongst other things a clerk to King Henry but also a leading spy, forger and a merchant in stealth who stayed within the confines of London and especially the palace itself. Thomas Burton knew more of what went on in the royal court than even Sir Richard, who cast his net further afield. The two men regularly shared confidences with Sir William Stokes, and both men conspired with Whittington, who in turn reported all directly to the king.

"Thomas, it is good of you to attend upon us at this late hour. Have you been offered refreshment?" Whittington asked, ever the genial host.

"No, thank you. I shall not abide long for I must return to other duties. Yet I have intelligence that is of the utmost import, and I suspect that it needs must be acted upon most urgently."

Whittington nodded, his senses on full alert. "Just so. Impart all, prithee," he said.

"I have just returned from clerking for his majesty, and with that the embassy from Burgundy was in audience. The meeting progressed for many hours, and in the course of it insinuations were strongly made of immediate action that was to occur in Paris. I fear that the Armagnacs are to be subdued or worse at the behest of the Duke of Burgundy. The more intimate details, were that if his majesty sided with Burgundy, he would be offered the hand of Burgundy's daughter, Catherine–"

"Wait, by God's grace. I have heard such rumour, but accounted it false. She was promised to Louis of Anjou, was she not? By the rood, the man has no sensibilities and no honour that he wouldst pawn his daughter's virtue as a drunkard his soul to gain what he desires."

"Just so. Yet here he asks for a lien upon the promise of his daughter's hand. I know not how that went, for I left upon the moment and stole into the quarters of the Burgundians. 'Twas well I did, for there was evidence there to prove this claim of uprising, sealed and hidden, yet it thwarted me not and all will be as I left it."

Whittington's eyes widened in interest as Burton continued. "They plan to rise up on the twenty-seventh of April and take Paris under Burgundian control with the dauphin as dupe and the king, well... we may assume that if he is sane, he too, will come under their thrall."

The horror of the words sunk into Whittington's mind. "The twenty-seventh? By Christ, we have not long. I must make immediate plans."

"I, too, must return afore I am missed," Burton acknowledged.

"One more point offers me great cause for concern; the missive that gave you the date – to whom was it addressed?"

"It was not, my lord. It was blank."

24th April, outside Paris

The two men rode side by side, with one of them leading

a pack horse. They were tired and aching after a long hard ride from Dunkerque. The journey had taken all of six days. The roads had thawed, leaving cold sticky mud where once had been frozen ruts. Rain had followed to hamper their journey even more.

"Hell's teeth, if there is one thing I abhor even more than the whoreson French, it is their godforsaken weather!" one man muttered, cursing once more as his hired horse slipped in the rutted road and nearly fell.

"Amen to that. I wish that I was back in Italy where the sun she would be shining, the fields starting to turn green and the figs ripening. How is it that Marco managed to stay by his dry and cosy hearth in England in the arms of a good woman while we must suffer thus?" He waved his hand around in a dramatic gesture at the chilling rain that slanted in from the north. The question was rhetorical, but it didn't stop Cristoforo from repeating it.

"Mark heard through others of his calling that wrestlers were being recruited clandestinely to form a new troupe," Jamie replied. "He was asked by Whittington to get himself selected as a member of this new group. We know not why they were being called or how." Jamie shrugged. He was secretly pleased, as he knew that Mark would only draw unwanted attention where they were going due to his size and the infamy he still carried from beating the French champion in a bout held at the court of King Charles three years earlier. They would hopefully not need his immense strength on this occasion, but as Jamie and Cristoforo travelled deeper into French territory, they became more nervous. They had moved down from the north, by-passing

Calais as they knew it would be heavily populated with spies, and all roads would be watched. They would be followed, he knew, at some point, but rather than curry suspicions they travelled openly using the Flemish direction as cover. Crowds thronged the roads, fighting through the mud, making it easier for them to fit in and immerse themselves in the sea of merchants and traders heading to Paris now that spring had arrived.

The queue for the north gates of the city was already tailing back along a road that was clogged with travellers who wished to enter the city. Carts, waggons, litters and horsemen fought for space and the right to enter.

"I have never seen the like of this," Jamie said. "What causes such disarray, I do wonder?"

A merchant in front of them who headed a retinue of baggage, animals and men, including two sharp eyed men-at-arms, answered them in the tongue of Jamie's father upon hearing Jamie's question asked with a Flemish accent, seemingly sensing a kindred spirit. "They are checking all passes, and tensions are running high it seems, by orders of the Duke of Burgundy who now runs Paris as his own personal fiefdom, God rot his eyes." This echoed all they had heard, for the duke was not a popular overlord, and Flanders and the Lowland countries were united in their dislike of him.

"Where are you bound, sir?" Jamie asked.

"I have a house in the city on the north bank whence I carry out trade. And you? By your accent, you are from Flanders."

There was a strong bond among the Flemish and accents were easy to define almost to within a district of a certain area. Jamie admitted that he was, choosing randomly the address of a relative who still resided there. He told the man that they were here on business and would seek lodgings and then trade with others in the town, including – and here Jamie ventured a risk – with the Duke of Orleans, for whom they had some orders.

"Then I wish you luck, sir, for though they be better than the Burgundians, yet they are cast of the same cloth." The man spat disparagingly to emphasise his thoughts.

Jamie passed the time of day with the merchant, and after some half-hour's conversation he learned much about the state of the town, including the Place de l'Hôtel-de-Ville, where the Duke of Orleans and Bernard VII, Count of Armagnac, were lodged. It was, he knew, not a great distance from the royal residence of Hôtel Saint Pol and the Bastille Saint-Antoine.

The lodgings so often used by Thomas de Grispere were available to them and they were welcomed as old customers. From here it was not too long a walk to the Hôtel-de-Ville, but due to the late hour when they had finally gained access and found their lodgings, they decided to leave it until the morning, as the Flemish merchant warned of bands of roaming solders aiding the Watch, who were ever more diligent.

There was a palpably febrile atmosphere to the town that was not normally present, and both men sensed it immediately.

"It feels like a tinderbox with sparks flying hither and thither," Cristoforo remarked.

"Certes, yes, it bears a tension that is ready like a canon

to explode with fire," Jamie agreed, and at that moment there was a knock at the door which he opened to servants bringing food and drink ordered from the landlord of the lodgings. Neither man wished to go abroad this night drawing suspicion upon themselves.

"I am right pleased that Lent is finished," Jamie commented, biting into a roast capon with gusto.

"Indeed. Tell, me what was that merchant saying upon the road today? He seemed very interested in all we did." Cristoforo's grasp of the Flemish tongue was poor.

Jamie frowned. "He was of my father's hometown and was lodging here in Paris for trade. We merely talked as two merchants. Come now, we cannot suspect everyone who speaks with us to be a spy or informer. I am sure that we are all watched with so much at stake and Paris in Burgundy's thrall."

Cristoforo said nothing and just shrugged in that Italian way that Jamie had come to know so well. "Mmm, your conversation was in Flemish, so I caught very little, but I am always wary of strangers abroad."

Jamie dismissed the notion, waving his hand that gripped the leg of the capon, and said nothing more.

Chapter Sixteen

The following day dawned with the promise of sunshine. It was still cold, but the rain had died down to a fine drizzle in the night, and the new day revealed a yellow light that promised the year might finally be shrugging off the harsh winter.

Paris was coming alive, and the thoroughfares grew busy as throngs of people crowded the streets, mixing with flocks of sheep and herds of pigs being ushered through to market. The animals left a trail of dung in their wake, to much cursing from the pedestrians, and the air was filled with the sickly smell of damp fleeces and the squealing of the pigs.

Jamie and Cristoforo gained directions for the Hôtel-de-Ville where the Armagnacs were based, and set off on foot for the north bank of the Seine and the Port au Ble' that ran along the whole of the northern shore of the mighty river. They passed by the Pont aux Meuniers and the Pont aux Changeurs that gave them access to the Île de la Cité, with guards at the bridges restricting access to the fortified island. No longer were the waters of the river frozen, and the new smells of spring began to emerge as the city came to life. Most citizens wore wooden pattens and scuffled along cobbles covered in the night's soil that was still to be swept down and out into the waters of the Seine. The stench had not yet become unbearable as it would in high summer, with the stifling heat and lack of breeze, yet it was enough to affect the senses of both men, who pulled up their cowls to filter the air that they breathed.

The beautiful cathedral of Notre Dame shone out in all its glory, its bells chiming terce of the mid-morning. They walked away from the river along the Rue Saint Martin, seeking the Hôtel-de-Ville. Turning right onto the Rue de Rivoli, they saw the palace before them. The flags bearing the Armagnac coat of arms flapped slowly in the breeze, showing the bright gules lion rampant snarling upon the argent shield.

The two guards at the gate were wary in this city of two powerful factions, both vying for supremacy. This was the building that housed the administration for Paris, and was perfect for the needs of the Armagnacs, who could dispense justice and laws with equal measure from within its walls. The edifice stood out as a constant thorn in the side of the Duke of Burgundy, and the Armagnacs guarded it well. The building itself was impressive, set within extensive gardens and surrounded by high walls that were as much for defence as ornamentation.

Unseen by the two men, a gently sloping shale beach led down to the Seine at the rear, which served as a private river port for wheat and other foods brought here for sale in the city.

Jamie and Cristoforo made for the guard house, wary of their reception, and asked to see either the Count of Armagnac or Charles, Duke of Orleans who was now head of the family despite his youth. Jamie had met the young duke two years previously when he carried out a diplomatic mission on his behalf, delivering a letter that helped stave off the Burgundian forces and repel their influence over the English throne. Jamie had been well treated, although he had been held as a virtual prisoner in Bordeaux, during which time he grew to be upon good terms with Charles, finding much in common. A mutual respect had developed between the two men, although Charles' rank far outweighed Jamie's station as a humble knight.

The guard returned with a steward who looked Jamie over with an expression of disdain upon his face. The man was used to dealing with lower orders and had little time for underlings or unannounced arrivals. "Do you have a message for my lord that I may present to him?"

"We do indeed," Jamie replied. "Yet it is for his sight alone, and what we carry in our hearts is of the utmost urgency and would be well received by your master, once he is made aware of all that we know."

The steward looked from Jamie to Cristoforo, saying nothing and rubbing his chin in contemplation.

Jamie sought to fill the silence with a final throw of the dice. "Sir, I should add, that I am a household knight to his majesty King Henry of England, and it is upon his business that we attend," he added. "The missive that I carry bears the seal of his most trusted servant and adviser, Sir Richard Whittington, and is sent straight from the Lancastrian court. I have a most urgent desire to seek an audience with your master, and can attest to the fact that it would be in his interests to humour me. We have met afore, and he is assured of my good will in all matters."

"I shall inform my master, Duke Charles, of your request. But he is unavailable at the present time and will return to the hotel upon the morrow. Now, messieurs, I bid you good day." With that the steward turned, giving no second glance nor opportunity for further discourse. The guards barred their way and the door was closed firmly in their faces behind the departing man.

"By God's legs the man is impossible, and I would teach him a lesson in manners," Jamie said. "Yet 'twould serve no purpose and there is naught we can achieve. We shall return upon the morrow and please God we are given an audience."

"Amen to that," Cristoforo muttered.

They wandered back to their lodgings in a foul temper, and with little to do that evening, they sought out a local tavern before the Watch came out in force. They were enjoying wine and food when the merchant whom they had met at the gates of Paris appeared, attended by a servant. He did not see them immediately, but upon sweeping the room with a glance, his gaze fell on upon their faces. With a beaming smile he moved over to engage them.

Jamie muttered quietly, "I would lief as not have company this eve, yet the man seems determined."

Cristoforo said nothing, and looked up with interest at the merchant and his servant came to their table.

"Ah, good sirs, this is indeed a fine destiny after our meeting yesterday. May I join you for supper and mayhap furnish you with more wine?"

They had little choice, for it would be rude to refuse the hospitality of the merchant, whose name they learned was Ekbert de Zoete. He was in a garrulous mood, which irritated Cristoforo all the more, as he was compelled to play the role of indentured servant. De Zoete kept the conversation going through dinner, seemingly rambling on all matters, yet each time it returned to Paris, he seemed enthusiastic and vehement in his denouncement of the Burgundians, sometimes looking around to ensure that he had not been overheard.

"Now, tell me, did you manage to achieve your audience with the Duke of Orleans this day?" he asked.

"We did not. He is away from the residence and will return." Jamie hesitated. He liked others to know little of his business. "But who can fathom the wiles of the French nobility? Mayhap in a few days' time we shall be lucky," he answered disingenuously.

"Ah, just so, just so. I, too, should like to trade with such men, yet I have failed to achieve an audience. I should love to know your secret," De Zoete responded with a smile.

"On this I must fail you, for the connexion is with my father, who has traded with the family for many years, and I with little guile, merely follow upon his lead."

"Well, I am sure that your father is most proud of you. Now, messieurs, if you will forgive me I am no longer as young as once I was and must retire. Thank you for your company." At this they bade each other goodnight and de Zoete left the tavern.

"Dost thou think that he sought to steal your trade? For his questions were most invasive." Cristoforo had not caught all that was said due to the fact that Ekbert had often switched from Flemish to French and back again.

Jamie pondered the point. "I'faith I know not, yet am right pleased that he left, for I was starting to find his company tiresome. Come, let us too depart to our beds, for I wish not to be abroad late."

They rose, settled their bill and left the inn for the chill night air as Jamie continued: "We shall rise afore Prime on the morrow, for I believe that the duke was in residence all this time and his steward is lacking in his duties by virtue of his own arrogance of position. I shall ensure the man's name is known to the duke when he realises the unnecessary delay in gaining our news."

Cristoforo grunted a reply. Both of them looked about instinctively as they walked the short distance back to their lodgings.

A few other revellers were abroad that evening; men returning to their homes, servants about their duties, yet both were uneasy.

"I like this not," Cristoforo said quietly, walking softly on the balls of his feet, ready. "There is a tension here, I grant you, yet there is more than that."

"Certes, 'tis true, and the sooner we reach our lodgings the happier I shall be, for never have I felt so alien in a land as I do here now. We could face great odds and I know not from which direction they will come. If Paris is to be aroused to rebellion as we suspect, it would be easy for two foreigners to be caught in the riots, their lives forfeit and lost without trace in the debacle."

They went to where the stables were located at the rear of their lodgings, passing through an archway. Here they saw a groom working by dim torchlight who had yet to bar the door for the night.

Once inside the courtyard, they turned to face the street and saw nothing untoward.

"Mayhap we have been living on a knife's edge for too long, and like children we begin to see dragons and nightmares where there are none," Jamie reflected.

"*Dio Mio*, if that be so, then my dragons have kept me alive so far and I shall not ignore them yet," Cristoforo declared.

Both men rose with the bells of Prime that woke them as neither man had allowed himself to slumber too deeply. They washed and dressed to make an early start, hoping to catch the Duke of Orleans before the day's events took him elsewhere. They broke their fast, buckled on their weapons and made to leave the lodgings.

They were no sooner out onto the quiet street, with Paris yet to fully awaken, when a familiar voice floated out into the morning air: "Ah, messieurs, good morrow. We are well met, I see. You go to visit the Duke of Orleans, yet I have another summons for you. For there is one who has long sought an audience with you, Sir James de Grispere, and Signor Cristoforo Corio, too, I assume." The portly figure of Ekbert De Zoete appeared from the side of the entrance. He was not alone; four men came from either side of the lodgings – men-at-arms, each helmed with a spear or sword, dark and determined in their intent. All bore the livery of the Duke of Burgundy. The eight men made to close in, hemming Jamie and Cristoforo in the confines of the street.

Jamie feigned surprise and an attitude of defeat, while Cristoforo remained as ever impassive, and caught Jamie's barely noticeable look, returning it with a twitch of his lip. Jamie knew enough Italian to command him as to what direction they should take, and each man knew his task. They had worked and trained together often enough.

"Ah, Herr Ekbert, why 'tis a most unexpected surprise," Jamie began expansively, opening his arms and smiling, noticing that he was at the outer reaches of the loose semi-circle of men-at-arms. "Now prithee, who is it that wishes our company?" he asked, moving one leg forward into an advancing stance.

The Flemish merchant gave Jamie a sly smile, puffing himself up to take control of the proceedings. "Why 'tis the–"

"Adesso!" Jamie snarled, his tone completely at odds with his demeanour. The party of armed men were confident; four against one was good odds, and their weapons were drawn and ready.

Cristoforo moved, dropping and swooping up to send a dagger flying at his first mark – De Zoete. The merchant had no time to reconcile the act with his own demise, coughing and crying out in the same last breath before slumping to the cobbles. The armed guards were distracted and looked on in amazement, their reaction times slowed by the shock.

Jamie drew his sword with speed, not even bothering to

come on guard. With the first outward sweep of the draw, the blade sliced into the right arm of the nearest man, taking his hand off at the wrist before he had even turned back to address the threat. Blood spurted from the wound, which Jamie did not heed, pushing the ailing man backwards to hamper his nearest colleague. With a straight overhead lunge, using the man as a shield, Jamie lunged straight into the face of the second man, killing him instantly.

The others started to recover their senses. The third man on Jamie's side tried to strike with his spear, which was encumbered by his two fallen comrades in arms. Jamie span outside the lunge, hating to turn his back on an opponent even for a split second, yet here he knew the move was apposite. With the turn, he slashed low at the man's legs and drove his dagger straight under the shoulder and into the exposed armpit with a killing strike.

Cristoforo had not been idle. After killing de Zoete, he drew his falchion from the sheath on his back and moved forward before the second spearman had brought his weapon to bear, driving the wicked blade into his neck. The man fell, spraying blood, and Cristoforo moved through to the next man. He parried the spear at close quarters and stabbed once, twice, into the chest, piercing the coarse links of the mail with heavy stabs of his dagger to reach the lungs.

The third man came with a sword, striking from middle guard, off the centre line to get round his comrade's body, which had fallen at his feet. The move took an extra second in his effort to close the distance and utilise the extra length of his arming sword over Cristoforo's falchion, while keeping his body safe from close attack.

Cristoforo ignored the body target, allowing the lunge to come, parrying the guard's blow at close quarters by stepping slightly to his right, now on the inside gate and seemingly disadvantaged for the next move. Yet instead of stretching and exposing himself for the larger target, Cristoforo drove upwards with his left dagger arm, driving the blade into the tendons and cartilage on the inside of his opponent's wrist, just as the sword was being withdrawn for a second attack. The weapon dropped from the now useless limb as the man howled in pain, instinctively clutching the damaged limb and unable to prevent the attack from the falchion that slashed horizontally into his exposed face, blinding him.

The fight had lasted barely a minute and there were now just two men left facing the foreigners they had sought to arrest. The two Parisians shared a glance, and as if by common thought, both turned and ran.

Jamie and Cristoforo looked to each other, still alert and aware that crossbow bolts could fly or more men arrive. The ambush had in the brief moments drawn a few onlookers who watched with horror at the carnage, which was extraordinary even for these violent times.

"Come," Jamie spoke, "we must away and not daddle. Those whoresons will return with more men, and we should be overwhelmed and lose our element of surprise."

Cristoforo nodded and walked forward to retrieve his dagger from the dead merchant's neck. Wiping it clean he offered Jamie a bleak look of satisfaction. "Truly there was a part of me wished to perform that deed the first time I saw the unctuous rogue," he said. "I told you that I durst not trust that man. Too desperate to denounce the scullion Burgundy."

"You had as ever the right of it in such matters. Florence was doubtless like this, and I should have paid more heed to your cynical view of men."

Chapter Seventeen

The two surviving men-at-arms rushed through the streets to Rue Saint-Denis and the Hôtel de Bourgogne. The striking building stood as a landmark on the Paris skyline, its huge Tour Jean-sans-Peur offering access to all levels of the palace that had served the counts of Artois and now served as the home of the Duke of Burgundy. The entire building was clad in ashlar stone and set in a walled garden within an acre of grounds, and a fortified gateway guarded the main entrance to the ducal residence.

The two men ran to their companions who were standing guard and hastily told their story, begging immediate entrance. They went to the main quarters seeking Raoulet d'Anquetonville, the henchman of the Duke of Burgundy. The man served amongst other things as an assassin to the duke, and it was he who had orchestrated the ambush of Jamie and Cristoforo as soon as he heard that they were currently residing in Paris.

As they almost fell into the private chamber of d'Anquetonville, they saw the duke's man seated at his desk. His dark looks creased into a frown, his lithe frame unbending from his seat. There was a feeling of deadly nonchalance about him. "Well? What news do you bring? Is the Englishman brought down or here in chains?" But he knew by their demeanour that neither was the case, and realised that he had once again, underestimated Sir James de Grispere.

"My lord, we beg your forbearance. Monsieur De Zoete is dead. He was the first to be killed, and from there six of our brothers in arms were slaughtered before our very eyes in only a few seconds," the man said.

D'Anquetonville snorted in disgust: "Explain yourself! Were more men faced against you than we had anticipated? And if not, prithee furnish me with an explanation as to how one knight, unarmed save for sword and gambeson, together with a servant who I understand bore no sword, defeated eight fully armed men from ambush?"

The two men-at-arms looked sheepishly at each other. "My lord, they were passing quick and the servant – who was not a churl from the marches of England as we supposed, but was an Italian by his speech – threw daggers with great celerity and was deadly, retrieving a falchion from about his person. Our comrades were dead in a few short heartbeats ere we could counter their attack."

"Enough!" d'Anquetonville roared. "You will tell me next that they sprouted the wings of the Devil and attacked you from flight. Scullions, away with you, fetch ten more worthy fighters and have the captain of the guard attend upon me immediately. Ensure that you have crossbowmen to aid you. Go now, and do not slink in here unmanned and mewling like a maiden."

The two men-at-arms, red of face at the insults, turned and left, the French assassin's words ringing in their ears.

D'Anquetonville seethed with anger now, knowing he would have to face the wrath of the duke, who would take this very ill. He went up to the duke's chamber and found him being attended by a clerk and Sir Jean de Kernezen, his spy and envoy.

"Your Grace." D'Anquetonville bowed.

Seeing the cast of his face, Burgundy waved away his clerk, knowing that he should not hear the report that d'Anquetonville was bringing.

"You bring tidings of de Grispere's capture, I trust?" he said in a calm voice that was more menacing than any shouting could achieve.

"I fear that I am in error, Your Grace. De Grispere and his servant, who was in fact an Italian from his description, are still at liberty."

The duke's face seethed with anger. "How many times now have you underestimated this knight? Twice in Paris last year – a perfect plan, you assured me, a crossbow bolt through his heart. And then again on the road to Italy, where routiers failed to capture or kill him. Like Lazarus, he comes back from your promises of death to thwart my plans so carefully laid. My best friend died at his hands – and de Berry was a better man with a blade than any I have ever seen – bested in the alleys of Paris. Now by Christ on the cross, send an army next time. I want his head on a spike. And do not underestimate the Italian. He is as deadly as de Grispere, and faster from your accounts. What do you plan?"

"By your leave, Your Grace, I have sent another armed mesnie to arrest or kill him, ten soldiers with crossbowmen hidden. Paris will be closed to them. Watchmen at all gates have orders to arrest any who accord with their description. Men are scouring the taverns, and I assure, Your Grace, that they will have nowhere to hide."

"What of the Duc d'Orleans? Is he still within the Hôtel-de-Ville?"

"He is, my lord. De Grispere tried to seek an audience with him yesterday and the Duc's steward, Lambert, turned him away. He is paid well into our service and will hold fast, blocking all access to the duke until after the morrow, when we shall hold Paris against all."

The Duke of Burgundy offered d'Anquetonville a bitter, tight-lipped smile that came nowhere near his eyes. Despite his lack of stature, he appeared to stand the taller of the two men, his eyes glittering at the thought of what was planned.

"None shall prevail until we hold the power in our hands. What say you, Sir Jean, is all in readiness?" The duke turned to his spy.

"As you say, my lord, we are prepared. Simon Caboche, the Butcher, has arranged everything and tomorrow shall see the dawn of a new power in Paris that will soon embrace all of France."

"Very well. In the meantime, take as many men as you need. Find de Grispere and his companion. Hunt them down. He will have nowhere to turn in the coming chaos, and the Armagnacs will neither find nor hide him. Why would they? Mayhap we can turn this to our vantage after all, and both men shall be made to disappear in the confusion," he deliberated.

Chapter Eighteen

Jamie and Cristoforo packed their belongings quickly and rode across Paris to revisit the Hôtel-de-Ville. They found stabling nearby and left their horses there, bribing the ostler to look after their war bags.

The same two guards were posted at the gate, and they looked upon them with less suspicion when they saw who they were. Jamie explained again that he sought an audience with the Duke of Orleans, and as before, one of the guards disappeared inside and returned with the same steward.

"Messieurs, my master the Duc is still not at home, you will have to return tomorrow," the steward told them dismissively. He turned and made to disappear back into the grand hall, telling them that only those employed in the government of Paris or of the mesnie attending to the duke or the Armagnac faction were afforded entrance.

Jamie and Cristoforo had expected such a response and were in no mood to be trifled with a second time. They reacted accordingly. Cristoforo, who had been feigning boredom, stood off to one side as the steward answered the summons, but as the man turned to walk back into the building, he was suddenly at his side with a dagger at his throat. "Cry out and you die," he hissed.

Jamie drew his sword to threaten both guards, who were nonplussed at the swift turn of events. No one, they reasoned, would dare to threaten the steward or force their way into the hotel in such circumstances.

They were wrong. Turning through the gap between the guards, Jamie raised his sword, covering any movement as Cristoforo manhandled the furious and frightened steward through the open gates. Once within, Jamie slammed the doors shut in the guard's faces. They found themselves facing an inner courtyard that was a-bustle with servants and lackies. Within the covered arch, nothing could be seen of the guards above in the fortified gatehouse. The men without the barred gates began to shout, and there came the sound of hammering upon the wood.

Jamie brought his sword tip to bear in front of the steward's eye. "Now, I shall demand this of you just once, for we have neither the time nor the patience to bandy words with you." The steward frowned and made to protest before Jamie silenced him. "Deny me and all shall hereafter call you cyclops. Where are the Duc d' Orleans and Comte of Armagnac? Before you answer, consider this. You will accompany us and at the first sign of falsehood, I shall gut you before we are taken."

"The...there, messieurs. The far corner of the courtyard, where the turret door rises upwards." The steward pointed with a quivering finger.

"Right. With me, and if any challenge us, Cristoforo's knife will find your heart. Now walk quickly, monsieur." At which they force-marched the steward across the courtyard to a few strange glances from passing servants and squires. None challenged them until they were nearly at the entrance to the turret staircase. Then a call of alarm came from the top of the gatehouse and one of the guards raised a crossbow, calling for them to halt from his high vantage.

"Wave them off with a smile," Cristoforo hissed in his captive's ear, swinging the Frenchman to face the gatehouse and the crossbowman. He did as he was bidden, waving that all was in order. No bolt came sloughing through the air, for no clear shot could be taken, but cries went up around the palace and all now were alerted.

Bustling the hapless steward into the turret, Jamie slammed the door shut and barred it. Now in a position of comparative safety, the steward began to resist and called out for a guard. Cristoforo punched him just below the ribs, his blow sharp and precise, with fingers bent at the second knuckle. The man cried out in agony, all thought of speech forgotten as the pain knifed through him. They hoisted the steward upright and half carried, half dragged him to the stone steps. When they reached the first floor they saw that the doorway opened out into a large hall where one man-at-arms stood on guard.

Jamie bolted the door once they were inside and called out to him. "Monsieur, we mean you no harm, yet we wish an audience with your master. Fetch the Duc d'Orleans or his uncle, the Comte of Armagnac. We have urgent news, and his life may be in danger."

Jamie and Cristoforo knew that their own lives were hanging in the balance. Through one desperate throw of the dice they hoped to pass their vital information to the duke before they were overwhelmed by odds they could not hope to overcome, trapped as assassins in the Armagnac court.

The guard's long-shafted halberd was still pointed in their direction, but indecision was written across his face.

"I order you to fetch your master!" Jamie adjured him. "Tell him I am Sir James de Grispere, household knight of the English crown, for he is of my acquaintance, and I have served him afore."

"Monsieur Lambert, what must I do?" the guard addressed the steward.

"Go!" croaked Lambert, Cristoforo's knife still at his throat. "Do as he says."

The man moved backward to the far door calling all the time for his companions in arms. A few seconds later the door flew open, and men-at-arms and knights appeared with their swords drawn, ready to kill all who threatened their masters. Behind them strode two figures, one much younger than the other. Arrogance and royal breeding oozed from both men.

Jamie recognised the older of the two as Bernard VII, Count of Armagnac and the nominal head of the family. The second man was much younger, little more than half his age, yet carried himself with the erect bearing of a royal scion of the noble house of France and nephew to the king. Jamie had last seen him two years previously in Rouen, when he had delivered a letter at his behest and had remained the duke's guest for three days on a mission crucial to the kingdoms on both sides of the Channel. He looked younger than his nineteen years, Jamie thought, and bore the same boyish, handsome good looks that had first won him the hand of King Richard's widow, now dead like her former husband. Jamie had heard that the duke had remarried Bonne, the daughter of the older count by his side, when she was just fourteen.

Despite his youth, the young man's voice was strong when he spoke. Never a coward, he appeared bemused by the scene before him, and spoke calmly with a feigned insouciance despite the tension in the hall. "I prithee messieurs, put up your swords, for this is indeed Sir James de Grispere as ever there was, and he is clearly determined to gain an audience with us.

"Now, Sir James, we are again well met, and we should be most grateful if you would release our most humble servant, for we assure you that no scathe shall befall you within our presence," the duke continued in his lazy and rather foppish manner.

Jamie nodded at Cristoforo, who released Lambert, at which the man sank to his knees rubbing his kidneys, clearly still in some pain.

Jamie took control, not wishing the circumstances to escalate once again. "Your Grace, I beg your pardon and crave your clemency for this trespass upon your presence, and I give my word of honour that we mean no harm to you nor any of your company here." At which both he and Cristoforo sheathed their weapons in an act of good faith.

The duke looked on mazed, readily accepting this pledge of honour. "Pray continue, for as before your unheralded appearance brings with it circumstances of drama that shall I am sure, divest the day of its tedium."

"As Your Grace pleases. First may I introduce my companion, Signor Cristoforo Corio, latterly of Florence and now a loyal messenger for the English crown." Cristoforo bowed with a flourish. The duke acknowledged the introduction with a flap of his wrist and a raised eyebrow. Clearly he had heard of Cristoforo. "We come upon a fiat of my Lord Whittington and the new King Henry Five who was, as doubtless you have heard, lately crowned this month to great rejoicing of the court."

"Indeed, and we offer our felicitations. We sent envoys to the ceremony, yet we were unfortunately detained here ourselves on matters of state."

"Just so, and I shall pass on your greetings upon my return. Yet 'tis upon matters of state that I wish to have discourse with, Your Grace. There is imminent danger not only to yourselves and all immediate to your court, but to Paris itself and the future of France," Jamie finished, allowing the words to sink in. He reached into his doublet, producing a scroll sealed in red wax and stamped with Whittington's monogram. Jamie passed it to the duke directly, and the two men before him shared concerned and surprised glances.

Breaking the seal, Duke Charles read it twice, his frown deepening as he did so. He passed the missive to his father-in-law with a hand that shook, the only betrayal of his inner thoughts. The two knights moved back to the duke's side, looking on expectantly, puzzled by the reaction of their lord. The duke sent the other servants and guards away, ordering wine and refreshments to be brought forthwith. Then, as if to occupy himself with an action of diversion he walked sedately to the fireplace that had a solid blaze burning in its vast hearth. The young duke gazed into the flames, his mind turning with speed as he considered all that he had just learned and its implications.

The Count of Armagnac looked up from reading the information contained within the parchment. His urbane voice full of command came across to Jamie: "This intelligence, is it of truly verifiable integrity?"

"Yes, for certes. Sir Richard's sources have yet to be proven false."

"Should these events come to pass," the count declared, waving the parchment, "it would be calamitous."

"I say amen to that, my lord. Yet the time is upon us, for if all is to be believed this rising in rebellion against the king is to commence on the morrow, the twenty-seventh. We know little more than that, other than the assembly has authorised the movement of the guilds, yet they were unaware of the full meaning behind the documents that are to be signed by your king in ratification of these acts. Time flies like a hawk upon its prey, my lords, and you have little time to prepare."

Spiced wine and doucets were brought on gilded salvers by the pages and placed before Jamie and Cristoforo, and the room was emptied once more of servants.

The Count of Armagnac continued: "We find it very hard to accommodate that there be such repine that the whole of Paris will in effect be overtaken by a mob of guilds, apprentices and merchants – effectively the bourgeoisie!" he exclaimed, dismissing the idea that the labouring classes could ever overcome knights and the aristocracy.

"My lords, consider. Burgundy is behind this planned outrage, whose *véracité* I do not doubt for an iota. The whole of Paris is open, there are few palaces or hotels as well guarded as here in the Hôtel-de-Ville. Mayhap the Burgundian stronghold or the Bastille itself would withstand the assaults that are most assuredly planned, but little else. The benefits of these actions would be immense to the Duke of Burgundy, for he sees his grasp upon the dauphin slipping away I am told. His majesty is much more himself in spirit, I hear," Jamie continued diplomatically. "To wit I prithee, give due cause and concern to this matter ere 'tis too late. The two royal residences of the Hotel due Tournelles and the Hôtel Saint-Pol are at best poorly guarded, especially when there are many ways to attack with force or even subtlety, by which time all would be lost."

"You truly believe that Burgundy is the architect of this rebellion?" the count asked.

Jamie explained the ambush that morning, telling them how they had been lured into a false sense of security by one of Burgundy's many spies.

"Of time, Sir James, why didst thou not alert us sooner to this proposed action?" Duke Charles asked.

"Your Grace, we came post-haste at best possible speed. We arrived with a day to spare and requested an audience yestereve. We were informed that you were not within residence, and we were refused entry by your steward here, as we were indeed this day, which explains the manner of our entrance. Were it not for our persuasion we would have been turned away yet again."

The duke turned to his steward who made to protest. "My lord, I did not understand the gravid nature of their cause and sought merely to leave you undisturbed," he grovelled.

The duke cast a piercing glance at the steward, undecided as to his course of action, no doubt wanting to believe that the man had acted in his best interests. He dismissed him with a wave of his hand, whether to later interrogate him or because he wished Jamie not to see dissent within the ducal meiny, he could not be sure.

"Sir James, we would ask your forbearance, for there is much here to consider ere we make a decision upon the course of action we should follow."

"My lord duke, I have a boon to ask of you, by your leave."

"As you wish, Sir James. We shall aid you as we may," Duke Charles offered.

"Our position has, I fear, become untenable. We were found in our lodgings and forced to flee. We have sought reprove at a local inn, yet if the Burgundian yoke is as far-reaching as we suppose and his spies are everywhere, we should be discovered and face far greater odds than before. My lord, I wonder therefore if we could prevail upon you for a cot for the night – even a dry stable will suffice if all is taken and you need to husband your resources."

"Such a boon is the merest of trifles, and we have every sympathy for your plight. We shall have arrangements made for your accommodation – and this time I shall ensure that you have clear passage to my halls when you return," the duke said with a wry smile.

"Your Grace is most kind. Now by your leave, we shall fetch our horses and gear."

"For certes yes, go to, and we shall see you this eve for supper. I will have men stationed at the gate to assure you of entry, and for now, I bid you good day."

Chapter Nineteen

Jamie and Cristoforo left the Armagnac stronghold accompanied by one of the duke's squires to give them safe passage, and as they passed the guards at the gate they were assured re-entry upon their return. They walked the short distance to the inn where they had left their war bags and horses.

"What say you Jamie, think thou that they will heed our warning?"

"I think they find the notion of rebellion too hard to believe, and will rely instead upon the feudatory duties of all and their adherence to the rule of law. More fool they, for all we aver it will come to pass, and the steward Lambert is caught in the coils of Burgundy I'm bound."

"*Ma guarde me!*" Cristoforo urged, gesturing dramatically with his arm the way he did in moments of stressed emotion and reverting to his native tongue. "The tension here is *palpabile!*" He shrugged, bringing his left hand up, fingers clasped into a point, jabbing his own chest. "*Dio Mio*, can they not see and feel it?"

"Part of them doesn't wish to and the other part considers it beyond belief." Jamie shook his head in resignation. "My concern is that we are able make our escape afore it all erupts. Our devoir is done, and the politics of Paris are not our concern. With the Armagnacs now alerted there seems little more we may achieve."

With this pronouncement they entered the inn, cancelled their rooms and made to leave – having been charged a small fee for stabling and storage, much to their disgust.

"Where do you go, messieurs, if not to my fine inn?" the landlord asked begrudgingly.

"We are leaving Paris by the east gate, and return to Flanders early as all is not well at home and matters of trade are pressing," Jamie dissembled.

The innkeeper looked at them suspiciously, but nodded and bade them good day.

"A groat gets a mark that the scullion sells us to a Burgundian spy if he has not already done so," Jamie remarked.

"You shall get no odds from me on that score."

"Come, let us see what occurs at the gate and how matters are attended to."

At which they mounted and headed for the east gate close to the Hôtel-de-Ville, deliberately passing its gates. As they approached the heavily fortified east gate the Bastille came into sight. With its eight huge towers and complex moat system it looked impregnable; a bastion against all comers from the east, which was the reason behind its construction in the first place. Jamie and Cristoforo saw the long queues of people trailing from the gateway, facing delays as all passes and baggage were being thoroughly checked.

"I was hoping to mingle with the crowds and mayhap escape and take our luck upon the roads heading south to Armagnac and Bordeaux. Yet we are followed, I feel it, and there is no longer the opportunity."

"Yes, certes," Cristoforo agreed. "We should double back to the Hôtel-de-Ville and seek shelter there, for the riots will last a number of days, and with our warning please God the Armagnac forces will set to and prevail or divide Paris. But for now, look yonder. The men-at-arms bear the livery of Burgundy and are present on the gates overseeing all."

"You have the right of it, Cristo. Come, let us make haste and return to safety."

With that they skirted the gate, heading north before returning through side streets to the Armagnac stronghold. They were relieved to find themselves readily admitted by the guard, and noticed that more men had been deployed to the gates and ramparts. Yet the curtain walling was not as high as a castle, and could be scaled in a determined assault. They were shown quarters that had been allocated to them along with other squires and the handful of household knights attached to the ducal household.

Bells were rung for Sext, chiming loudly around the palace from a chapel tower in one corner of the buildings.

"Now if Marco were here, he would declare himself dying of hunger and demand to be fed," Cristoforo joked.

"Aye, that he would. I wonder how he fares. There was a new commission abroad seeking wrestlers, and he was going to explore the muster. From which quarter the commission came he knew not, yet others of his Cornish brethren had informed him of the opportunity offered by a secret patron. I wonder who that person might be?" Jamie mused, his mind taking on new concerns as he had an inkling of the dangers that this latest turn of events could present to the English court and king.

"I am sure he will flourish, for he is ever in demand, and rarely have I seen him bested. He is a force of God with the strength of three normal men," Cristoforo opined.

"Amen to that. Come, let us spy out this palace. I wish to know its weaknesses and strengths and routes for a possible escape, as I have no wish to be trapped."

They moved out of their quarters and explored all corners and aspects of their temporary billeting. Like many Parisian halls and palaces, it had been assembled over time, incorporating existing buildings or land and amalgamating all under one domain. The Hotel-de-Ville included civil offices for the administration of government as well as accommodation for the Armagnac faction. There would be weaknesses in its ability to withstand assault and opportunities to be exploited through secret doors and hidden access points. Jamie made a mental inventory to report to the duke and count over supper.

As Vespers rang out, Jamie and Cristoforo entered the duke's large dining apartments. The two nobles were both attended by their wives: the Countess Bonne, still a handsome woman at forty eight years, and her young daughter, also named Bonne, who was now married to Duke Charles. At fourteen, she held the promise of great beauty as she developed into full womanhood, and even now she had a presence that was far in advance of her immature years. She would make a perfect consort for the young duke, Jamie decided, if they lived long enough to enjoy the fruits of old age. Other household knights were also in attendance; the chief lieutenants and high-ranking knights of the Marmousets, as the Armagnac faction was known within France. Among them were the Chancellor of France, Sir Arnaud de Corbie, and Jean de Garencieres of the Royal Council.

With the introductions made the meal began, and Jamie and Cristoforo were treated to a sumptuous feast of many courses accompanied by fine wines from Bordeaux.

It was at this point that Jamie asked the question that had been plaguing him since earlier that day. "Your Grace, my lords, have you given further consideration to that which we imparted earlier this day?"

As the senior member present, Bernard, Count of Armagnac cleared his throat softly in an ominous manner before beginning to explain their thoughts. "Sir James, we greatly appreciate the effort extended by you and your companion Signor Corio in overcoming all that you have done to warn us of a potential uprising." He emphasised the word potential. "We are of course greatly indebted to you both. We have reflected upon the matter and have taken certain exigencies to ameliorate the eventuality. Yet in truth, we do feel that the situation is exaggerated and will dwindle to naught."

Jamie tried one last time to persuade them of greater

measures to be taken. "If you will forgive me, my lords, I have been remiss. To wit, I was specifically asked to enquire after their majesties at the behest of King Henry, who is all concern in this matter."

The final words were left hanging in the air, and the room became tight with tension as all conversation stopped. White lines of anger appeared at the corners of the mouth of the older count, who felt that his authority had been flouted.

"Sir James, I repeat, we have ensured that measures have been taken, and we are grateful to you for your advice." These final words were uttered in a manner that brooked no argument.

"My lords, forgive a sely knight his tongue, albeit in good faith. For I wouldst not seek to teach my betters their trade, and shall seek solace in the knowledge that I but did my devoir and shall, as you proscribe, let the matter sleep and proceed with seemliness."

The duke nodded in satisfaction, and Jamie knew that the die was cast.

Chapter Twenty

The following morning the chamber began to stir as pages brought water and the knights and squires rose from their cots as the bells sounded for Prime. Jamie and Cristoforo washed and dressed hurriedly with an ominous feeling for the day to come.

They broke their fast on bread and salted cod with buttered eggs and one of Jamie's favourite dishes, fried *Let Lardes*. He saw the green and yellow slices on a serving platter and made for them, tucking into the fried curds, eggs and lardons, coloured with saffron and parsley with relish.

"Mark will be so envious, for only in Paris do they do this to perfection. I have seen him consume a whole platter," Jamie remarked.

"I like them myself, and I agree that these are the best I have tasted," Cristoforo stated, licking his lips and returning to the serving trestle that held the platters of food.

Once they had finished, they left the hall and made for the ramparts to look out over the streets. A grey curtain of cloud hung above the town, blocking out the sky, and when the sun had burnt it away it left a strange, bright haze that hurt the unshielded eye.

Cristoforo squinted into the distance some streets away, seeing a darker vapour rising above the tallest buildings, from which he noticed two more spirals of colour billowing upwards. "Look there!" he said, motioning to Jamie. "Smoke. It does not bode well," he prophesied. "There, more." He called out, as more clouds of smoke rose across the city. Houses were on fire, and suddenly the noise of a mob came to their ears and flames shot up as a thatched roof caught fire two streets away.

Jamie acted immediately, running the length of the rampart to the main gate, whereupon he lent over the crenulations and shouted down to the guards. "There are *rif-et-raf* running through the streets. The bourgeoisie have rebelled. Come within and bolt the gates, I adjure you, be quick!" The two guards looked at him and then at each other, hesitating. "Hurry, I bid you, don't daddle," Jamie urged. "For if you hesitate you will be caught and killed."

As one, they turned to run through the gates opened by their comrades-in-arms from within who had heard Jamie's shout. They acted not a moment too soon, for the city began to echo to a hum of shouts and cries of anger as two hordes approached from either side of the street beneath, formed into coherent spearheads of well-armed men all bearing the white caps of their common uniform.

It was a swarm of the deadliest kind, Jamie concluded. This was no disenfranchised gathering of malcontents, but a well organised army disguised under a banner of anarchy. He watched in horror as crossbows were brought to bear, ducking down behind the crenulations and pulling Cristoforo with him. "They are well armed with mail, swords and shields. This is the well-rehearsed insurrection we were led to expect."

The clang of steel on stone sounded above their heads, and one unfortunate guard who had positioned himself ill, felt the thud of a quarrel as it sloughed through the air to find its mark. He cried out as he fell backwards to the courtyard below.

"Come, we can aid no one here. We must report back to the duke and the count and ensure that all entrances are bolted against the attackers." At which Jamie called to the squire who had escorted them yesterday, ordering that he get all men-at-arms to the ramparts immediately. The sound of trumpets was heard from around the walls. The plague of Burgundy had begun!

Then as they made to depart the wall they heard the cry go up from below: *"Cabochien! Cabochien! Cabochien!"* the chant went up.

"What is this Cabochien?" Cristoforo asked.

"I know not, yet t'would appear to be their rallying cry. Come, let us away and report to Duke Charles." As they did so the chant grew louder and hammering began upon the wooden gates.

They reached the main hall of the hotel and the residence of the Armagnacs, which was separate from the administrative part of the accommodation that housed officials who would be unlikely to attend their offices this day.

As they entered, they saw the Duke of Orleans issuing

orders to his household knights and captains of his guard. Upon seeing the two men enter, he made last minute demands and awaited their presence before him. "Messieurs, I bid you good morrow and admit that we should have heeded your warning more strongly. Were it not for you I am sure that the gates would have been breached and the hotel already taken. We are again in your debt, Sir James. Even now we are heating oil and sand to throw down upon the rabble," he finished, the anger clearly apparent within him – both at himself and the impudence of the mob outside.

"Paris is burning, Your Grace. They have set fires and that sweep eastwards. Have you any news of their majesties? Were they informed of the possible incursion?" Jamie asked tentatively, aware that he was on dangerous ground.

"Spies and messengers were sent out yester eve, yet none returned," the duke finished lamely, his hands clenched in impotent rage.

"Your Grace, I wonder to that end if I may speak with your steward, Lambert?"

"How will that profit our situation?" the duke snapped, defensive of his own household.

"My lord, I fear deception is at work here to the detriment of our position. To this end I would question Monsieur Lambert."

"As you wish. I believe he is about his duties in the western quarter where he went to ensure all was secure there. For it houses the quarters given over to the administration of Paris. It is part of the original *maison aux piliers* with a number of small courtyards and squares that open out to the street on the western side."

"By your leave, Your Grace," Jamie uttered, fearful of what he would find. They had yesterday seen the pillared sections of the western apartments that gave the original building its name before it was bought and extended to encompass the whole hotel.

"Hell's teeth, I fear the worst," Jamie muttered as he and Cristoforo ran to the western side of the building. He spied the squire who had given them safe escort yesterday talking with a sergeant-at-arms and called to him: "Edouard, we make for the western quarter and fear intrusion into the hotel with treachery at work to undermine us. Would you and the sergeant join us ere we find ourselves overrun?"

It was the work of a few moments to recruit the sergeant and Edouard de Breudeport to their numbers, and with them half a dozen men-at-arms, all mailled and ready with spears and kite shields bearing the Duke of Orleans' coat of arms of an Or and Argent quartered shield with fleur-de-lys and serpents shining forth.

They passed through a studded door, entering a walled courtyard with separate doors off each end offering access to the rest of the interconnected buildings. Jamie immediately recognised it as a weak point, and then fear struck his soul, for at the far end between two buttresses was a postern gate of solid construction that was currently barred. Before it stood Lambert, the duke's steward, and a servant pulling the wooden bar from the shackles that locked it in place. Even as they watched and Edouard shouted for Lambert to hold, the beam was freed and span upon its pivot bolt and horror was released as the white-capped men surged through.

Knowing it would be too late, Jamie turned to the last

man-at-arms. "Return bolt that door and get men at the *chemins de rondes* with crossbows. Now!" With a final thought he added, "leave me your shield."

The soldier obeyed with alacrity and the sergeant nodded in agreement at the action, hefting his shield and preparing to die in battle rather than let the mob overcome the hotel and take his lord. The door behind them slammed shut with an ominous thud.

"Form a wedge on me. Cristo in the middle, for you have no shield or armour." With reluctance the Italian obeyed, knowing that it made sense. Then the battle madness took Jamie as the mob came forward, their weapons raised, shouting their chant of *Cabochien!*

Jamie replied with his old battle cry: "An Umfraville, an Umfraville!" running forward with the men-at-arms in a tight wedge. This was no battle, but a tightly packed melee similar to the skirmishes he had fought with Sir Robert de Umfraville on the Borders. Like the Scots, the Parisians were lightly armoured, if at all, although some carried spears and the long knives of the butchers who made up many of their number. There was a concussion as Jamie's shield smashed into the leading rank. The force crushed a man's nose, driving him backwards, his upraised arm poised for a slash downwards with his sword. Like any experienced fighter, Jamie knew the point beats the edge in such situations. Jamie's sword point bit the soft skin of his opponent's neck in a spurt of arterial blood and the man's cries for his nose were silenced as he fell backwards under the impetus, hindering his nearest companions.

Twice more Jamie found gaps and jabbed hard with his

sword, driving through aprons and gambesons to open deadly wounds. A man appeared to his left, a nail studded club poised to drive downwards. Jamie raised his shield in time to ward off the blow, taking the full concussion through the wood and hide as he drove his sword forward into the exposed belly, jerking it sideways upon entry for maximum damage and to release the suction from the blade. As the man's belly was ripped open all thoughts of attack disappeared, but in that moment of exposure, another attacker came on from his right. The man was better arrayed, clad in a mail habergeon, a buckler in his left hand and a sword in his right that snaked out to pierce Jamie's torso. There would be no time for Jamie to bring his shield or sword to bear and parry the attack, and he prayed that the stiffened black fabric of his gambeson would protect him. The point met his stomach with a hard thrust as the opponent lunged, and the gambeson tore but held against the blade. The attacker's arm disappeared as a falchion caught him in the face, turning it into a scarlet mask.

A wall of bodies grew at their feet as they slowly but inexorably drove the mob backwards towards the door, stamping or stabbing on the supine figures beneath them, to ensure no one faked death or injury to rise up in surprise at their backs. There began a chaos of cries, sprays of blood and desperate attempts to overcome the defenders, yet training and better arms finally showed through. It was bloody work with no quarter given, and soon the sweet metallic stench of blood mixed with sweat and loosened bowels filled the air. The defenders were aided by the confines of the courtyard which meant that they could not be surrounded from any attack through the narrow door to the street that impeded a fast surge of men to replace the dead and dying. Soon they pressed the attackers to the archway leading to the street, with two of the men-at-arms driving spear tips into all who blocked their way. Then finally Jamie heard the whistle of crossbow bolts through the air, bringing with them death from above. At this close quarters the sheer power of the bolts drove men backwards as though plucked by a giant hand, and the disheartened attackers retreated to the street. Heartened by the slough of bolts, the men-at-arms, directed by the archers above, rushed through the door behind them to aid the small band of defenders throwing their weight to close and bar the door to the streets beyond.

Heaving for breath, some with hands on their knees, the small band ceased their combat. In reaction to the proximity of death and with the primeval struggle over, they momentarily relaxed to look at the dreadful carpet of dead and dying men at their feet. Two of their number had succumbed to the lethal onslaught. The ground was liberally pooled in red that soaked into the beaten earth, and the white smocks and caps of the anarchists were smeared with blood, creating a strange panoply of red and white streaks, macabre in the aftermath and the stillness that always followed combat. Many of the defenders bore grazes and had bloody faces, or wounds that bled from torn mail or cloth.

Cristoforo looked to his shoulder where his gambeson had been sliced. He had not felt the wound, but now it bled copiously. It would need stitching, he discovered, and he would have to instruct Jamie on how to do it to his satisfaction. He bent to retrieve a thrown dagger from a dead opponent, cleaning it on the man's white cap.

"Cristo, I am in your debt. 'Twas well done when you skewed that whoreson," Jamie offered, gently squeezing his friend's good shoulder.

Chapter Twenty-One

The cries from the street were becoming more subdued. Crossbowmen from the *chemins de rondes* and the small brattices secreted about the wall, had wreaked havoc on the closely packed mob, and the rebels had moved on to find easier prey. In the infirmary off the kitchens in one of the main buildings, a bowl of hot water sat infusing with herbs from Cristoforo's pouch, and a friar looked on with interest as Jamie and the seamstress by his side washed their hands – the girl in puzzlement – then poured coarse cooking brandy over them before drying them with a clean linen cloth on Cristoforo's orders.

"Why do you take such care with washing and cleaning the hands?" the friar asked.

Cristoforo explained that his ancestors had been instructed in the Holy Land and the lore had been passed down through his family for generations.

"You take instruction from heathen *saraceni*? Is that not the Devil's work?" the friar asked, using a Latin expression.

Cristoforo frowned, used to this response from the western lands. "I do. The healer was a good man who aided my great grandfather in many ways, offering teachings from the Greeks that have long been forgotten. You may scoff at and deride his methods, yet they are wholesome and have saved many lives since he imparted them in good faith. The herbs are from God; as is the grape that provides the brandy; the needle is steel, no different to the blade that cut me. The honey that I use to aid closing the wound comes from bees that God placed upon this earth. Why do you see only superstition and the Devil's work?"

The friar was suitably admonished: "I shall pray for you as you work."

"Do so, Father, for in that we are as one, and only differ by acceptance of knowledge, not devotion."

At which he instructed Jamie to remove the needle and thread from the bowl of boiling water with a wooden spoon and place it on the cloth to cool, then showed him how to hold the lips of the wound together while the bemused girl began to stitch it shut.

"Fear not, my lady, for my soul is clear and so now is the wound. 'Tis but a few pricks of the needle and your work shall be done," Cristoforo said, bestowing upon her his most fetching smile. For a moment she lost concentration, nearly stabbing Jamie as she took her eyes from her work.

"I beg pardon, my lord." She stumbled, re-focussing upon the task at hand.

"Aye, just make sure you stab him, not me." Jamie chided her good-humouredly. "I've had enough of French steel pricking me this day."

Cristoforo smiled at her again, putting her at her ease. "Fear not, *cara mia*," he told her. "His bark is much worse than his bite and his senses are dulled to the point where he feels nothing."

The seamstress understood that the teasing was good natured enough, and returned to her duties, causing Cristoforo to take a sharp intake of breath as the needle bit and the thread did its work.

"There, my lord, I'm finished," she said eventually.

"Why 'tis most neat and pretty, I shall know where to return when I am in need of beauty and solace," he said, flirting with her.

The seamstress dropped her eyes coquettishly under her lashes and bobbed a saucy curtsey which brought a glare from the friar. She turned and skipped from the room, swaying her hips suggestively as she did so, looking over her shoulder in a beguiling way before she disappeared through the doorway.

"May I see the work?" asked the friar.

"By all means," Cristoforo agreed, pouring more brandy from the costrel over the wound, allowing it to evaporate.

"And this will not putrefy?" the friar asked, amazed at how neat and clean the work was.

"Please, God no. For now I will bandage it with a poultice of herbs and when I am sure there is no infection, I will add honey to aid the healing of the flesh."

"By the good Lord, 'tis remarkable and I wouldst speak more about such methods if there be time ere you depart."

"Most assuredly, Father. I will seek thee out in due course."

Dressing once again in a silk shirt and gambeson, Cristoforo left with Jamie to attend upon Duke Charles, who asked them to speak with him in his private chambers.

The man before them looked haggard and drawn, clearly shocked by the events of the morning. No stranger to conflict, the duke had been amazed at the speed and power of the forces arrayed against him and the liberty of all Parisians. It reminded him of the assassination of his father in the very streets of Paris not far from here, again at the behest of the Duke of Burgundy. Since that day all the male family members had sworn vengeance against John the Fearless. "Messieurs, we are in your debt, and I must console myself with the knowledge that the hotel still stands and that we are safe inside. We pray to God that this insurrection is soon dealt with, and that the armies of France shall put down this revolt and deal with the bourgeoisie swiftly and mercilessly. We are to send messengers to muster our forces from outside Paris. To wit we shall achieve what we failed to do this day two years ago when we were thwarted by Burgundy and indeed your country's armies, who aided the Burgundian cause on that occasion." The duke's speech finished with a barb directed at Jamie, who shrugged it off.

"Your Grace knows only too well that I am a sely soldier, bidden to go hither and thither at the behest of the crown, performing its ministering as a leaf upon the breeze and no stranger to conflict for all that. The politics of the court are a mystery to me, and I durst not enter that arena of chivalric devoir for fear that I should drown in its vat of intrigue and duplicity."

"That is as maybe, but for now we let us consider

ourselves as allies in this conflict brought about by Burgundy as you prophesied. Yet I do wonder if even he, with his hand so firmly upon the bridle of power, can harness the forces that he has mayhap unwittingly unleashed upon not just this great city, but the person of his majesty."

"Do you fear for their majesties, my lord? Are they within the palace of the Hôtel Saint-Pol?" Jamie asked nervously, for if they had been taken or slain, their mission would have failed in the eyes of Whittington and others.

"The *rif-et-raf* moved eastwards from here, and are even now burning and looting towards the Bastille, leaving the palace of the king in their wake." The young duke's eyes burned with anger at this terrible calumny upon the French aristocracy.

Jamie felt impotent; they had warned them all and given them sufficient time to act, but he doubted they had taken the information seriously. He wondered whether they had informed King Charles or the young Dauphin Louis, who was married to the Duke of Burgundy's daughter Margaret, and whether they would give any credence to such a warning. Jamie questioned if he would have the strength of mind to rebel against his powerful and domineering father-in-law, or even consider him a threat in the first place. He knew the answer without confirmation – he would not. He brought his mind back to their present predicament. "My lord duke, is there aught else that we may do to aid you? For I hate to be idle here. It serves me not well."

The duke's lips compressed into a tight-lipped smile: "Sir James, you are a goodly knight, and we thank you with our hearts and forgive our trespass against your countrymen, for much is done in battle that is regretted in the aftermath. 'Tis not possible I fear, yet I would have news of the king."

At this point there was a knock on a side door and the squire, Edouard de Breudeport entered, begging an audience with the duke. He was still dishevelled from the fight in the courtyard, his jupon bloodstained and cuts upon his face and leg. "My lord, forgive my intrusion, yet we considered it expedient to obtain all intelligence that we could from these bourgeoise, and I have news. Two were taken alive and information was extracted regarding the leader of this revolt, who is one Simon Caboche, a leading member of the *écorcheurs* who directs them in all matters. Their aim, it seems, is to take all of Paris, demanding more rights and privileges for the bourgeoisie and in particular the academics, who wish to reduce the power of the king and give more control to the *États généraux de Langue d'Oil*–"

"What? By God's legs, this cannot be. Butchers taking over Paris and making demands of the king of France? We shall crush them and put every head on a spike," he cried. "What else did you learn?" Duke Charles enquired, when he had calmed down and gained control of his emotions.

"My lord, the man we captured was a self-styled captain of their army and knew more than most. This Caboche, it seems, is an agent of the Duke of Burgundy, and with papers put before the assembly in February, none knew the full extent of what was being proposed. They seek..." Here, de Breudeport's courage failed him as even he could not conceive of such a thing happening. "They seek to force the king to sign these ordinances that were originally drawn up by those advising the Duke of Burgundy."

The duke swore under his breath, unable to accept what he had just heard. "So the whoreson Burgundy aligns himself with plebs and the Parisian *boucherie*? I wish to speak with the captain of their forces."

"Unfortunately, my lord, that will not be possible. He died under torture and the wounds he sustained in the debacle within the courtyard. For which messieurs..." He turned to Jamie and Cristoforo. "I am deeply grateful, for without you we should have been overcome this day and the hotel would have been taken."

Jamie and Cristoforo bowed their heads in acknowledgement of the praise.

"Your Grace, by your leave we should like to see to ourselves and reconcile our position here and see what aid we may give in any quarter," Jamie said.

"Prithee do. Proceed as you wish, you have carte blanche. All that I seek is news of his majesty and the dauphin, yet that is not possible with the streets as they are."

The two made to leave and did not speak until they could not be overheard.

"The palace of the king will fall, it is poorly protected. 'Tis a palace, not a castle, and only the Bastille could withstand a determined assault." Jamie shook his head in disgust. "I wouldst know that their king is safe, for without him all may be lost with Burgundy at the reins to incite this terror to greater heights – mayhap in the direction of England."

Cristoforo smiled wickedly, enjoying the moment. "Then let me venture forth this night and see what I may. Under the cover of darkness I shall be little disturbed and shall mingle as an apprentice of the Italian silk guilds, of which there are many here, or mayhap as a banker, for again many of my countrymen take this role. I would cast the least suspicion, and the night, she is my friend."

"No, I could not allow you to go alone," Jamie decided.

"*Dio mio*, am I a child? For you would encumber me and stand out more than I would alone." Cristoforo snorted.

"I do not care to face Alessandria should aught happen to you."

"Fear not, all will be well, please God. Now I have a thought upon which I would act. Many of the dead in the courtyard wore those ridiculous white caps and aprons, marking them as Cabochiens, as they styled themselves. We shall secure at least one, mayhap two bodies, and have them cleaned, for I would dress as one of them this night."

Cristoforo slipped off to find the whereabouts of the dead men and their garb, with Jamie shaking his head in his wake and he turned his mind to how he might help guard his friend's back.

When the bells for Vespers sounded, Cristoforo was dressed as never before, wearing a white apron and a cap upon his head. For the rest he was dressed in black. "This will serve, I feel." He offered a smile, his teeth flashing in the dusk.

He removed the apron and folded it carefully, tucking it inside a length of knotted rope that he had wound around his waist. He took off the cap and placed it inside a hidden pocket within his cloak. "There now, I shall be one of them if caught, and all will be well."

"Where will you exit the hotel?" Jamie asked, nervous for his friend, who would be heavily outnumbered if set upon.

"By the gates that lead down to the river and the port there. For it appears always to be noisy and will provide a good place to merge with the others of the bourgeoise."

"I have found two tabards in the Burgundian livery sequestered from the officials within Paris, one of which I have asked the seamstress to make larger for me so that I can accompany you on this errand," Jamie declared.

"Nay, Jamie, to what end? Burgundy himself may be in the palace, which is but a short distance eastwards and a few minutes' walk. You will be far more prominent than I, and a Burgundian servant or squire supporting a Cabochien directly and alone? No, it will not do. I can arrive and quietly slip into the Hôtel Saint-Pol and see what I am able to procure by way of intelligence."

"I shall consider the matter. When do you leave?"

"In half of the hour, when all will be dark, and the drinking and looting will have begun. I must also await a missive that is being prepared for me by the friar within the hotel here, closed with a fake seal addressed to his majesty King Charles. If all goes well, I shall gain an audience with the king and learn all that I may."

"I will see you at the river gate ere you leave," Jamie concluded.

Chapter Twenty-Two

The half-hour passed and the two men were due to meet again at the harbour gate leading to the shallow beach that sloped down to the Seine. Parts of the river beach had been raised to form jetties and other sections were enclosed by a low wall that ran as an esplanade joining the river to the Port au Ble and the Place de Grève. Here mobs had gathered during the daylight hours, causing havoc and raiding the incoming boats, stripping them of their cargoes which were then distributed freely amongst the anarchists. With noise levels running high, large groups still shouted and ranted in jeering voices under pools of torchlight. As cheers rose at some unseen horror, the river gate postern was opened within the frame of the main wooden structure. This was narrow and only four feet in height, set into the wooden planking of one of the main double gates and almost indiscernible even in daylight.

Jamie was waiting for Cristoforo to arrive, and the lithe

figure of the Italian emerged before him from the dark shadows in the lee of the curtain walling.

"*Amico mio*, by the gods why are you dressed so?" Cristoforo asked when he saw that Jamie was clad in a tabard bearing the Burgundy coat of arms. His left arm was in a sling that bore an ominous dark patch upon it near the shoulder. Under the tabard he wore a knee-length French mail habergeon, and at his belt his own small buckler was hooked at his side. On his head he wore a padded coif over which was a Franco-Burgundian sallet helmet pointed at its conical top that had separate brow and tail plates, the latter hinged in the Burgundian style. On each side was painted the distinctive red Cross of St Andrew, together with the firesteel, sparks and the Golden Fleece that Duke John had chosen as his personal emblem for the war against the Armagnacs.

Cristoforo was in his customary black from head to toe, his cloak at this moment swept back to reveal a thin diagonal leather strap running from shoulder to hip that supported the deadly crossbow upon his back.

"I shall accompany you to the palace," Jamie said. "For with me as an escort we shall not have to jump at every shadow and can travel more openly, you in your guise and me as a whoreson slave of Burgundy – for I do look the part, I believe."

"You do. I was about to lift a dagger and take your life thinking we were overrun!" Cristoforo joked.

"Now, should we encounter trouble, leave me and achieve what you will, for there is much at stake here and the king must be reached at all costs and intelligence brought back to the Armagnacs."

Cristoforo nodded in acknowledgement.

The postern was then quietly opened, drawn back on oiled hinges to permit the two men to leave the Hôtel-de-Ville. They moved quickly away down towards the Seine across the gravelled square into the baleful light of the torches, where a vision of hell met their eyes.

The gibbets and stocks were full. Bodies swayed in the night air, two still kicking, gurgling as they died while the mob brayed and cried in a drink-fuelled blood lust and hatred of anything Armagnac. The voices of the hanged cut dry rasps as they gasped out their final words, their tongues lolling as they heaved and breathed their last, defecating down their legs, bringing further cries of laughter and mockery from the crowd, who had placed bets on whose bowels would be voided first.

Both men were inured to the horrors of battle, yet somehow the sight of these innocent bodies being strangled slowly by the hangman's noose struck home deeper than any conflict on the field of war. They passed unchallenged, heads held high as they marched forwards to the bank of the river, Jamie arrogantly forcing a path through the ranting Cabochiens. Here were worse sights, for at the stocks were others, their clothes ripped from them, taunted and stuck with swords and knives. In their number women pleaded for mercy as they were abused by the drunken mob. Both the men balked at this and wished to stop and somehow aid them, but they could not. To do so would bring death upon themselves instead.

They stopped their ears and moved closer to the shoreline and the route away to the east, where they found three men blocking their path, white caps upon their heads. The leader, belligerent with drink, demanded: "Who are you and where do you go?"

Jamie replied in a Parisian accent, easily adopting the arrogant tone of these men whom he despised, and shouted, "Out of our way, drunken oaf! We are the duke's men from the Hôtel de Bourgogne on our way to the Hôtel Saint-Pol on his grace's command, where we shall serve papers upon his majesty for terms of finance from the House of Lombardy and the bankers' guild."

"Finance, is it? Do you carry coin? Mayhap some silver would aid us, too," the leader asked aggressively.

Jamie stepped forward, and as he did so his sword flashed out, the point suddenly at the butcher's neck. "I trade in steel, monsieur, and my day has been long and tiring. I was wounded at the assault upon the Hôtel-de-Ville behind us here, which rankles ill with me, for the whoreson Armagnacs still hold fast there. Doubtless you were drinking and preying elsewhere upon easier targets, for I did not see you in our company." Jamie knew that subtlety would not suffice with the drunken men before them. Before the man could respond, Jamie countered again. "Wouldst thou accompany us hence? We will happily return with you to the duke's presence where you can explain why you halted an officer of his inner court performing his duty."

The man became sober, but the aggression and light of battle was still in his eyes. "Mayhap I shall, yet what if I called my brothers in arms here to aid me? Where then would your precious duke be with his demands? For we now rule Paris and shall with new laws control all the Assembly, and perhaps we shall be greater even than my lord Duke of Burgundy. Perhaps we shall give John the Fearless something to be frightened about." He finished, sarcasm rich in his voice.

"You could call them, and I shall ride down to hell on your blood-soaked trail, for you will be the first to die, you and these two dullards with you."

The two other men baulked at this and made to move, despite the drawn sword. Then one found a dagger at his throat, pricking the skin and sending a small trickle of blood down the side of his neck. He stayed very still. "My companion here deals in steel as well as silver," Jamie said, "and I would not be the one to upset his temper, for it is short as is our time. Now do we pass, or shall we prepare to depart for hell together?"

The leader moved aside reluctantly, muttering under his breath.

Cristoforo moved on as Jamie waited and watched their backs disappear into the darkness to half heard threats and curses. He was aware that they were watched still, and did not trust anyone not to mount an attack.

"Come, Cristo, let us not daddle, for I durst not trust them, and they will sally forth again upon finding their courage I'm bound, with our murder as their revenge."

"The lust for blood is roused to further heights by drink," Cristoforo agreed, and the two men sprinted on into the darkness, seeking the esplanade to the Qual de le Greve that ran alongside the river Seine within the city walls.

They moved up a side street and waited, steadying their breathing, certain they were being followed. The moments passed and then a gaggle of coarse voices came to their ears accompanied by the sound of footsteps as the three men who had sought to waylay them appeared, accompanied by a group of some ten or fifteen more men, all roughly armed with knives and cudgels and the odd captured sword, their white Cabochien caps easily identifiable in the lights of fired buildings and torches that illuminated the roads. They were met at a street corner further east by a second group, who by the sound of the conversation knew well the leader of the group from the Place de Grève.

"You haven't seen them? Two men, one an Italian of the banker's guild, the other a Burgundian captain with his arm in a sling, so?" The leader motioned, copying Jamie's apparently wounded arm.

"No men of that likeness have passed this way, for we have the road," the reply came, slurred and surly with drink.

Cristoforo, cowled in black, peered out around the corner to assess how many there were. He spotted another group lit by the flames of a burning house, seeing the ruddy, slab-like peasant face of the speaker who led the newcomers, belligerent in his manner even to a supposedly friendly member of his guild.

The churlish man continued: "Why do you seek them so fervently? Have they bested you in some way?" He sneered, seeing the truth of the matter.

"Nay, yet there was something amiss that I cannot fathom. Aid us, spread out and let us find these two for there is something ill-formed."

"Find them yourselves, for we have discovered these two pretties and would have some sport ere we go hunting for more." At which the leader motioned to two women who shrieked in terror as they were held fast by others of his group. Their eyes were wide in horror of the fate that would no doubt befall them as anarchy and hell ruled the streets of Paris. One of the men grabbed the younger woman's hair, pulled back her head and forced a kiss upon her. She tried to wrench her head away, and attempted in vain to slap him. He came away laughing. "This quarry is sweeter than chasing two men through the streets on a fool's errand."

Further grunts and laughter greeted his words as they dragged the two women, screaming and kicking to a broken-fronted house that had been looted earlier to meet their fate. Their wailing and cries of anguish lanced painfully into the hearts of the two men lurking in the shadows, their honour and chivalry torn by the scene that they were so impotently witnessing. Jamie thought in vain that if there were no mission and he were in full harness and mounted on Richard, he would ride into their midst and slaughter them, despite the odds stacked against him. Yet he was forced instead to skulk away like a coward.

Cristoforo stepped back into the street, shaking his head and motioned for them to retreat northwards away from the river before it was too late.

They moved up the Rue Fauconnie, passing more ruined and looted buildings. The street was littered with broken possessions and dead bodies, and the smell of charred wood and soot fouled the air, with smoke hanging in palls before their eyes. Then a sweet tang similar to that of roasting pork assailed their senses, and they both recognised this smell of old as charring human flesh.

They continued north along the Pas Charlamagne that led them to the wider Rue Saint Antoine that ran from west to east in parallel to the Seine. Here they were forced to halt, for mobs comprising both men and women were openly controlling the street. Their victims were men, women and children, who were being herded into a central square, passing through a line of faggots and kindling. Dogs howled and barked at the scene before them, scenting fear and unrest.

"They mean to burn them alive?" Jamie shook his head in anger, his right hand going to his sword hilt, drawing the weapon.

"No, Jamie, it will avail us naught and bring us certain death."

As they watched, a man was pulled up by his neck on a rope attached to an overhanging dragon beam, crying out for mercy and asking what his crimes had been. The mob heeded him not and continued to stretch him upwards, laughing and jeering as they did so.

Cristoforo pulled down his cowl and placed the white cap of the Cabochiens upon his head to show his apparent solidarity with the crowds before him. "*Madonna*, my countryman wrote of this, and now it comes to life in front of my very eyes, the Ninth Circle of Hell." Cristoforo crossed himself and grasped the crucifix at his throat.

Jamie's voice was barely recognisable, sounding strained and harsh when he spoke. "Come, let us leave this hellish mob to its atrocities."

The two moved off eastwards along the wide street bordered on either side by spectacular buildings of three and four stories. They pushed forward through the mobs of people, brushing off drunken fools and peddlers who sought to sell goods and food as if this was some form of carnival. It was a macabre scene, conjured as Cristoforo had said straight from Dante Alighieri's epic poem.

They turned left down Rue Saint Paul and then left again into the side street of Rue Neuve Saint Pierre which brought them to the main door of the Hôtel Saint-Pol. This, they had been informed by the Duke d'Orleans, was the main entrance that led directly to the apartments of Queen Isabeau. The palace was not a single building, but was composed of three separate buildings purchased at different times and integrated by means of linking galleries. The queen's apartments were set in the centre, with the children's rooms to the north and the king's own quarters to the south. They had wanted to approach from the river entrance directly to King Charles' apartments off the Quai des Célestins, yet had been prevented from doing so by a group of suspicious watchmen who had attempted to follow them.

Before them was a new horror, and they realised that their mission might well be in vain, for either side of the gateway that offered the main entrance to the palace lay piles of dead men, left in careless heaps, listless and broken in death, their limbs askew, their eyes glazed. Crows and vermin were already picking at the corpses. The birds cawed and flapped their wings, accompanied by the snarling and tearing of foxes and the squealing of rats.

Chapter Twenty-Three

Jamie and Cristoforo looked at each other in dismay.

"*Dio Mio*, have we truly entered Hell on earth?" Cristoforo said. "Is the Book of Revelation come to haunt us? For I know not where I have seen such carnage as this."

"I have seen similar, yet only on a field of battle. Mark me, they all wear the royal livery or that of Armagnac. 'Tis a charnel house, by God's legs it is," Jamie swore.

They wrinkled their noses against the rising stench of the dead, moving to approach the gates in the sputtering light thrown by the brands in their iron sconces. The gates were open, and at each side stood rough looking men with ruddy faces, their heads bearing the white caps of the Cabochiens. Two held swords at the ready, though to Jamie's eyes they looked unskilled in their use. One was swaying, and Jamie observed he was drunk to the point of falling over.

Jamie had his sword unsheathed and Cristoforo walked cat-like on the balls of his feet, ready to fight or flee. When they saw the white cap upon Cristoforo's head and the tabard bearing the Burgundian arms, the guards relaxed a little.

"Hold, what is your business here?" called a guard, who was apparently their leader.

"We come in the name of his Grace the Duke of Burgundy, I to escort this man of business from the House of Lombardy who bears papers for the king to sign," Jamie answered, hoping that he would not receive the news that the king was dead.

"The House of Lombardy, bankers? What place do they now have in the town of *écorcheurs?* For we bow to no man, not even to Burgundy himself."

"Beware then, for his grace's wrath is great and will brook no rebuke in this matter. You have sacked the town, yet who will pay to restore it? Who shall give you fiscal reward for your efforts? The bankers of course, or you shall be lordlings of little more than a funeral pyre with naught to recommend you save your pride.

"Now inspect our bona fides and let us pass, for I have seen enough death this night and would not add your bodies to the tally," Jamie finished, raising his sword to emphasise the words.

At this point a captain of the guard arrived, also in Burgundian arms. This is what Jamie had feared, for whilst the Burgundian army was large, most of the captains knew of each other, at least by sight.

"What is this? Who seeks audience with the king and on what business?" he demanded, catching the tail end of the exchange.

Jamie explained again their business and added, "I was

offering my wisdom to this malapert, yet he seemed disinclined to heed my words." This was said deliberately to provoke the man, who would have to fight or back away from the conflict with a captain-at-arms present.

The captain looked closer in the lights of the flambeau. Jamie's blood ran cold. "I know you not."

"I am of the duke's personal retinue, brought from the Low Countries to serve his grace loyally here." Jamie maintained a haughty demeanour and inflected his words with a Flemish accent.

The guard peered at him suspiciously, then snorted in dour acknowledgement as Jamie and Cristoforo both breathed a barely concealed sigh of relief.

The captain considered all before him and then shrugged, seemingly agreeable to the explanation. "Come, follow me. The palaces are a rabbit warren of rooms and passages."

They passed under the archway into an enceinte surrounded by buildings with many doors leading off, some of which had been broken inwards and hung on bent and shattered hinges. Set out before them were ornate flower borders and gardens, now trampled and ruined. More bodies lay here in a tangle of death, arms at unnatural angles, faces stark and unmoving. Fired casements still smouldered and the sound of raucous voices echoed around the space, resonating from the rooms above them and interspersed by shrieks of some hapless maid caught in their web of terror.

Jamie saw the captain shake his head in disgust: "This..." The captain motioned with his left arm. "...is far worse than anything that even the whoreson English would do. I loathe to see my countrymen so debased."

Jamie nodded and looked at Cristoforo, who offered a Latin shrug in response. They continued towards the river, entering first one building then another. Groups of guards lounged at doorways, and upon recognising the captain they straightened up and moved aside to grant access. Each apartment was desecrated and had been ripped apart, and beautiful hangings lay smouldering or shredded upon the floors. They passed the queen's own private chapel, empty now of the rich chattels that had once graced the alter. The door hung at a strange angle and dark stains were spread about the floor in sticky pools where someone had forfeited their life's blood.

They passed down a long corridor that opened onto a beautiful vestibule that had mercifully not been desecrated. Two ornate carved chairs stood either side of an immense oaken door, each decorated with statues of gold and silver. In one sprawled another captain of the guard, while two Cabochien rebels stood drinking in the corner by a long trestle table.

Upon seeing their guide, the captain stood and passed words with him, and Jamie and Cristoforo were motioned to wait beyond hearing distance of the whispered conversation that took place.

The new captain looked suspiciously at Jamie and signalled for the two men to come forward. When he spoke relief flooded over them.

"I will take you to his majesty, who is under house arrest on the orders of the duke. Follow me," he snapped. "And sheath your sword in the king's chambers, for you will not require it unless you too wish to take his life. I have sent two Cabochiens to Hades already this day and shall spare nothing in his majesty's defence for all that might seem otherwise." A hard questioning look came into his eyes and Jamie obeyed with alacrity, returning his weapon to its scabbard.

The captain called for the large oak door to be opened, barking a command from outside, and once Jamie and Cristoforo were inside it was slammed shut with an ominous resonance. The atmosphere within the chamber was sombre, but at least it lacked the charred smell of burning wood and the sickly aroma of death.

The hangings were still present upon the walls, complete with embroidered pearls and gold filigree. This they knew had been the life's work of King Charles V, the current king's father. Another corridor led down to some steps, off which they saw a beautifully panelled library that had been the old king's passion. A guard stood there, and they saw to their relief that all had been left untarnished, with not a book out of place. To Jamie's mind the connected rooms resembled a series of small villages, each with its own character, locked within a mystical and fabulously appointed town.

Jamie made trite comments along the way, but their new guide, a man by the name of Louis Sancerre, turned to Cristoforo. "You speak not at all, Italian," he said. "Where do you reside?"

Cristoforo looked back at him as one who had but latterly awoken from a dream, seemingly lost in thought. "I? Why I have quarters with my master at the Pont au Change."

He named the main congregation of money lenders and bankers in the town, most of whom were either Jews or Italians. "He is from Lombardy, though I hail originally from *Firenze,* of a banking family there. We seek our position here as money lenders to the great lords and royal families – who of course include his grace the Duc of Burgundy and his majesty."

"Why the king at this moment?" Sancerre enquired.

Cristoforo shrugged dismissively as though any fool would be able to put together the pieces of the puzzle. "The duke needs funds to furnish his campaign and through that course needs must open a conduit to the king. Money will change hands to ensure the safety of the king, and we shall provide the funds. 'Tis a simple process." He finished with a hint of arrogance, as though explaining to a simpleton.

Sancerre scowled, halted and snarled at Cristoforo. "Take not that tone with me, Italian, for I am not a goky to be trifled with!"

Cristoforo affected complacency and bowed his head. "No insult was intended, signor. I deal in silver, you in arms. Each to his own account."

The captain muttered something and moved on. "Now we come to the royal apartments. His majesty is lodged here, barricaded with his family and a few retainers who managed to escape the slaughter without."

He called out once more, and the doors were opened by two men in the livery of Burgundy. Upon seeing the captain they bade them enter.

Once Jamie and Cristoforo were inside, the captain said

that he would wait outside the doors to escort them back to the queen's apartments in the Hôtel du Comte d'Étampes.

A squire at arms appeared in the outer chamber: "I am Pierre Aycelin, squire to my Lord of Jaingy, Sir Arnaud de Corbie. Whom do I have the pleasure of addressing?" The squire was courteous. Whatever else had befallen the king's party, the manners and mode of the court were still in place, Jamie and Cristoforo were pleased to see.

"I am, as you see, of his grace's meiny, attached to his guard duty from the Low Countries. I bear a gift to his majesty from this Italian banker who has funds pledged, I believe, and there are matters that need to be seen by the king and documents that must be signed," Jamie replied, deliberately obtuse in his meaning. He then asked in Latin if he could take him to his master.

The squire looked slightly puzzled at the change in language, but understood perfectly and replied in the same ancient tongue. "Of course, yet do you choose this tongue for a purpose?"

"So those that serve the Burgundian cause may not comprehend matters that are for the king's ears only."

Pierre Aycelin caught on quickly, glancing at the two guards, who seemed bored and obviously had not understood a word.

At which Cristoforo chimed in. "Is there anyone of rank within that serves Burgundy? For if none, then our timing is auspicious, for there is much that we would impart to his counsel and those who would advise him."

"There are those who may give cause for concern, and I will endeavour to smooth a path for you. Follow me."

They did as they were bidden, seeing more elegant rooms bedecked in a superior way, with finery, gold inlaid tapestries and marble statues that stood as sentinels at each doorway they passed. They entered a high-ceilinged chamber that would have been fitting for the King's Council. Elegant panelling graced the walls in light oak, darkened little by age since the interior had been completely renovated by King Charles V.

A beautiful throne stood at one end, around which milled various courtiers, knights and pages. The smell of frankincense, sandalwood and sweet lavender scented the large chamber, and all the windows were tightly shut against the night, rendering the room a little stuffy. A febrile atmosphere pervaded the air, as each figure seemed intent upon the other, some with bandaged wounds from the debacle of the previous hours. They had, Jamie surmised, clearly been caught off guard, which meant that no word of warning had reached them from the Armagnacs – or if it had, it had not been heeded.

The squire presented his master.

"I am Sir Arnaud de Corbie, Lord of Jaigny," said the older knight before him, his manner haughty and dismissive. "Whom do I have the honour of addressing?"

Jamie sketched a bow in response. "My lord, I am Sir James de Grispere, household knight to his majesty King Henry Five of England. And this is my companion, Cristoforo Corio, lately of Florence and now in his majesty's employ as a Royal Messenger."

The lord before him changed in his demeanour: "An English knight? Here? Yet I see that you bear the Burgundian colours. How came this to be? Furnish me with an explanation forthwith, I prithee, or your life shall be forfeit!"

At the French knight's subtle gesture, men-at-arms of the king's guard moved forward, wary now as was the squire, Pierre Aycelin, who acknowledged that he had been duped.

Jamie held up a hand, knowing that his and Cristoforo's lives hung in the balance. All present were strung as tight as bow strings and the slightest irregularity would sign their death warrant.

"I beseech thee, sir, hold. For we have lately arrived from the Hôtel-de-Ville, where reside the lords of Orleans and Armagnac, who have scribed a missive here for your eyes and those of his majesty the king. We have braved much to venture here and warn you of all that has occurred, and would not wish this to be wasted upon a misunderstanding. Cristo?" Jamie gestured to his companion, who produced the scroll from a pocket within his cloak and passed it to the knight before him.

"This is sealed with the ring of the Duc of Burgundy," the knight queried, at which point Jamie began to lose patience.

"Would you have us travail through these murderous streets carrying a missive that bears the seal of the one man whom all would seek to destroy? We used this false seal to protect ourselves from the rabble, and now we receive a similar threat within these royal walls we have striven so hard to attain," Jamie snapped.

The knight's visage darkened. "I trust that your message is better prepared than your manners," he retorted.

"I'm sure that is indeed the case, sir, yet I have not come

to bandy words or manners with those who, if they had been better prepared and heeded the warnings I myself carried from England, would not be situated as they are. Now, do you wish to read this and hear what we have to impart, or shall we be on our way and leave you to your fate?" Jamie concluded.

Cristoforo for once was the calmer of the two, and proceeded almost languidly in his speech. "Signor, I have fought hard adversity to reach you here, and for the love of your king, I would beg that you heed the contents of the letter. As my companion attests, it bears a false seal to ensure our passage through what can only be described as hell upon earth, and we have yet to return through its untamed streets. Yet you will see upon close inspection that the seal is not a true representation, merely one that we conjured up in the hours before we left the hotel. I can testify to the fact that it was written by his grace the Duc d'Orleans, and would ask that you break the seal and see for yourself."

Suitably mollified, and pleased to be distracted from Jamie without losing face, the Lord of Jaigny broke the seal and read, his eyes widening as he took in the words. He hurried to the bottom and saw the signature of Duke Charles and by its side, that of the Count of Armagnac.

"By God and all his Saints, you speak the truth. I shall arrange an immediate audience with the king. I would offer an apology, as I now see that your coming here was a mission of the utmost import, and fraught with danger to your persons. I thank you for your courage. His majesty is much discomposed and tried in vain to escape to the Château de Vincennes. Yet the whoresons had cut off our escape there and have taken the Bastille as well, with the Provost of Paris, Pierre des Essants taken prisoner. I pray to God that he still lives."

Jamie and Cristoforo exchanged glances. Both fortresses taken, even the Bastille! This was a nightmare. "I had bethought the Bastille impregnable, Sir Arnaud. How came this to happen?" Jamie probed.

"'Twas so indeed, and still should be, yet they were betrayed from within by traitors posing as friends. There is but a small garrison there which was easily overcome once the gate was opened to the bourgeoisie."

Jamie shook his head: "The same plan was afoot within the walls at the Hôtel-de-Ville, where the duke's own steward turned traitor, opening a postern gate to the rabble. Only by good fortune did we counter the attack. It was a close run thing with the hotel so nearly at their mercy."

"I trust his head now resides upon a spike at the gates?"

"No, my lord, for he escaped in the melee and could not be found."

"I prithee wait upon the court, such as it is, and I shall beg an audience with his majesty that you might impart all that has happened and direct as you have been instructed by his grace the Duc d'Orleans. On a point of order, I would ask that you relinquish your sword before I bring his majesty forth."

Jamie nodded his assent and passed his sword to Pierre Aycelin, and with that Sir Arnaud left through a doorway to another chamber.

Chapter Twenty-Four

The king, when he arrived, brought with him the still strikingly beautiful Queen Isabeau trailed by six of his remaining children who continued to share the palace with him, including his heir, the sixteen year old Dauphin Louis.

Jamie studied him with interest. Despite the late hour and being raised from his bed, the dauphin showed more intelligence than his father, even when the monarch had his full wits about him. There seemed a greater strength of character that all assumed had been inherited from his mother, whose lasting beauty and command of the Council had withstood all ravages of time and circumstance.

For all that, the king seemed to have control of all his faculties, and his sharp, beady eyes took in all before him in an appraising manner. At forty-five, the once golden hair had turned a light brown and his attempt to grow a wispy moustache and beard to cover the weak chin was ill-conceived. His voice when he spoke was light and almost feminine in its tone.

Once seated on the wooden throne, he addressed Jamie and Cristoforo: "We would ask that you come forward and be recognised, for we hear that you did us a great service this day."

The two men bowed three times and moved before the king. Jamie saw two of his household knights move forward, ready to protect their monarch if any move should be made to harm him. Nobody was taking any chances on a day such as this.

"Your Majesty is most kind to indulge us at this precarious moment, and we would offer our heartfelt prayers that Paris soon comes once again under your royal control," Jamie offered. The king nodded, seemingly pleased with the response, encouraging further explanation. "Majesty, if we may, we would furnish you with all details that have led to the unhappy circumstance that sees us here before you in your most gracious company."

"Just so, pray continue," the king replied.

Jamie gave a full account of all that had occurred, from his briefing in London to their arrival here and the terror that had overtaken all of Paris beyond the palace walls to their horror-filled journey to the French royal court.

"And you say that the Duke d'Orleans and the Count of Armagnac rally at this moment, with hopes of raising an army to counter these ravages upon our fair city?"

"We do, Majesty. They look to find ways of contacting troops further afield outside the walls of Paris. Once an army is raised, they shall remove the pestilence of this Cabochien revolt in which you have been so terribly involved. The true trial lies in finding a way out of the city, for the gates are barred and most closely watched, with all expecting an attack by the Armagnac forces. Without the palace mass slaughter has occurred, with killings and fearsome acts against any who may even be suspected of sympathising with the Armagnac cause."

Here the courtiers frowned, considering that the information might be too much for his majesty. The king wanted to believe that his subjects loved him and would not rebel. The dauphin and the queen realised the horror of what had occurred more quickly than the king, and while his face showed surprise and dismay, their expressions displayed contempt and anger. Jamie wondered if the scales been lifted from the young dauphin's eyes as the king raised a scented lace handkerchief to his face as if to ward off the horror of Jamie's words.

Queen Isabeau spoke with icy calm. "We have witnessed some of the desolation of which you speak, and would wish no further scathe to occur. To wit we are informed that our cousin, whose very name we cannot bear to mention, is to present ordnances that will limit his majesty's powers and offer more to *Les Etats Generaux de Langue,* which we must assume includes the bourgeoisie and more particularly the Cabochiens, as they have styled themselves.

"To this end we shall play whatsoever game they wish, all the while holding steadfast and praying for the day that the armies of our lords of Orléans come to our relief. For your part in this sorry affair, we thank you most heartily, and would pray for your safe delivery back to the Hôtel-de-Ville. Is there any means at our disposal that may assist you in your endeavours?" she offered graciously.

"Majesty, there are two matters that may aid us, if I may be so bold. The hour, whilst late, still encourages the rabble to plunder and terrorise in a drunken rampage. We would ask that we may trespass upon your hospitality a little while longer and escape within the early hours of the morning, when I pray all shall be asleep or nursing sore heads, sated of their lust for debauchery and violence."

The queen nodded her head: "We should readily acquiesce to this demand. And the second boon?"

"I would ask Your Majesty for bona fides granting safe passage for myself and my companion, Signor Corio, to travel through France. The land may well be in turmoil and a royal warrant would suffice in safeguarding our fate should we be apprehended by French forces."

"It heartens us greatly to see that you still hold our power in such esteem as a talisman against forces of evil, and I pray that your faith be justified should you be captured as foreigners by forces that are loyal to us."

Queen Isabeau called for parchment and ink to be brought by a clerk, and a royal warrant was then transcribed and signed by both their majesties. The seal was bright with newly melted wax and cooled to a duller sheen as the royal party made to leave the hall.

Queen Isabeau called Jamie closer. As he did so, he saw the strain in her face showing in the lines etched around her large eyes. She was still regal and aloof, yet somehow appeared vulnerable at the same instant. "We believe this to be the second occasion that you have come to the assistance of France. It shall not be forgotten." Her lips were soft, with an essence of mint that floated to his senses as she spoke. Her voice had a husky Germanic accent that Jamie found alluring. He could see why this woman had captivated so many men's hearts. "Other than our warrant of guarantee, we dare not entrust any missives to be found upon you should you be caught. However, let us have no ambage here, for we fervently support our lords of Armagnac and would have you register this intent with them. We shall have to bow to pressure to sign our cousin's ordinances, yet they are easily revoked, and with such action we shall enact a great and terrible revenge upon his person and his supporters. We adjure you to pass these sentiments onwards to our cousins."

"As Your Majesty pleases, consider it done."

"Now you must excuse us, for we are poor company and needs must retire."

As one last parting gift the queen offered her hand for Jamie to kiss, which he did with grace and aplomb, bowing over the outstretched arm. "Majesty."

Queen Isabeau looked at Cristoforo, who had remained silent during her exchange with Jamie. "And you, Signor Corio, we thank you for your bravery and courage." Cristoforo offered her a deep bow. "I now bid you goodnight and Godspeed." With that she swept away, leaving both men enveloped in a gentle and alluring scent of jasmine, bergamot and orange blossom.

"She is indeed a queen," Cristoforo said, "and one who is well worthy of the title."

"Amen to that," Jamie agreed, clearly still captivated by her charisma.

In the early hours of the morning, with the sun not yet risen, Jamie and Cristoforo slipped out of the palace to the

Quai des Célestins leading to the Seine. The captain of the guard had been put off twice from relieving the royal party of their charges. He was told that they were drafting papers of finance, and seeing evidence that the two men were still present he went away, each time more suspicious. When they were ready, they left by a side door with no guards to witness their departure.

In the darkness all appeared quiet and calm. Jamie and Cristoforo both knew that was a common aftermath of a disorganised rabble, fuelled on hate with little left to orchestrate the rioting once the night's excesses had ceased. As the rioters slept or fell unconscious with drink at the celebration of their success, only the watched gates and walls were a problem – and as ever the city's weak spot was the River Seine.

The river gate closed behind them and they made their way to the quaysides, which were showing signs of life. This part of Paris never seemed to sleep, with new cargoes being brought in constantly, and a sense of order was returning after the night's pillaging of incoming craft. Groups of boats of various sizes had formed a fleet and anchored themselves in the centre of the river, suspicious of coming ashore, but traders and excise officials were being rowed to and from the group, allaying fears and encouraging them to disembark their wares.

Jamie approached a boatman who was roping his cargo of what looked like barrels of wine brought up from Bordeaux. The League of River Merchants had been granted special dispensation by King Philip VI and paid a sum for each cargo that they brought. He had ordered a new landing point built at the Port de l'Ecole, to which the barge was heading past the quay at the Place de Grève. Jamie and Cristoforo would disembark from there and make the short distance to the back of the Hôtel-de-Ville.

For a few coins the bargeman agreed to transport them downstream to the next quay. Thankfully the sun had not yet risen, as there was nowhere to hide on the open barge, but it would still be safer, and they were less likely to be challenged on open water. A small bench offered them an opportunity to sit against the barrels.

They wrapped their cloaks around them against the night, Cristoforo shifting awkwardly to accommodate the small crossbow that still hung upon a single strap across his shoulder. It was a cumbersome way to carry it, but he had not wanted it seen by the guards or the Cabochiens in the streets whom they passed. Now he brought it to sit upon his lap with the strap behind him, checking the deadly device for any damage or malfunction. Testing the cord and feeling for the three quarrels secured underneath, he was satisfied, and he and Jamie sat quietly, lost in their own thoughts, their eyes straining to pierce the dark streets and alleyways for any sign of threat as the sky gradually grew lighter from the east.

The garrulous bargeman asked questions and gave a running commentary of all that had occurred. Flaming brands acted as warning lamps to other river craft and in their flickering light they saw the dead hanging from makeshift gibbets and heard the cries of the dying. Some of the Watch were heaving bodies into the river, carelessly disposing of them. The terrible smell of death filled the air.

As time passed the lapping of the water changed as the bargeman steered his craft towards the shore.

"You are certain you go no further, monsieur?" Jamie asked, realising that they could if they wished make their escape all the way to the sea by such a way, once they had imparted the king's news and the queen's assurances to the Duke of Armagnac.

The bargeman had been silent, watching the events on shore and casting the odd suspicious glance at Jamie and Cristoforo, wondering no doubt exactly whom he had picked up for passage. "*Non, monsieur.* I regret no, I stop here then return upstream as soon as the wind favours me once more."

No amount of coin would dissuade him, and the two men offered to help unload, posing as steves for the man's wares. They bought two small barrels of wine for their own cover of purpose and moved up the quay in the direction of the Hôtel-de-Ville. It was here they knew that they were at their most vulnerable, caught between the Cabochiens on the beach and the guards upon the walls of the Hôtel-de-Ville, for whom they would no doubt look in the dark like any other rebels seeking to assail the fortress.

Macabre dark shapes swung in the early breeze, testament to the brutality of the previous night. Ropes creaked under the weight of the corpses as they spun to and fro in the morning breeze. Groans were heard from the ground too, as drunken groups sought to combat the ravages of drink upon their bodies. Some called out, demanding to know who they were or asking them for another drink from the small tuns they carried. Jamie and Cristoforo ignored them and walked ever closer to the gates of the hotel that loomed out of the darkness above them, blacker against the skyline that was even now changing as the soft light of dawn started to filter through. This was their moment of greatest peril.

A figure appeared upon the *chemins de rondes* on the gated tower above. "Away, or we shall loose upon you!" the guard snapped.

"We are friend, sir. I am the English knight, Sir James de Grispere. Fetch Edouard de Breudeport – and hurry, for we are exposed and needs must enter."

The guard's shout carried far in the quiet of dawn, but at the same time a cry went up from the groups behind them, calling for them to identify themselves and state their intent.

Jamie and Cristoforo put down the tuns of wine and prepared to face the onslaught that they were certain was coming. They watched as figures unravelled themselves from their makeshift beds upon the shale of the beach and stood, coming to alert and roused to action by the promise of more sport and death. One man identified himself as their leader, and walked forward.

Jamie recognised him as the aggressive watchman from the previous evening as he strode into the middle of the group. Flambeaus were being lit and raised high, throwing their light forward. "Why 'tis those two rogues from last night! Take them or kill them, bring crossbows to bear," the Cabochien shouted.

Jamie released his cloak, drew his sword and placed his buckler upon his left arm; while Cristoforo unbuckled the strap on his chest, pulling around the crossbow, cocking the weapon and placing a deadly quarrel in its tiller in one fluid motion. He sighted and let loose a quarrel that hummed its deadly way towards the target.

The loud-mouthed leader flew backwards under the impact as the bolt thudded home and sprouted from his chest. He landed gasping his last breaths like a fish upon the beach where he now lay.

Cristoforo wasted no time and began re-cocking his deadly bow, looking to his next target.

Another figure appeared, bearing a full-size crossbow of his own. He bent to put his foot in the stirrup, hooking his belt claw to pull back and cock the draw string of the more cumbersome weapon, but as he did so a second quarrel whistled through the air, bringing death. The impact killed him instantly, taking him backwards as the string of his own bow released and twanged harmlessly at his feet. Then from above came the sound of more bolts flying, and the remaining rebels fell or ran crying for their lives at the deadly onslaught launched against them.

"Never was I so glad to hear the twang of bowstrings – yet what I would have given for a good English war bow and bag of arrows." Jamie sighed. At which the locks were slid back, and the postern gate swung quickly inwards.

"Come, quickly afore the *rif-et-raf* gain new courage," called Edouard de Breudeport. "Hah, and you return with fresh wine! Never were guests so welcome!" he joked, as Jamie and Cristoforo picked up a tun each and moved within the protection of the walls.

Chapter Twenty-Five

Council Chamber, Palace of Westminster: May

The king was presiding over his first council meeting since his coronation. All the new council members sat around the large table with their new monarch at its head. They were expectant, and wished to see if their expectations were to become reality.

"My lords, it is gracious of you to attend upon this auspicious day as the first official presentation within our new Council and government. We pray to Almighty God that sees a new reign of prosperity to our realm and that we may all move forward as one. To build upon our promise of unity and harmony within the kingdom, we are proposing to be merciful and release our cousin Edmund, Earl of March from house arrest, and mayhap return in due course his estates that were confiscated."

There were mutters around the table and exchanges of glances. It fell to Bishop Henry Beaufort to voice the combined fears of the other members of the Council. He stood before speaking: "My lord king, if I may?"

"Pray proceed, my lord bishop, we are ever eager to hear from our ecclesiastical brethren."

"I thank you, sire. I have concerns upon this move, lord king, and I would not wish to decry any commands that you wouldst give. Yet I am sure that we all here are only too aware that the Earl of March is a direct descendant of our great grandfather, and therefore has a direct right of inheritance to the throne, being senior even above your majesty. With this in mind, if I may venture, is it wise to release a proven traitor and rebel who may turn upon you with an army at his back to seek the crown for himself?"

The speech was well phrased as all knew the circumstances, but the way in which the bishop spoke highlighted his own royal lineage, offering a more personal view than any other present would dare to.

The king grew tense and turned a little pale, before he visibly relaxed, not wishing to cause controversy at his first council meeting. He took a deep breath and began his response. "My lord bishop, we are as ever grateful for your concern and comments upon such matters of state. However, we feel that the earl has learned his lesson and we wish to be merciful, sowing mayhap a future that is without the discord that emanated from the previous reign of our dear father. Ours is a new reign and we would reconcile old enmities, to wit we shall continue with our plans of amnesty." The king's words were spoken gently, yet gave no room for manoeuvre or negotiation. The king by his tone was adamant.

"As Your Majesty pleases," the bishop responded, bowing to King Henry. He resumed his seat, outwardly calm yet inwardly seething.

"Upon this moment we shall send out writs this day and call for parliament to meet upon the fifteenth day of May. Let it so be known, and we shall meet our new government with a clear heart and conscience."

×✤× —

Bishop Beaufort was in his private house north of the river close to the palace. It was well appointed and hidden from any major throughfare, discreet in its own grounds to the rear of Le Straunde. He was in a private meeting with Sir Thomas Chaworth. "How was Sir John when you saw him at Cooling Castle?"

"He was in fine form, Your Grace, and ever confident that he would withstand the winds of change when placating his majesty as to his spiritual beliefs."

"Was he indeed? Well from what I have witnessed this morning at Council, I am of the persuasion that he may have the right of it. For the new king seems intent upon forgiving all and saving us with his prayers, ensuring that we are all forced to wallow in his piety."

Again Chaworth was struck by how vehement Beaufort was in his denouncement of the new king.

"You believe, my lord bishop, that the king will agree to this new heresy?" he asked. "For I'll warrant that Sir John has sided with us and served us right well in France these two years past, and he is of the Royal Household. Yet will this foundation be enough to withstand the gale of blasphemy that blows against him? I wonder at it."

"We shall see, and betimes we shall do all we can to upset the apple cart of intimacy between the two. For Richard Courtney too lurks within this ring, and none forget his part in raising Oxford University against the king. A worse band of idolators I have not the disgrace to encounter, save a Saracen.

"And to speak of such, I hear that Whittington's mawmet de Grispere has been absent from court and is rumoured to be in France. Have you heard aught?"

"Only the same rumours as ever, my lord. Nothing of a more substantial nature."

"I like it not when that knight is abroad, for it bodes ill to some and we are often the target. Very well, go to and report if perchance you hear news or intelligence of import – and stay close to my Lord of Cobham. No doubt we shall see you in the Palace upon the recall of parliament ten days hence."

Palace of Westminster: 15th May

The Lords and Commons sat before the king in his first official parliament. They were only too aware of pressing matters of finance, and granted him taxes on all wool exports for the next four years as well as a lay subsidy, the main form of taxation in England. This was done in an effort to cement their relationship with their new monarch.

Yet the Speaker asked for quiet to make clear a very salient point, given the past history of how monarchs had treated such largesse. "Your Majesty, we would add that in the past, the Commons had requested good governance on many occasions and their requests had been granted, but our lord, the king, was well aware of how this had been subsequently fulfilled and carried out." Here he paused, allowing the words to carry their full import.

The king knew full well that the Speaker was alluding to the fact that his father had promised much and delivered little.

The Speaker continued to push the point home, bringing pressure to bear upon the new king. "Howsoever, since God has endowed the new king with good sense and many other bounties and virtues, we are assured that he would practice and maintain good governance."

With this, King Henry knew that he would have to keep up with his obligations or lose the faith and support of the Commons. "My Lords and Commons, we thank you for your concessions, which we shall put to good use in the protection and safety of the realm, both here and in Europe," he replied. "To wit, those concerns and criticisms that you may have regarding the future, we should ask that you put these in writing to us for consideration."

. . .

Two days later a list had been drawn up and the king read it in his private chamber, with the Lord Chamberlain, Lord Chancellor, Lord Chief Justice and his clerks present, together with his private financier, Sir Richard Whittington, who was the last to read the list. He raised an eyebrow as he continued: "Why, my lord king, this is worse than we thought. It covers Wales, Ireland, the Scottish borders and Calais, which is to be expected, but also Gascony and the raising of a navy, together with good governances and provisions for new laws of peace. Why 'tis a prison of finance. No concessions that have so far been given will reward you sufficiently to make good all these ties and demands. You shall have to look elsewhere to fill the crown's coffers," Whittington said, flicking a dismissive hand at the parchment as he did so.

Bishop Beaufort, the Lord Chancellor, caught on immediately, inwardly gleeful that this would now mean that the king would have to come cap in hand to the Church – a Church that was vehemently against all forms of Lollardy and was even now bringing actions against the nominal Lollard leader, Sir John Oldcastle, the king's friend and household knight.

Whittington continued: "Our greatest concern, my lord king, is the sea and the trade routes to the Low Countries and Gascony, for our trade, as his majesty is aware, is strongest in these shipping routes."

The king merely nodded in acknowledgement, his mind in turmoil as to what his next steps should be. He knew that finance was imperative for the throne to function, and the Commons must be appeased at all costs. Henry knew that he had bought himself time to consider all planned demands and work out a new route to take that would lead him to the Church and its financial help, and with it, the balance of friendship with his old ally.

A clerk to the king came through the side door, and Sir Richard saw that it was none other than Sir Thomas Burton. He walked up before the king and bowed: "I earnestly beg your pardon, Majesty, yet I have grave news that bears the telling upon this instant."

"Prithee continue," the king adjured him.

"Majesty, I have received terrible news that confirms the rumours from France. Paris has fallen to a revolt. They say that a group of plebs have risen up, in particular the butchers, calling themselves the Cabochiens. All is in chaos, with slaughter on the streets and assassinations of Armagnacs and their followers."

King Henry looked across at Whittington, who paled at the fate that may have befallen Jamie and Cristoforo.

Chapter Twenty-Six

L'Hôtel-de-Ville, Paris, June

The atmosphere in Paris had been worsening for days now – if such a thing were possible, Jamie thought. Drunken groups of men and women roamed the streets accusing anyone who fell short of their standards of being an Armagnac supporter. No one was safe, and even the Burgundian lords travelled about the city with a full armed escort of twenty men or more, their crossbows at the ready. The bourgeoisie had become indiscriminate, drunk on alcohol, power and the lust for death. Whole streets had been burned and ransacked. The Bastille was fully in the hands of the mob now, and the king had signed the *Ordonnance Cabochienne* prepared by the Estates General earlier that year. Full power was now in the hands of Burgundy and Simon Caboche, the crude butcher who ran the mob. They defied all authority, answering to no one but their own crude methods and their courts of death.

Jamie and Cristoforo looked out again at the shale beach

behind the hotel leading down to the Seine. They had been prisoners within the hotel for days now, unable to venture forth for fear of capture. Twice they had tried to pass through the gates or make it to a wall that offered an easy drop to possible freedom, and each time they had been thwarted. Patrols circled the walls at intermittent times, and camps of followers had set up guard posts for any who tried to escape. The hotel was locked down like a trap waiting to be sprung.

They had deemed that the only way to escape with any hope of success was via the river, using a bargeman to take them west to freedom. Each day they had looked towards the river port to see what barges or boats came into dock and if any of them were making ready to head downstream for Versailles, from where they could flee south on horseback to English held Gascony, using their documents from Queen Isabeau to protect them. But no barge so far had been observed carrying on downstream with a full cargo; all had turned around and headed back upstream, inland towards the centre of France, from where escape would be impossible. It was frustrating to see their potential route to freedom consistently barred to them. But on this day, just after midday as the bells for sext rang from the chapel tower, their luck seemed to change as a low slung skiff appeared heading upstream, its twin sails billowing in a breeze that blew inland from the west.

"There!" Cristoforo pointed, his keen eyes taking in the full sails, the foremost of which was a smaller triangular canvas straining at its rope lines, as it came steadily upstream towards the quay. "Look, see how she floats low in the water?

She is fully laden, I'm certain," he declared, becoming excited at the prospect of a possible escape route.

"I do hope that you have the right of it, for I am heartily sick of our stay here and wish to be homeward bound," Jamie replied.

"Amen to that. Let us watch and see what occurs."

They continued to observe carefully as the fully laden craft made its way slowly against the current. As it finally turned towards to the jetties that sprouted from the quay, they saw the crew of four plying the bow lines back and forth, emptying the sails of their wind as the master skilfully brought the skiff to lie alongside a jetty. One sailor jumped the narrowing gap, line in hand to secure the bow. He then took an aft line, pulling the craft in and mooring it tightly to the wooden structure. A harbour master came forward from his office, which was no more than a single storey wooden structure. The guard at his side looked bored, and performed his duties in a perfunctory manner. With the cargo being unloaded the skiff's captain and the harbour master walked back towards the office, undoubtedly to check and sign any necessary papers.

"We needs must find where he would sup, for it will be close to the port, yet I've never known a mariner who did not wish to visit a tavern upon reaching dry land," Jamie affirmed.

Cristoforo nodded in agreement, and sure enough, after two hours had passed, the master of the skiff left the wharf and made for the nearest streets like someone who knew the way, accompanied by his three crew members.

Nones was rung as Jamie ran down to a side gate,

managing to avoid the patrols and moving quietly from the hotel. He wore the tabard and helmet of the Burgundian colours as before and looked exactly like what he pretended to be – a man-at-arms seeking wine at a tavern. He was pleased that the boat master had chosen a local tavern, l'hostel du Barbel, just a few hundred feet from the hotel. Despite the disguise, Jamie felt vulnerable and exposed.

Venturing into the tavern, he saw that it was filling up with those who worked the boats and a fair number of Cabochiens, distinctive with their white caps and coarse features. Many eyes turned towards him as he entered. It was no time for timidity or subtlety, and as such he cloaked himself with an imperious expression and an arrogant demeanour, striding forward with a swagger to his step, left hand on his sword hilt, emphasising who he was and the authority that was still invested in him despite the encroaching takeover of the town by the rebel mob.

The master sat at a table with his crewmen around him, drinking ale from a flagon and looking around at the Cabochiens, probably wondering what had happened to Paris since their last voyage there. Jamie approached them, siding up to their table. The men looked up suspiciously at the armed presence before them.

"Monsieur, are you the master of the skiff that has just moored at the quay?"

The master was wary. He had seen the destruction and mayhem first hand in the town, and now an armed soldier was approaching him. He became concerned that his boat was to be impounded – or worse. "I am," he replied curtly, licking his lips and looking to his shipmates for help if trouble began.

Jamie responded genially: "Ah, the harbour master directed me to you. Do you travel back downstream soon?"

The boat master relaxed a little realising that there may be some profit for him here. Jamie saw the tension leave his shoulders. "I do. I await the tide, for the river is treacherous to those that know it not. There are shallows unseen, and many a craft and unskilled master has fallen foul of them," he responded, emphasising his skill to raise his price, Jamie thought, smiling inwardly.

Jamie sat down and began to engage with the man. At length he negotiated for a cargo that would be brought before Vespers that evening and loaded for shipment.

"Oh, there is one other matter," Jamie continued, as though he had absentmindedly forgotten. "His grace insists that I should accompany the shipment with mayhap a servant to aid us at Versailles. Will there be room to accommodate us?" Jamie watched as the wily captain saw more silver to be added to his fee. He rubbed his chin in the manner of all those who wish to strike a bargain. Jamie had seen such a gesture many times as a boy at his father's side when travelling to trade.

"Well, I'm not sure. Two of you, you say? That will cost you four silver marks, my lord." It was an outrageous sum, Jamie knew, but he would pay it willingly to escape Paris.

"You drive a hard bargain, master boatman," he said gruffly.

"Those be my terms, soldier. Take them or leave them."

"I accept, and I will bring with me my papers of passage

and my servant afore the tide turns." Jamie left the inn and moved first left then right down a maze of side streets, keeping his bearings but heading for the Burgundian headquarters at the Hôtel de Bourgogne that was coincidentally not that far from l'Hôtel-de-Ville. He ducked quickly into a pie shop that was on the point of closing and bent swiftly as though to pick a coin from the sawdust upon the floor. As he did so he saw a figure dart past, dark and cloaked against recognition. Smiling to himself, he slipped quietly back out again, much to the bafflement of the shop's owner. Within minutes he was back at the side door of the hotel, and with Cristoforo on watch and waiting for him, he slipped in quickly to the security of its walls.

"How did you fare?" Cristoforo asked anxiously.

"We sail west on the evening tide. We must now procure a handcart and prepare to leave."

"I shall be at the smithies, for I have found a whetstone and needs must attend to my blades."

An hour later Jamie looked into one of the lean-to sheds that faced inwards to the outer enceinte and found Cristoforo seated upon a rough wooden bench, carefully and methodically running the stone lengthways along the blade of the wicked-looking falchion that usually resided in a scabbard at his back. The dying rays of sunlight twinkled from the newly honed blade. "The damned *crapaud* steel nicked the blade, and it took me an age to hone it thus."

Jamie looked upon the weapon. Slight compared to a broad or arming sword, the falchion suffered from time to time when pitted against heavier steel, yet Cristoforo set his attention to honing an edge with which he could shave.

Cristoforo had shown Jamie the sharpness of the blade once, holding the weapon edge upwards and asking that Jamie drop a piece of silk across it from shoulder height. The weapon had sliced the feather-light silk in half under its own weight and impetus. The falchion had been formed of the best Damascene steel. Now, satisfied with his efforts in the fading light, Cristoforo wiped the excess oil and flipped the weapon in the air, catching it by the handle to rotate it by the wrist, twisting left and right in a butterfly action, testing as ever its balance and feel. A wicked smile appeared as he felt whole again and returned the weapon to the sheath at his back.

"No daggers?"

"I tended to those whilst you were away. The mail blunted one, but all are sharp again. Now, did you manage to procure a cart?"

"I did so with the aid of Edouard, and we leave by the north gate and approach the quayside from a different direction along the Port au ble."

They took their repast at the kitchen tables, not wishing to cause comment in the main hall, before loading the handcart, covering their war bags and other gear with several bolts of material and spare clothes.

They bade their farewells to the Duke of Orleans and the Count of Armagnac, who had prepared letters to be delivered to King Henry explaining the situation and asking for his forbearance. They promised they would uphold the Treaty of Brétigny as soon as they were returned to power.

"When next we meet, the circumstances may well be different," the duke said ambiguously.

"I fear they may, my lord, for we are separated by terms and differences that honour alone may not breach. For a storm is gathering and clouds of war are strengthening in their intent."

The duke nodded. "So be it, and may it please God that we do not meet upon the field of battle, for I should hate to kill so valiant a knight."

"And I a duke, my lord," Jamie countered, a thin smile upon his lips.

The duke raised an eyebrow and smiled back. "May the Lord have you in his keeping, Sir James, and you, Signor Corio. We wish you health and Godspeed."

"And you, my lord. We shall pray for the deliverance of Paris." They bowed and left the hall.

Édouard was there to see them off, now a brother in arms. Having fought together, they had formed a bond. "Fare thee well, Sir James, and you, Cristoforo. A safe journey home."

They bowed to each other, and leaving the hotel, Jamie and Cristoforo moved through the streets, their senses on high alert, ready to be stopped at any moment, unsure if they had been betrayed or followed after Jamie's meeting at the inn.

The cart creaked through the streets, and twice a group wanted to see what the cart held, hoping for easy plunder. Jamie drew his sword and they slunk away, but each time the chances of discovery grew greater. Finally, they turned left towards the river and the city walls that bounded the bank. Dusk was falling as they approached the quay and made for the waiting skiff.

Two guards saw them coming and made to bar their way. "What is your business here?" the guard challenged. "'Tis late for loading and time for sailing."

"I am on his grace the Duke of Burgundy's business, I have my bona fides here signed by his grace. Do you seek to bar me from my duty?" Jamie produced his papers but doubted whether the fool could read.

Then a voice called out from the harbour master's office. "Georges! Leave them be, they sail with Maurice upon the tide."

And so thought Jamie, *they have paid him his pieces of silver. Coin will oil all wheels whatever its stamp.*

"Come now," called the master of the ship as he appeared from the bow cabin, jerking his thumb upwards, "I've held as long as I may. The tide's turned and we needs must be off."

Jamie nodded in agreement and the two men loaded the goods aboard.

"Not much, is there?" the master asked suspiciously.

"They are valuable tapestries that my lord wishes removed from here to his home in Versailles."

"Very well." He shrugged. "The coin?" At which he held out his hand palm up expectantly.

Jamie reached for his purse and counted out the marks to add to the amount he had paid earlier. The master bit each one and they disappeared into his leather purse. He inclined his head for them to come aboard.

They settled on the wooden cross planking of the skiff that served as benches and felt the vessel lurch as the lines were cast off and the skiff caught the current and began to float off downstream. They were finally leaving Paris and all its horrors behind.

Jamie muttered in Latin to Cristoforo. "I am relieved, yet I fear the bridges may be guarded, even though the boatman said they were never stopped. Please God that we shall reach Versailles by daylight."

Cristoforo nodded in the darkness by way of acknowledgement, still alert to any lurking danger that remained. Both men knew that the landward route was some seven leagues, but by boat it would be twice that distance, making it a four-to-five-hour journey. As they passed downstream they heard the sound of more rioting as the night's conflict floated out across the water. Fires were lit and houses burned, and screams of agony once more pierced the night air.

Chapter Twenty-Seven

Versailles

The small riverside village of Versailles had two short jetties that reached out into the mighty Seine, together with a half harbour enclosed by a semi-circular rock wall where fishing boats and cargo barges were tethered, rising and falling in the river's gentle swell. A few nightlights were still burning, warning of the treacherous shallows for which the Seine was infamous. It had been testament to the boat master's skill that Jamie had observed Cristoforo, his fear of water never as bad on rivers as it was at sea, standing in the middle of the boat to see how he twisted and turned the vessel in seemingly benign waters, heeding the calls of the two crew who tested the depths at the bow with fathom weights.

The master explained in his coarse French. "The river, she is a bitch of a whore, changing her mind this way and that, seducing you to follow and lure you into shallows that will rip out the keel. No trip is ever the same, and many's the time I have seen boats cast upon banks of shale where no bank was previously." He coughed, heaved, and spat over the side to express the love-hate relationship he had with the river.

Eventually they bumped against the jetty, wood to wood contact prevented as the fenders took the brunt of the collision, rubbing and squeaking as lines were slung to pull the skiff in against the wharf. Looking at the dawn skyline, Jamie saw two prominent buildings standing proud above the low-lying plain and the cottages of the villagers.

They fetched their war bags and other gear and stretched their aching muscles, looking around warily, still not fully believing that they had escaped. They had cat-napped on the skiff, each keeping watch as the other slumbered, leaning against canvas and curled against the cold damp air.

They made to unload their small cargo of cloth and other goods that had been transported, supposedly at the behest of the Duke of Burgundy, along with the other cargo being moved from the skiff.

The master called to them as the lines were untied. "Good luck to you, masters, whoever you may be and wherever you are bound." He sketched a wave as the ropes were untied and the skiff drifted out into the waters of the river once more.

"Now to find horses and food. I would wish to bespeak a bed and rest, yet we are too near to Paris and Burgundy's influence here, and I wish to put more miles between us."

"I agree. We are no strangers to privation, and 'tis better to be tired than dead," Cristoforo agreed, pulling in his belt tighter. Both men were gaunt and had not rested properly in the days since they had first entered Paris.

A watchman came down to the wharf, with a dog on a leash by his side. It growled at them from deep in its chest, then stopped as Jamie bent to stroke its head. The rough coat reminded him of Forest, and he felt a pang of homesickness.

"Who be ye, and what is your business here?" the man asked gruffly.

"We have travelled by skiff from Paris and wish to ride south. Is there a place where we might procure two horses and a mule to provide for our needs?"

"Aye, go to the castle when the sun rises. There's an ostler near there, and he'll have what you need. If'n you need a feed, my wife runs the tavern yonder she'll be up and about bakin' soon enough and she'd set a repast for you," he offered. "I hear there be terrible unrest in Paris, with the town in uproar and rebellion. Be that true?"

They confirmed that it was, not wishing to be drawn too much in that regard, and thanked him before moving up into the town, leaving the bolts of cloth in his care until they returned.

"In truth, I care not one wit for them, and would soon as leave them to that watchman as payment," Jamie declared. "Our funds are running low, and we need to find a banker who will make good on a promissory note. Once we are with horse we shall ride to Orleans. It is not the most direct route, yet I fear there will be many on the road who follow Burgundy. Let us hope the word is not yet out that we have escaped. From there we shall cross southwest into Gascony then make west for the coast and take a ship to England."

Jamie and Cristoforo progressed well on the four day journey to Orleans, although they were tired and worn down by the constant need for vigilance and the fear of discovery. They managed to find an inn for their third night's stay where they finally felt secure, and arrived at the Armagnac heartland and the town of Orleans the fourth day after they'd set out from Versailles. There they discovered that a great army was being mustered ready for the relief of Paris. With a letter presented into the Duke of Bourbon's hand, they were well received. The captain of the guard at Orleans and the Duke of Bourbon, who had paid homage to Prince Thomas the previous year, grilled them for whatever information they could provide. They were now tenuous allies, bound only by the Treaty of Bourges. Their treatment was civil and better horses were provided for their long journey up to Cherbourg Cotentin, made longer by the need to stay within the safety of English held territory.

 —

London

Henry Chichele, Bishop of St David's, moved forward to stand before his new king. "Sire, I bring the memorandum that you asked to be prepared for negotiations with King Charles," he said. "It encompasses all that you desired, with a dedicated reference to the Treaty of Brétigny in the year of our Lord 1360. We would pledge this document as desired upon your majesty's behalf to continue the truce with the French crown, whilst holding those lands in Gascony that have been secured by your brother, the Duke of Clarence and Sir Thomas Beaufort, Earl of Dorset."

By his side was Bishop Henry Beaufort, who was to serve with the embassy when it was despatched to France. He looked on impassively, secure in the knowledge that both he and his brother were to play an important part in England's future – both diplomatically and martially.

"We thank you, my lord bishop, for bringing this forward and wouldst give full consideration to the document for our signature in due course. There is of course a current impediment to a journey to meet with King Charles, to wit Paris is still in the throes of revolt of the so called *Cabochiens*. Though we are advised that new armies seek to conquer the bourgeoisie with aid from our Armagnac cousins, the premise would still be true that Burgundy will continue with his power over the king and indeed France. It is therefore him with whom we must treat.

"The Low Countries are of course within his domain, and here is the greatest pattern of trade, so peace should be kept at all costs to aid our fiscal deficit."

"As Your Majesty pleases," Bishop Chichele agreed.

"To wit, my Lord Chancellor, how goes the conscription of more ships to fight piracy and aid clear transportation?"

"My lord king, the figures from William Caxton, your new appointment as Clerk of the King's ships, make for poor reading. The tonnage is down from the previous year, and we have..." Beaufort consulted a document before him. "The tally is just some one hundred and sixteen vessels, ranging from balingers and barges to scaffs and spinas. More vessels are to be arrested to service with the minimum tontight payable. Yet I fear that it will still not be sufficient unto our needs, and more funds need to be made available for new ships and crews as demanded by parliament. We await new reports from master Caxton within the month."

The king nodded in assent, his mind turning to matters of how he might raise more funds to fill the royal coffers.

"Sire, if I may bring to your attention another matter that relates to France?"

The king nodded warily, sensing a trap was about to be sprung, and his other advisers – including Sir Richard Whittington – paid great attention to Henry Beaufort's next words.

"Word has reached my ears," the bishop and chancellor continued, "that representations have been made to the Avignon Pope concerning the Lollard heretics, and have gained sympathy in that regard, receiving praise and encouragement from certain factions within France. It bodes not well, my lord, and the sect and all its teachings permeate our society here, invading guilds, scholars and places of learning as well as certain feral elements of the Church, I hear."

The king looked in alarm at Richard Courtney, aware that he would have to ask the next question, knowing full well the answer. The clerks waited with bated breath, their quills ready to scratch and record all that was questioned and answered.

"From where comes the catalyst of this insidious movement, my lord bishop?"

"My king, it pains me to inform Your Majesty, yet I fear

the instigator alleged to have incited such heresy is Lord Cobham, Sir John Oldcastle."

The king had schooled his features to this reply, and no movement of his facial muscles betrayed his innermost thoughts. He continued calmly. "Very well. We thank you, my lord bishop, for your information and assure you that we shall take steps to resolve the impediment to the ecclesiastical unity of our realm."

The bishop nodded, pleased with the outcome of his discovery.

Other business was concluded, and the meeting was brought to a close. Then, as all members were bowing and filing to leave the royal presence, King Henry spoke quietly to his trusted clerk, Sir Thomas Burton. "Ask Sir Richard Whittington and Archbishop Arundel to attend me presently in my private chambers."

The clerk and spy nodded his assent and slipped out to pass on the summons discreetly.

The king stood in a smaller chamber, a room that was comfortably furnished almost as a solar, rather than a place of commerce or business. It was accessed by two doors, one off the main council chamber and another off a small corridor, one of the many that riddled the rabbit warren of the palace. Through this lesser path the two statesmen were led by Burton, and all now awaited the private audience with their king.

"My lords, we are greatly distressed, for as within our father's reign, God rest his soul, the sword of Damocles hangs above us waiting for the cord of financial disaster to be severed. That this fate should be closely intertwined with that of the Church and indeed our friendship with Sir John, Lord Cobham, brings us to the impasse that now presents itself so plainly." The two men nodded, letting the king speak. "We must encourage and maintain trade with the Low Countries and the importation of wine from Bordeaux, which is currently within our control as well as between Iceland and Scandinavia. To do this, we needs must secure the seas with good ships and strong crews, and as ever France approaches like a thorn in our side, always ready to attack should we prove weak or vulnerable. In particular, Harfleur is most often used against our ships as a base for piracy by any other name, and indeed to aid the traitor, Glyndower.

"To make such provision secure and present a united front, we must have unity with our realm and funds to secure the seas. The Church, my good archbishop informs us, is able to provide the deficit of our funding at a price of our friendship with one who purports to divide the realm." The king paused again and both Whittington and Arundel nodded in agreement to his summation of the facts before them, while Burton remained in the rear, standing impassive in shadow. "The balance of the scales therefore outweighs any bond of service or friendship. We should like you to begin proceedings to interrogate Sir John Oldcastle on his faith and proclivities in that direction, for we cannot have dissent and a fractured realm."

Archbishop Arundel agreed, a gleeful look in his eye, pleased at the turn of events. "In which case, Majesty, I can assure you of full ecclesiastical support, both morally and financially. We shall debase all rumour and scour the realm of any foreign presence."

"Thank you, my dear Archbishop. We welcome your assurances. We shall of course endeavour to meet with Lord Cobham as a final throw of the dice, to see if we cannot dissuade him from his current course. If that fails, we must continue with ecclesiastical proceedings and arrest him in that regard, for which we are persuaded that you can have all documents and evidence prepared. Now would you excuse us? For we have matters of finance to discuss with Sir Richard."

"By your leave, sire." At which the elderly prelate bowed and left the chamber.

Once he had departed the king turned to Sir Richard Whittington.

"What say you, Sir Richard?"

"Your Majesty chooses a wise course, one that would attempt to prevent conflict and strife within the realm. Yet should that fail..." Whittington paused. "Why then the courts and prosecution would seem to be the only way in which to stem the tide of Lollardy and all the uncertainty it brings."

The king was not fooled by Whittington's careful words, and probed deeper: "Think you that Sir John will acquiesce and fall to our side, relinquishing his heresies? Fear not, for you will not rouse us to wrath. We require a fair answer."

Whittington was aware of Sir Thomas Burton's presence, and knew that in private they would have discussed this very issue. He pulled at his ear in a familiar gesture, head tilted slightly to one side as he considered his answer, delaying the response and giving himself time to think. "Sire, I believe in my heart that a favourable outcome is unlikely," he continued carefully, "despite Your Majesty's best endeavours to persuade Sir John."

"And should your worst fears come to fruition?"

"In that unhappy circumstance, I have a contingency in mind. It is far reaching, and palls upon my conscience, but it will greatly aid us in our provision. Yet I do earnestly pray that it will not be necessary."

The king looked at the ruthlessness of his financier and spymaster with steely eyes. Wishing not to hear confirmation of all that might hang in the balance, he changed the subject slightly with a prescience that bespoke a keen mind: "How does the situation in Paris?"

"Majesty, we had word via a pigeon message that was by its very nature brief to the effect that the Armagnacs now have King Charles' blessing and most importantly that of the young dauphin, who has rebelled against his father-in-law, the Duke of Burgundy. It bodes well for us and possibly ill for the duke, for it will cause a division and weaken France for all that."

"Just so, just so. Then it appears that Sir James was in time to alert them as we had hoped. Is there any news of him and his Italian companion? Are they alive?"

"Sire, e'er it please you, we have received word that they are safely arrived at Cotentin and seek passage from a ship to transport them back to England. Yet none may sail by direct order without two warships as escort – and of course a favourable wind."

"So far?"

"Yes, Majesty. It seems that they consorted with the Armagnacs, escaped Paris and fled to Orleans. They tarried there until they could make their way across France to evade Burgundy's clutches."

"Then we would know what devious plans you have in mind to aid us if Sir John proves false," the king finally declared.

Part Three
England

Chapter Twenty-Eight

Cooling Castle, Kent

The private gymnasium at Cooling Castle was covered in rough mats to aid the breaking of a fall. Ten pairs of men clad in the rough cotton jackets of the Cornish wrestlers heaved, writhed and sweated in the late July heat, despite the open casements and the low lying floor that was always cooled as the surrounding moat drew heat from the walls.

They were all engaged in a series of practice bouts, trying new moves, throws and holds. The blond giant was matched against someone of nearly his own size. The man was not as strong as Mark, but he was nimble and fast. They moved backwards and forwards as though linked mechanically, each feeling as much as seeing what the other did, then as Mark's opponent's right foot moved back, hardly off the floor and in perfect balance, Mark pulled hard from a shoulder grip. The foot stopped moving and drove down with his opponent's full weight upon it, seemingly immoveable. But now his feet were apart, his left leg forward, and in that instant Mark went with the direction of resistance, driving back and hooking his right foot inside to sweep at that leg whilst he was momentarily off balance.

As expected, the other man lifted his foot up and out to avoid the sweep. His legs were further apart with the move, the right foot forward and leaning slightly to the fore, still in balance. Mark jumped at the opportunity, hopping in as he turned his back, landing on his left leg, his right bent to engage with the right of his opponent at the shin. Mark sprang and heaved, driving backwards as he did so. The hapless opponent flew upwards, both feet off the ground, and Mark rotated, bringing him crashing down to the matting with a heavy thud.

To avoid injury, and as this was but a practice bout, Mark avoided landing with his weight upon his opponent to break a rib or an arm, taking the weight of his torso just short of such a crashing fall. The fallen opponent had put his arm out to help cushion his fall, yet was still winded and shaken as his head had rocked back onto the hard matting.

"By the rood, Mark, that was hard to break. Where did 'ee learn that? Not in Cornwall, I'm bound." The man spoke with as thick an accent as Mark, as did many of those attending the practice at the castle.

Mark shook his head with a smile. "No. I fought a deadly lumpen ox in Scotland who tried to blind me, and 'twas against him that the move came to me, which I have perfected till now."

"That be the same man as cut your face?"

"Aye," Mark agreed, rubbing the scar upon his cheek that reminded him of the cold winter days in Edinburgh, grateful as ever to Cristoforo and his healing ways. A clapping broke through his reverie as he thought of his Italian friend, now gone some weeks with no news save rumours of riots and revolts in Paris.

"Bravo, Mark, that was as fine a throw as ever I've seen." The speaker was Lord Cobham, Sir John Oldcastle, a tall man in his early thirties, fit and well-muscled. The strongly featured face was framed by naturally wavy light brown hair that fell back in a helmet shape from a broad forehead that bespoke intelligence. The hair followed the jawline to a full beard and moustache. The shoulders were broad and their misshape of muscle defined him as a man of arms and the knight that he was. By his side was another that Mark recognised, the man's nephew by marriage, Sir Thomas Chaworth, the knight Jamie had mentioned in the Nottingham plot.

"You shall make a fine present for his majesty when we surprise him in August hence," Lord Cobham added, in a strong deep voice that resonated across the gymnasium.

The king, as all knew, had forgone all forms of entertainment for a respectful period of time during his mourning, and had only buried his father at the end of June after awaiting the return from France of Prince Thomas.

Mark, along with other Cornish wrestlers, had been recruited to come and train at Cooling Castle with the promise of bouts and payment as a reward. All had at first seemed above board, but the journey there had been a little sinister in its clandestine nature. They had been closely watched since their arrival, with none being allowed to leave the confines of the castle without escort and then only to nearby Rochester for ale and a night's entertainment. They were only permitted to leave in parties of three, supposedly to cause less comment within the town and thereby keep their presence a secret. Mark had cynically reasoned that one might disappear, two might conspire, but with three there would always be the odd one out who would report any departures or talk of discontent with their masters. With three men one never knew who to trust completely. This fostered a slightly febrile and suspicious atmosphere amongst the normally steady camaraderie of the wrestlers.

The recruitment was done under the guise of a 'surprise for the king' to please and support him following the death of his father and to 'bring him out of languor and mourning', Sir John had said. The word had gone out along with a promise of coin and sport, without knowing who the sponsor was. Mark had fortunately informed Sir Richard Whittington of the approach, yet knew not if it would be acted upon or if he would be in time to alert him to all that was occurring. He wished that Jamie would return, for he would, Mark was assured, know what to do and how to act. For all his recent experience, he missed his friend's direction of purpose and understanding of the wiles of the court. He now looked on suspiciously, seeing Chaworth present once more in Oldcastle's company. The two knights moved off in unison, speaking with their heads close together and not affording Mark the opportunity to hear their conversation.

"Now, Sir Thomas," Oldcastle said. "Prithee tell what news you have of the court?"

"The king proceeds as we thought, and needs must secure more funds for campaigns," Chaworth replied. "Yet he is caught in a cleft stick, for he cannot manage the deficit upon those funds alone through Parliament. He turns to the Church, I hear, and that news is confirmed by Bishop Beaufort and rumours from the Council. Yet I would adjure caution, my lord, for I hear that Arundel was in private conference with the king and that can only mean one course: your summons to appear before the synod to answer calls of heresy."

"Fear not, Sir Thomas. I have texts and tracts of my own to counter their arguments, and they will find it hard indeed to prey upon me with tales of heresy and witchcraft, for I have the Lord on my side – and mayhap soon a king.

"I have clergy who will vouch for me from Hereford, London and Rochester, and the net grows ever wider. The Scots are to keep my account and I theirs, for support from them will accomplish much with the pope in Avignon. We have strong backing amongst the guilds of London, and that I hear is growing daily. Soon it will be too late to stop the momentum that has been started. So whilst King Henry would seem to summon me to his side, 'twill in the end be me who allows him to mine."

×✶× —

Kennington Palace, London

Sir Thomas Burton slipped through a side door a minute ahead of the embassy that he knew was approaching the king's private chamber. "Majesty, 'ware the approach of Arundel and others," he said. "For they seek an audience on urgent business pertaining to Lord Cobham."

The king grasped matters quickly and asked: "To what end?"

"Papers and documents were discovered in the hands of an illuminator housed on Paternoster Row. He has admitted to being in the employ of Sir John, and these tracts were his and his alone."

"Very well. Go to and attend with the other clerks, and be invisible," the king ordered, waving his hand to a bench where the others laboured, scribing matters of state into documents.

A page knocked upon the door of the king's chamber, asking if Archbishop Arundel may enter and have an audience with him. The king agreed, and moments later a flustered Arundel entered together with the Lord Chief Justice, the newly appointed Sir William Hankford, Bishop Chichele and the chancellor, Bishop Beaufort. Other lords followed, including the Earl of Warwick.

King Henry appeared unamused at the invasion of his privacy as if by ambush. He raised an inquiring eyebrow, the only outward sign of anger other than the whitening of the puckered scar upon his cheek. "We were informed that only Archbishop Arundel was to be present," the king said.

"Majesty, we do humbly beg your pardon. Yet this matter upon which we are now instructed has such dominion over our thoughts and actions that we could in all conscience not delay."

"Pray tell us what is amiss?"

"My lord king, we have documents here ordered by Lord Cobham, Sir John Oldcastle. They are documents, tracts of scripts pertaining to doctrines of Lollardy and other matters of heresy. The provincial synod has read this terrible libel against the Mother Church and felt the need to make your majesty aware of the nature of them and the curse upon our realm they bring." The elderly prelate finished breathlessly.

"May we see these documents?"

"Majesty, as you please." The archbishop called up a clerk who produced scrolls that were passed to the king's own clerk.

Minutes later the king laid down the final document before him, his face white with anger. "Never have we seen or read documents of such an abhorrent nature. We consider them and the conclusions drawn from them to stand against our faith and our Church. We shall commission an order for Sir John to attend us here and explain the meaning of them, if they truly belong to him.

"Now, my lords, we wish to be alone with our most spiritual advisor and beg that you leave our presence – all save you, my lord archbishop."

Chapter Twenty-Nine

Windsor Castle, Early August

The meeting between King Henry and Lord Cobham, Sir John Oldcastle had started amicably enough as they found common ground, but when the king directed Oldcastle towards his views on religion, he was disturbed at what he found.

"My lord king, I once called you blanchemain and wouldst continue to do so in my heart despite all that you have risen so high to be a just and fair monarch," Oldcastle said. "Our Lord knows that we have fought together, shared blood and bile upon the field of battle and survived to tell our tales of victory."

The king responded gently: "Indeed, and our complaint, such as it is, is not that of discourtesy or lack of faith, yet rather a matter of faith itself, for that is what seems to divide us at this juncture." Throughout the meeting so far, the king had kept his voice even, imbuing his words with all the inflections of friendship that he could muster.

"Sire, then let me say upon all that is holy and in the grace of our Lord God, that I pledge my unequivocal friendship and support to your majesty." He paused. "Yet I cannot in all conscience accept the Pope's authority on certain tenets of Christian teaching which I have read and studied in the Bible, and which would seem to contradict the dictates of the Church, or at best be equivocal."

An icy silence fell between them as the king sought to master his speech. "Sir John, we cannot countenance this view. Certainly there may be areas of religious doctrine where interpretation is ambiguous, yet you go much further and denounce the teachings of the Church. That, we cannot condone, and we wouldst rail against such views. We are ashamed that you should interpret the teachings of the Mother Church so, and we can no longer call you blanchemain or accept you as a knight in our service." The king clenched a fist and shook it at Sir John, continuing in exasperation. "Your actions will drive a wedge through the kingdom and divide brother against brother if you persist in preaching such heresy. It must end forthwith!" The king shouted these final words, lost in a white hot rage at Sir John's blatant obduracy.

The knight blanched at the venom of his sovereign's words, and without a by-your-leave he turned and left the chamber, fearing for his safety that he might be arrested on the spot.

King Henry turned away and let out a long breath. Composing himself, he called to his clerk: "We leave for Westminster upon the hour, and will brook no delay."

Later, in his private chamber, the king held an audience

with Sir Richard Whittington, Sir William Stokes, his financial spy, and Sir Thomas Burton, all of whom waited expectantly as rumours of Sir John Oldcastle's abrupt departure from the court had spread like wildfire.

"My lords, it is with great regret that we must now denounce Lord Cobham. Upon speaking with Sir John, we found him to be intractable and recalcitrant beyond belief. It is with regret that we shall be instructing Archbishop Arundel to begin proceedings and summon him to an official hearing." He stopped for a moment, realising that his next command would set Whittington's ruthless plan in motion. "Sir Richard, so great do we feel the depth of this heresy has spread and its roots invaded all society, that it is with regret that we feel this next course of action shall be necessary. We shall sacrifice a pawn to bring down a knight. Implement the scheme and we shall see what we net," he commanded.

"As you wish, Your Majesty." Sir Richard bowed.

"Now go to, and with Sir William's help we shall use what means we can to halt this insidious sect."

 —

The Thames Estuary

The cog and the two warships that had accompanied it upon its long journey from Cherbourg sailed steadily up the Thames, a benevolent wind aiding their progress. Jamie and

Cristoforo had been plagued by bands of *routiers* as they crossed France, causing them to divert from their planned route more than once. It had taken them three weeks to gain the comparative safety of Cherbourg, and they arrived there to find no ship waiting for them. All had been sequestered and refitted or were acting under new orders by direction of the new Clerk to the King's Ships, William Caxton. Everyone considered the head of the navy to be painstakingly slow in his work, and his methodical outlook was proving a hindrance to trade and progress.

After a full audit of warships and private vessels, he had allowed half the fleet to set sail again while the remainder were refitted for war and ordnance or seized for the use of the crown. The two warships had sailed down to Bordeaux accompanying the cog, which had filled its hold with wine and commenced its return journey, hugging the coast of France. The wind had been capricious, and it was only through this ill-fortune that it had been delayed sufficiently to offer passage to Jamie and Cristoforo. The small convoy had been forced to seek shelter at Cherbourg when the wind turned, and here they had lain dormant for three days until a prevailing south-westerly had allowed them to continue their voyage to London. Jamie and Cristoforo had managed to gain passage, although Cristoforo had been seasick for most of the crossing, and was even now looking green in pallor as he struggled to focus on the banks of land that bordered the wide channel to each side.

Jamie smiled as his familiar homeland hove into view. The scenery was more verdant than France, and the familiar shape of the houses – their thatching, grey now against the burning sun of August – faded to a well-worn hue. The smell of freshly cut hay floated across the water to him, mingling with the sweet tang of the sea. The white dots of sheep and the distant orchards added to the panoply of England as they glided past, offering succour after the horrors of Paris and the uncertainty of possible discovery on their journey through France.

As Tilbury came into sight, the banks of the river rose appreciably where they had been raised to reclaim the marshes and create a port for unloading and distribution before London. A small ferry sailed across the channel at this narrow point, linking Tilbury with Gravesend on the southern bank, the little craft dodging the paths of the mighty sea going ships.

An hour or so later the contingent made port in London itself with a creaking of wood as the large vessels bumped and groaned against the wooden wharfs, the last of their momentum halted by strong cables of hemp that were secured by the proud piling heads thrusting upwards from the wharf. Cristoforo breathed a sigh of relief, crossing himself and saying a prayer.

The gangplank was thrown down to cross the gap as the large craft nudged against the quay, the steves readying the wooden cranes to swing outwards, cargo nets ready to unload the fine barrels of Bordeaux wine. Hoisting their war bags and arms, Jamie and Cristoforo strode across the plank, with Cristoforo grasping the railing tightly in his right hand and breathing a sigh of relief when his feet finally touched the firm land of the dock. He was about to tell Jamie how glad he was to be back on solid ground when a group of ten men-at-arms hove into view, led by a captain of the guard who looked purposeful and determined.

"I bid you good morrow, sir. Are you Sir James de Grispere, knight of London and attendant to his Majesty King Henry?"

"I am, captain," Jamie confirmed. "How may I assist you?"

"Then, sir, I arrest you in the name of his Majesty King Henry Five. You are accused of high treason, consorting with the French to aid and abet them in overthrowing King Charles and inciting powers to rise against the crown of England. Will you come with us willingly or must we use force?"

Jamie was shocked beyond measure and Cristoforo squinted in anger, dropping his war bag and relaxing in that familiar way that his friend knew only too well. In seconds three men would be dead, Jamie knew, and he would add to the tally, leaving the others leaderless and ready to be killed. Yet what purpose would it serve? A mistake had been made, and these were honest English soldiers after all. Jamie and Cristoforo had done nothing amiss, and had served the crown too well for such an accusation to be taken seriously. Something was awry, and there would be no need to shed the blood of his fellow Englishmen when a simple summons to Sir Richard Whittington would doubtless undo this wrong.

With an almost imperceptible shake of his head, Jamie prevented Cristoforo from attacking, and at that moment some instinct made him look skywards to the ramparts of the gatehouse guarding entry to the city, where two crossbowmen stood alert, weapons cocked and ready for any trouble from either of them, eyes sharp and merciless.

The captain followed Jamie's gaze, a tight-lipped smile appearing at his mouth. "A guarantee, if you will. Your reputation precedes you, Sir James, and others have underestimated you to their cost. We have been watching for ships and noting the tides. All craft were watched to await your arrival."

Cristoforo was angry at this insult and cut through the discourse. "I would know where we are to be taken," he asked, his anger becoming apparent as crowds gathered, sensing the drama that was unfolding before their eyes.

The captain turned to Cristoforo, looking at him disdainfully: "The warrant bears only Sir James de Grispere's name, not yours, Italian. You are not a citizen of this realm, so no treason is possible in this regard. Your companion's destination is the Tower. We are bidden to deliver him for incarceration until a date for his trial can be set."

Cristoforo was relieved yet also perturbed. Something was amiss, and this whole sorry business puzzled him.

Seizing the moment, Jamie spoke out. "Go to, Cristo. Gain an audience with Sir Richard and tell him of my plight, then attend Lady Alice for she will know what steps to take."

"That will avail you naught, Sir James, for upon this warrant there are two signatures that seal the document – and one of those..." The captain grinned through gritted teeth. "Is that of Sir Richard Whittington."

Jamie felt as though he had been struck a body blow by an axe. "By God's legs, Sir Richard is cosignatory to this warrant?" He was dumbfounded by the news.

Cristoforo, too, was shocked. "I shall inform Lady Alice, Jamie, fear not."

At this, the men-at-arms encircled Jamie and the captain demanded his sword. Complying to the request, he unbuckled his sword belt and handed the weapon to Cristoforo, who was looking on with anger apparent in every fibre of his being.

Jamie had expected to be boarded onto a barge or lighter as the Tower was only some seven hundred yards downstream, and with all the foot traffic it would be the most efficient way to transport him. Yet it was not to be. A common cart was brought forward, and with his hands bound by rope he was loaded onto its wooden bed. This to his mind was the biggest insult, for only convicted felons and those sentenced to death were transported thus in public. It drew attention from everyone it passed, with many jeering at the sight of what appeared to be a bound villain, off for incarceration with perhaps his life at forfeit. Some threw rotted fruit and vegetables at him, and the disgrace was absolute in Jamie's eyes, made worse by the fact that he knew he was innocent of any crime.

The route ran parallel to the river along Billingesgate, Petit Walles and then at the end the street made a sharp left turn by Watergate up to join with Tourstrate, where before him rose the ominous shape of the Tower, its stone still white against the grey of others around it. The smell from the river was stronger here, infused with rotting sewage, waste and the odd corpse that washed up with the tide. The outer moat had been dug by Edward First over a hundred years earlier, yet everyone still called it the New Moat. It linked the Tower with the new defences at King's Wharf to the west of the main hexagonal structure. It was wide, nearly one hundred and fifty feet across, and protected what was now the outer curtain wall that had also been raised by King Edward.

Smoky tendrils of fear etched their way down Jamie's spine. What had at first seemed like a nightmare from which he would soon awake was becoming terrifyingly real. He remembered how intimidated he had felt by the walls and the smell of fever when he had visited Black Rhys in the final days before his execution three years earlier. Even then he could not wait to be free of the place, and the memory left a dark shadow on his soul. His only consolation today was that he spotted Cristoforo following the spectacle his journey was creating, discreet and unobtrusive as ever. His presence and the knowledge that Jamie had a friend on his side in the outside world offered some small solace to his soul. Steely-eyed guards armed with spears and shields cast a watchful eye upon his progress, nodding brusquely to the captain of the guard as he passed through with his charge.

The cart passed under the Barbican Gate, which was still in a state of disrepair, then clattered across the second drawbridge that crossed the inner moat to the strong walled Outer Bailey that had also been improved by King Edward. It was a seemingly impregnable fortress with much history attached to it, and had seen off many revolts and sieges in its times. Although built as a palace, the Tower now served more as a gaol for important prisoners than a stately residence.

At the inner gate, the captain of the Tower came out and

motioned for the procession to halt. "Who goes there, and who is the prisoner?" he called gruffly. He was mailled and helmed, a man-at-arms at his side and two crossbowmen alert on the ramparts above, looking down upon them.

"I am captain of the guard serving his majesty, and present you with a new prisoner to be held until his trial. Here is the warrant."

The captain broke open the seal, noting the king's stamp and that of Sir Richard Whittington. He raised an eyebrow and read the words slowly. "Sir James de Grispere of the king's household? You are now fallen low to treason, I see. Well, this shall be your new home until you are adjudged. Yet I would adjure you to make your peace with God, for few leave here as free men." He offered Jamie an evil smile then turned to the sergeant at his side, making to allow them through.

Moving inside the walls to the inner bailey, Jamie saw the St Peter in the Bailey chapel off to his left and shuddered at the crosses and headstones of the graves that stood starkly to attention, marking the last resting place of those who had met their fate within the walls of the Tower. In front of him stood the four-square bulk of the keep, the White Tower with its surrounding guard rooms and great hall.

"Jump down, Sir James." The captain of the men-at-arms sneered. "For this be your new home now and we'll find you a snug bunk to settle in. Your new companions shall be rats and mice and you'll treat right well with them, I'm bound, for they, too, care not whom they betray to get what they want." He seemed convinced of Jamie's guilt, as most of those who heard the news of his arrest would be. He was grabbed by the guards and pushed forward towards the tower before him.

The Constable of the Tower, Sir Robert de Morley, was waiting for them at the top of the steps. He was a bluff soldier who was well known to Jamie, having been at court for some time, and now served this new king in his tenure. "Sir James, this is a sorry affair, and it gives me no pleasure to see you thus accused of treachery and treason, and of conspiring with the French. I am ordered to hold you in custody here from the time of your arrest and I shall do my devoir as bid by his majesty."

Jamie stood tall, schooling his features and looking to all the world as though he had not heard the constable's words, for no recognition did he give. He began to build a wall around himself that none could or would breach. The only sign he gave was a brief nod of acknowledgement, then he cast his gaze into the middle distance, staring through eyes that neither saw nor focused upon anything.

Chapter Thirty

Cristoforo left the scene, the sight of Jamie being taken prisoner and publicly paraded through the streets in a cart still embedded upon his eyes. *In a cart, porca miseria!* he thought. He walked westwards along Tourstrate, his mind in turmoil, planning as he would for an assassination, considering all possibilities and outcomes, realising that nothing was to be gained by continually watching the Tower. He moved carefully in case he was being followed, trusting no one given the circumstances.

He avoided the most direct route up Garscherch Street, and went instead to the small church of St Nicholas Acum that linked two thoroughfares of St Nicholas' Lane and Abechirchelane, both of which led to Langburnestrate. He knew the church well and used its rear door to exit into Abechirchelane, and went from there to St Mary Wolnoth church, which was vast and full of pillars and dark areas. He had been taught by his father that darting between churches was a perfect way to conceal a route or show a following presence. Nobody needed a reason to enter a church, and such buildings often had many exits and offered the cover of darkness and places to hide. It was also a good place to watch and observe unseen. He passed a chapel entrance and moved into a sacristy that was unlocked – for who would steal from a priest in a church? Here he dropped both war bags that he had carried from the port and readied himself. A small spyhole was drilled into the intricately carved marquetry, utilised by priests wishing to see who was coming to confession – after all, forewarned was forearmed.

Cristoforo waited and was repaid for his patience when he saw two men-at-arms enter and look carefully around. They had been present at the wharf when Jamie was arrested and had been skilful enough to follow Cristoforo from the first church, but now their efforts fell on fallow ground.

One growled a curse and was silently admonished by a passing priest who scowled at him, raising a finger to his lips in annoyance. The soldier nodded. "Sorry, Father," he muttered.

With that the two men left, and Cristoforo smiled to himself as the bells began to chime for sext. If they were sufficiently well informed he knew they'd have a good idea of where he lived, but he never liked anyone to know his exact whereabouts – or more importantly his business. With this in mind he hurried off, changing direction now and heading directly for the rear entrance to the house of Alessandria's uncle, Signor Filippo Alberti, where they currently resided.

He moved quietly through the rear stables and into the servants' quarters. Finding a groom, he bade him take his war bags into the house, and to tell his mistress if he should see her, that Cristoforo had returned safely, but that he had an urgent fiat upon which to attend.

Certain that he was no longer being followed, he made his way to Jamie and Lady Alice's house on Le Straunde. He discovered that Lady Alice was at home by seeking entrance from the rear door of the servants' quarters so that he would not linger or be seen by chance on the street.

The steward of the house, who knew Cristoforo by sight, bade him enter. "Signor," Cristoforo said. "I beg you, please say that I am here as a messenger, for if it is me alone, Lady Alice will fear the worst as to Jamie's fate and suspect him dead, yet that be not the case," he assured, as he saw a flicker of concern pass across the steward's face.

The steward nodded and agreed to this course of action. He returned swiftly. "My lady will see you now, Signor Corio, please do follow me."

Lady Alice was in her private solar with her maid, Nesta. She put down her sewing and stood, smoothing her gown with her hands, expecting to receive a royal messenger, curiosity written upon her face. When she saw Cristoforo she gasped, her hand rising to her mouth: "Oh, Cristo! Where is Jamie? Is he hurt or...?" The words would not come to her.

Cristoforo crossed the distance quickly bowing in his stride and grasping her hand that was cold to the touch. "My lady, fear not, Jamie is alive. Please do not bestir yourself on his account I beseech you, he is well. That I speak true upon my word of honour."

"Then where does he reside?" she asked querulously.

"My Lady Alice, pray be seated," he replied, and turning,

he addressed the maid. "Nesta, some wine for your mistress, prithee. There is a long tale to tell. Have a fire lit, for she is cold, and fetch a shawl."

"We have all heard such rumours and horrors of Paris and wondered at your fate. To see you so, alone, my first thought was to consider the worst, entering as you did under a veil of mystery," Lady Alice said when she had recovered from her shock and accepted Cristoforo's word that Jamie was at least hale in body.

"For that lack of thoughtfulness, my lady, I must apologise," he continued gently, still holding her hand in comfort, "but I considered it the most propitious way in which to find an audience with you with none seeing me enter."

"Cristo, I know not of what you speak, for as ever you disarm me with riddles. Now, whatever ill tidings there may be, pray furnish me with the truth, for I am composed and would hear all, no matter that I be poorer in my soul for it."

"My lady, you rally as ever, and I am in awe of your spirit."

At this, a servant returned with the wine and proceeded to light a small fire despite the August heat outside the house. The kindling took instantly, and reassured by Cristoforo that he would attend to it, the man left them alone with Nesta.

"Now, my lady, I have shocking news of ill tidings as you suppose. While no harm has come to Jamie, he is fallen upon unfortunate circumstance." He explained all that had happened since Paris and their arrival at London to his arrest.

She was silent, then a vehemence entered her voice as her spirit came to the fore: "There must be some mistaken cause, for Jamie would never be a traitor. He is honourable and was ready to shoulder any burden in favour of the crown and his country. What says Sir Richard, for 'twas he that sent you both upon this fiat?" she demanded.

"My lady, that is the worst of the news, for it was Sir Richard Whittington whose signature was placed beneath his majesty's upon the warrant for Jamie's arrest."

Lady Alice stood now, unable to keep still or silent. Her fear was quickly replaced by anger. "Then he shall answer my questions, for I shall instruct my father to approach him without delay. We have long had dealings with that cause, and Jamie serves Sir Richard well and faithfully. I would also see Jamie and shall make plans this instant to attend upon him. Nesta, have the grooms prepare a carriage. We travel to the Tower."

Cristoforo raised his hands palms outward. "My lady, await me and hear what I offer as advice. I have come here from seeing my own love, and she awaits me even now. Let me be secreted in your carriage and let us visit first Alessandria. She will accompany you to Jamie, and with her shall go grooms to protect you. Have coin too for the guards, as they respect only that currency, and for Jamie's sake and benefit, will provide more in his direction if they are offered coin to do so."

Cristoforo's reunion with Alessandria was as emotional as had been his meeting with Lady Alice, albeit in a different direction. As used to the ways and wiles of court from being schooled in Florence, that town of deadly rumour and plotting, she gave much thought to all that had been said. She paced the room in silence, which Cristoforo knew to be a bad sign. Her hot Latin blood normally ran fast and furious, demanding instant action, yet in silence, she was more deadly and more to be feared than ever.

"*Va bene,*" she said at last, as though making a decision. "We shall enjoy a light repast while guards and an escort are prepared. I shall advise my uncle to visit Sir Richard as a matter of urgency and endeavour to find out what rumours swirl abroad. From such a public exhibition of arrest many will now know all that has occurred." At which she flicked her fan to and fro gently in front of her face, her mind turning all before her.

"I must attend upon Jamie's family, for as you say, untruths will spread with rumour and turmoil, and I should like them to hear all that has occurred first from my own lips," Lady Alice offered.

Kennington Palace

The court soon discovered that the new king favoured Kennington Palace above his residences in Westminster or Windsor. Lying south of the river and slightly west of Westminster Palace, it served almost as a respite for King Henry – for here, with his favourite courtiers surrounding him, he could meet the challenges of his new reign and gain views and ideas from all who came to seek audience in these less formal surroundings.

The main hall of the palace had been built by his great-grandfather Edward III, and at nearly a hundred feet long was a vast and impressive space in its own right. To the east of this lay the Prince's Chamber, three stories high and nearly as big as the main hall. It was here that the king entertained and felt most at his ease amongst courtiers and dignitaries alike.

He had been entertained this day by jesters, harpists and mummers, and the proceedings were coming to a close when one of the heralds took a position by the open door, summoned by a page, and blew his horn. As the finishing notes died out he called forth:

"My lord king, Lord Cobham, Sir John Oldcastle begs an audience with your majesty pleading obeisance and bearing a gift of entertainment. May he be seen and come forward to your majesty's presence?"

The king looked to his household knights, the Chamberlain of his Household and Richard Lord Grey of Codnor, and at a sign from him nodded his assent, privately hoping that this may prove to be a token of servitude and a change of heart on behalf of Lord Cobham. "Pray let him enter in goodwill and at our command."

With that the doors were opened to permit entrance not only to Sir John but also to a procession of matched pairs of wrestlers. Sir John came forward, striding proudly and swept three deep bows before his sovereign.

"Majesty, e'er it please you, I have this day a surprise gift, to wit ten matched pairs of wrestlers, all loyal and tutored to the point of perfection in order to provide entertainment on this auspicious day."

The king nodded, a smile changing his whole countenance from stern warrior to benign sovereign, keen to seek peace within his realm.

The court relaxed perceptibly, with small cries of joy or encouragement coming from the ladies as the volume of the conversation swelled at Sir John's announcement.

By his side, Sir Thomas Burton whispered: "It is as we expected, Majesty, and we have been well advised by Mark of Cornwall."

The king said nothing, but offered a slight nod, a smile fixed in place as he prepared to enjoy the entertainment before him. He loved wrestling and was an able practitioner in his own right. Pages and servants brought forth mats at Sir John's direction, and these were laid out in a rough rectangle in preparation for the bouts to begin.

Sir Thomas moved up behind Sir Christopher Urquhart, one of Henry's knights and a friend to both Jamie and Mark. Sir Christopher was betrothed to Jeanette and a close friend of the de Grispere family. "Sir Christopher, seek a private word with Mark if you can," Sir Thomas whispered. "I would know anything that he may have to impart that may be to our favour. Approach him openly, as if by coincidence, and repeat to me all that is said."

Kit looked slightly puzzled then nodded, moving off to engage with Mark, whom he knew well, having fought with him at the battle of Smallhythe when the English forces had recaptured the king's ship *Juliane* and defeated the pirates of Sir William Longe.

"Sir Christopher," Mark responded as the knight hailed him by name. "This is well met, and you will be entertained this day, I'm bound. Does Jeanette accompany you here for the sport?" he questioned jovially.

But as he spoke, Kit noticed that his eyes were roving carefully about, stopping briefly upon the figures of Sir John and Sir Thomas Chaworth, who were themselves both carefully watching the hall and all their charges who were to partake in the wrestling. Kit braced himself as Mark's huge hand landed upon his shoulder in a show of familiarity. Knowing the strength that lay there he winced, even within his battle hardened frame. Keeping a smile upon his face and speaking low he muttered: "Burton did ask if anything should be amiss this day concerning the king's safety?"

Mark had been treading a fine line in duplicity since his inclusion into the Lollard's group. He waited until a throw occurred and then clapped and roared with the rest of the crowd, who were delighted with the sport. Then while all were distracted he replied quickly: "Do not let the king wrestle. It is a trap, and blades are here secreted. None are concerned for their fate. They see themselves as martyrs to the Lollard cause and would assassinate the king. He will be dead upon the instant and rebellion will swiftly follow. This be a test to find a weakness, if naught else. Many are here not marked as Lollards, yet they follow the faith. Bid his majesty take great care, I adjure 'ee!" Mark's words were spoken in a low whisper, unlike Mark's normal manner of speech.

The crowd quieted for the next pair, and no more opportunity arose to speak of such matters. Kit and Mark exchanged platitudes in full view and within the hearing of all, with Mark congratulating Kit upon his coming nuptials. Then as planned, a page arrived to relieve him with a summons at which he bade the giant good day and moved off back to the king's side to speak briefly with Thomas Burton as ripples of talk began to spread through the king's immediate meiny.

Kit broke off again and hurried back to Mark who turned, puzzled at his return. This time the conversation was of more note, particularly to a suspicious Sir John Oldcastle, who waved Chaworth closer to overhear what was said.

"Mark, I have grave news that even now travels upon the wind of rumour. Jamie has latterly returned from France, and he has been arrested and taken to the Tower, where he is imprisoned under close arrest as a traitor to the realm."

"What? Nay, this cannot be," Mark responded, incredulous at the news. "He has returned this day, you say, and was taken immediately into arrest? On what grounds?"

"High treason and consorting with the French against the crown."

"By the rood, I shall not give this credence. The Tower? How can this be? Upon whose orders?"

"They say 'tis upon the direct orders of the king – and Sir Richard Whittington."

Mark was shocked into silence, shaking his head in disbelief. "I should go and see what may be done," he said eventually.

"Nay, stay here, for you may aid him more here and find out what you may to assist the king."

"Aid the king, you say, when he imprisons my companion who I would call blanchemain, one who has saved my life as we dealt in the blood and steel of battle? I will not."

"Do so, Mark, for it will serve all better to aid Jamie's cause."

Then Mark's mind turned to consider another matter. "Cristoforo left with Jamie. Did he return with him, and does he, too, reside in gaol?"

Kit shook his head. "The two returned together, but there was no mention of Cristoforo, and I can only assume that he was not arrested. I will find out all I can and meet with you this eve at the house of de Grispere. But now I must go to watch the king and keep him safe from harm." At which he strode away to return to the king's side.

His place next to Mark was taken by another knight, Sir Thomas Chaworth. "What ails you, Mark, for you look much distressed and of ill humour?" he asked.

"My lord, I have received ill tidings concerning the fate of a good companion, who has been arrested and taken to the Tower, accused of High Treason."

"By the good Lord, who is this unfortunate?"

"Sir James de Grispere."

"De Grispere? I bethought him in France upon a royal fiat."

"Just so, yet he returned this day and is even now imprisoned in the Tower falsely accused."

Sir Thomas was clearly shocked, and the news covered all other suspicions that may have entered his head. He left as Mark was called to begin his own match upon the matting. Mark walked out as though in a daze, moving his arms to loosen them in the time-honoured fashion, yet giving no consideration to his bout, which was against the man whom he had thrown at Cooling Castle.

Returning to Sir John Oldcastle, Chaworth passed on the news.

"What, de Grispere at odds with the king and Whittington?" Oldcastle said. "This is news, indeed. Go to and find all that you may, for this could be to our vantage in the fray ahead."

The stickler called the opponents to wrestle, and Mark wrenched himself back out of his trance to treat with his opponent. It was in vain, and the contest was seemingly one sided. Mark was easily thrown twice in succession, rendering him the loser.

Theirs was the last bout, and Sir John came forward full of confidence and charm, stopping before the king and sensing a tension about him which he strove to ignore. He had fought as a warrior in many battles, and did not lack courage, and he took heart with his plan. "Gracious Majesty, I trust that we have pleased you this day in honour of your dear father and that you have found the sport entertaining? To wit I wondered if Your Majesty would grace us with a bout of your own to show us the error of our ways?"

The ghost of a smile flitted across the king's face, knowing now the trap that was set ready to spring. A part of him was sorely tempted to best the forces against him, for he, too, was a warrior who had never in his life shirked a fight. Yet he also wanted to play the game to see where it led. "Lord Cobham, we are as ever most pleased to see thee and of course are much diverted by this most excellent display of skill and prowess. Whom would you have me tumble with upon this fine day?" At this, sharp glances were cast in the king's direction. Many of his closest confidants knew by now what was planned. If he were to close with any upon the mats, his life may be forfeit.

"Why Majesty, I could find a lusty fellow to engage with you, yet what of myself, for we are well matched, are we not?"

"Hmm, indeed, and yet upon our last encounter we retired from the arena with no decision made. We believe that there should be more resolve in that regard and must gracefully, yet with regret, decline the offer of combat this day. For we have also sustained an injury to our shoulder with sword and buckler and could not do justice to such a worthy opponent as yourself or any other of the good fellows here on such a day."

With these words, Oldcastle recognised that his fate had been sealed, and made to retire gracefully with his liberty intact. "As Your Majesty pleases. Mayhap another day when we are both in finer fettle. By your leave, sire, I would retire and see to my men."

"As you wish, Sir John, and we thank you for the entertainment."

Both men knew the merit of the other and that the game of chess had just begun, with far more to play for than the stakes of a wrestling match.

Chapter Thirty-One

Evening had fallen, and with it everyone's spirits. The Tower had closed with no visitors being allowed to enter – particularly any who were related to Sir James de Grispere.

"We were repelled by a foul toad who holds his office by virtue of greed and fear," Alice cried, her small fists clenched in rage and futility. "No access? My father shall deal with this and with that scullion Whittington, who sends good men to their deaths and then upon their rallying against all odds commits them to a grave of dishonour."

Mark and Emma had met Lady Alice, Alessandria and Cristoforo at Thomas de Grispere's house. Jamie's father sat slumped in a chair at the head of the table, all the fight gone from him, so shaken was he by his son's incarceration. His large frame seemed stooped and much older this night, lacking in the bulk that normally gave him such gravitas.

Jeanette put a comforting arm around her father, and by her side Sir Christopher Urquhart, who had brought the terrible news, stood unbelieving at all that had transpired.

"This cannot be. Sir James is most faithful of all who are loyal to the crown and all it stands for. He is a knight of the royal household, and such a fate does not bear the thinking of," he said.

"He be steadfast in his loyalty, and I have never heard him speak a word against his masters or the king," Mark opined. Emma reached out and took his clenched fist in her hand, which looked childlike in comparison.

John was as puzzled as the rest, yet he knew the court, having travelled and fought with Henry's father, and had seen first-hand how fickle were the ways of kings. "'Twas ever thus and is not to be marvelled at." He grunted. "The tide of loyalty ever broke upon a shore of shifting sand to roll back another way and join a sea so deep that none could fathom it."

All looked in amazement for it was rare that he spoke so fulsomely except when instructing in arms or combat.

"My uncle too was thwarted in his efforts to see either the king or Sir Richard," Alessandria said, "both of whom have given him audience with good heart in times past. Yet here now we stand halted at the gates of Hades unable to enter and draw back our own from Cerberus' guard."

At this Cristoforo crossed himself and pleading a headache made for the courtyard behind.

"*Hai una malle di testa?* Fie on you, for we all suffer so," Alessandria admonished, and he rattled back a reply in Italian, waving his arm in a dismissive gesture.

John frowned and commented quietly: "He looks unwell, I should see that he is not too affected." He slipped out to the courtyard as the others continued their conversation. Once outside his eyes quickly grew accustomed to the gathering gloom. In the light of a brand set in a sconce by the postern gate, John spotted a servant lifting a bar to unlock it.

Three strides on his long legs and he was there on almost silent feet – yet he was not quiet enough for the figure in black before him, who span with lightning speed to stand coiled as a snake, ready to strike.

"Hold, Cristo, 'tis only I," John said. "You did not fool me as you did the others. I would accompany you, for I believe I know where you venture, yet my old bones are not as fleet as yours, nor are my skills in the darkness as fine as they once were. Yet have a care, I adjure you, and make matters not worse for Jamie."

"Worse for Jamie? Not I, yet others must look to themselves this night," he hissed, his voice more deadly than any threat of bravado.

"Amen to that, and may God go with you."

Cristoforo nodded and slipped off into night.

"Or the Devil more like," John whispered to himself as he saw the gate was safely barred before turning to rejoin the company inside.

×✤× —

Sir Thomas Burton stood before Sir Richard Whittington in his private solar away from the eyes of the palace, reporting all that had occurred at court that day.

"Now tell me of Lord Cobham and his party of wrestlers."

"It was as we had suspected. Praise God that Mark of Cornwall was able to aid us in that regard. His is a most valuable commodity to stay so close to one so dangerous, hiding in plain sight. For the troupe entered as Mark had advised, yet none suspected the ruse of an assassination of the king in the presence of all. Yet as to that we should have, for a similar fate nearly befell his father – but then to mummers, not wrestlers."

"Not just on that occasion," Whittington remarked. "For three times with poison and steel did the whoresons seek and plan his death, and that counts for naught the outright plots and schemes so woven to be almost a solid cloth of treason wrapped around a prince brave enough to oust a dissolute monarch for the sake of the country, causing him to be badly treated and badly thought of by some who were unfair in their judgement, by court of emotion not facts. Yet I digress. Continue, I prithee."

"As you say, certes yes. Then at the end of all, Sir John challenged the king to a bout, but he too cautelous, led him on and in no uncertain terms let it be known they were no longer friends until Sir John came about and confessed all and stood once more a good Christian man. All this while the king's life was hanging by a thread and would have been forfeit had he entered the fray of a match."

"Just so, for Mark is worth his considerable weight in gold, and ever the scales should accord such a king's ransom. And say you that the court was abustle with rumours of Sir James' arrest?"

"Aye, that they were, for by all accounts his was a most public arrest, and Mark above all was shocked to hear the news. It will not go well, I fear, yet there is naught I can do.

"As you say, Sir Richard. Yet Mark is in Oldcastle's favour, and although back in London may well be called upon again now that he has shown fair favour to him."

"Indeed, and we must plot to stay ahead of Oldcastle's machinations if we are to protect the king from all comers."

"I must now away, for the night falls quickly and I have matters to which I must attend," Burton said. He picked up his light cloak from the table where he had carelessly draped it and moved towards the door. With a final thought he turned to Whittington once more. "Have a care, Sir Richard, for this goes far deeper than once we thought, and many are the forces that are darkly gathered against us. From reports that I hear, this talk of Lollardy has infected the guilds, the priesthood and other knights, who collect now to act with force when the moment is propitious. Never had I thought to see such a day."

"I shall fear not, yet I shall take double my servants when I move about the town and in the palace."

"And what of here?" Sir Thomas spread his hands and raised his eyebrows.

"The doors are bolted, and my servants are to hand. Fear not, for I am secure in my own house." Whittington finished with a smile.

Sir Thomas pursed his lips in a gesture that bespoke concern and doubt, yet he had said his piece and it was all that he could do. He bade Sir Richard a final goodnight and slipped out through his doorway, hearing the bolts drawn across from the inside as he left. He moved carefully along Paternosterstrete and then took a side street, cutting through the churchyard of St Michael de Paternoster and doubling back upon himself via Paternosterlane. He was well practised and moved silently, coming to a halt in the shadows where he could have an unobstructed view of Whittington's house. The evening air, although much cooler here, chilled by the river that lay some hundred yards to the south, still would not show his breath. Thus satisfied he waited, concerned for his companion in the king's service, sword ready by his side. Some instinct told him that all was not well. He watched as candles were ignited in the upper rooms and shutters pulled across, the scrape of the metal locking bar audible in the still night air.

For half an hour he waited as church bells struck in the adjacent tower, yet nothing stirred or looked untoward to his eyes that were now accustomed to the night. He watched as the last shafts of lights disappeared from around the shutters as the candles were blown out in the upper rooms that he knew to be Whittington's bedchamber. He shrugged to himself, yet remained alert. His instincts were rarely wrong, yet he could not stand guard until dawn. He moved off carefully into the night, heading south towards the river, following his nose towards the Thames and the summer stench that rose with its currents to Wynwharf, where he knew that he could secure a wherry for the journey upstream to the palace.

. . .

In Sir Richard Whittington's house, the nightly creak of timbers played its habitual tune as the structure cooled and settled after the heat of the day. Sir Richard had dismissed his servant girl and said his prayers for his wife, Alice, dead these three years and whom he still greatly missed. He turned to settle, realising that he had become over warm in the night, and in that movement he felt the cold touch of steel at his throat. He froze, seemingly unable to breathe.

A voice hissed in the darkness, foreign by its accent. "Do not move or cry out, or your life shall be forfeit. You should have heeded your friend more carefully and shut your house up tighter. He stayed watching from the street for near an hour as a good friend should, solicitous of your life. I am not your friend, and I wish to have answers, *capisce*?"

The Italian, Whittington perceived. *Cristoforo Corio, I underestimated him as many have done before.* The thoughts came unbidden, and he surprised himself that even as his life hung in the balance his mind should yet strike for rational thought.

"As you wish, Signor Corio," he rasped, aware of a sticky warmth at his neck below the blade.

"Let us not fence, for I shall not tarry long, and I shall leave either a corpse or an honest man behind. Why did you have Jamie arrested? Why was your own hand upon the document that sealed his fate?" With hardly a pause for breath he continued in a venomous tone. "Why, when he has served you faithfully in France, risking all to turn the French against the bastard Burgundy? All of this and more he has done for you and for the king, and how do you reward him? A stinking cell in the Tower," he spat. "Why?" In his agitation the dagger bit slightly deeper, causing Whittington to flinch back into the bolster.

"I prithee, Signor Corio, be not over-hasty. I can explain all from the vantage of my position and that of the crown," he croaked. He had not been inured to the friction and terror of combat, and he knew that before him crouched one of the most skilful killers he would ever meet; completely amoral and single minded, his only point of balance being loyalty and friendship – and he, Whittington, had crossed the Rubicon on both counts.

"Then strike a light for a candle and speak plainly, spymaster. Speak or I shall take your fingers one by one so that you shall never again pull the strings of a mawmet and juggle with the lives of others. I shall let you sit up, yet do not cry out, for though you may call in that instant, it will be your last action and I shall be away afore any come to your aid, finding you choking like a landed fish from the river yonder."

Whittington, feeling the dagger removed, pushed upwards with his hands to gain a more upright position, his movements steady and precise. He struck a flint and the candle spluttered into life.

"'Tis true. I had Sir James arrested, yet for a purpose not immediately apparent," he said. "You were there and witnessed the act. Did nothing seem odd to you? Suspicious in your nature as you are, did you not wonder that so public a display should be enacted in the street afore all? It was rehearsed to be so, the arrest made with a drama that would be remarked upon and that rumour should spread as fire through a thatch."

"Why? To what end?" Cristoforo snapped.

Realising that he had reached the assassin, Whittington inhaled slowly. "Much has occurred since you left the kingdom. New lords are in place and new orders given, with many vying for power and consequence who see the new king as weak and able to be swayed at worst. His show of piety, whilst applauded in some quarters, is yet seen as a weakness by others. You will have seen that ships are being arrested and navigating the seas has become of paramount import."

"Come to, I wish to know the cause not hear your diatribe on court politics." Cristoforo snorted impatiently.

"Just so, just so. You will be aware of what Sir James told you regarding the Scots and the false Richard. Well, there is another faction in England far more deadly as it holds all ranks in its sway and gains ground prodigiously quick. Lollardy raises its head again, this time to greater heights."

"Porca miseria!" Cristoforo swore, crossing himself.

"Indeed. Sir John Oldcastle is at the root of it, linking Wycliffe's teachings with the Scots, who care not one fig for anything other than their own gain, and the Avignon pope, who seeks the same ends as that of France with his master. Yet Oldcastle has already run afoul of the king and sends out deeper and deeper tendrils to insinuate himself into society on all levels whilst fomenting rebellion as he goes." Whittington explained in detail all that had happened. "Even if Oldcastle should be arrested, there are many who would continue to act treasonably. We need someone with inside intelligence who can inform us upon the ringleaders. To gain credence to such a position I needed a man who would carry such public denouncement as may be heaped upon a stalking horse, inveigling himself within the sect and so informing upon all. This is why I did not have you arrested too. I wished you to be on the outside of all and aid us as you could."

Then Cristoforo saw it all: "And you would ruthlessly use surprise as the best cover, as with genuine fear and anger upon our miens we played your part right well."

"For that, *mea culpa*. I needed a thorough ravaging of Sir James' character and position to make him a perfect foil for Oldcastle's followers to use. Anything less and he would have been suspected and the danger to him would have been greater if he were recruited directly. His reputation is too good and loyal, and something radical needed to be implemented."

"Yet why the Tower? Why not the Palace or house arrest?"

"That will come in due course with much planning. Yet I needed a public denouncement, his reputation in tatters. The Tower? Why that will mayhap aid us and him in due course if Oldcastle is arrested and secured there, as I suspect he will be." Always the chess master, Whittington had thought many moves ahead in his game of courtly intrigue and was seeking to gain all advantage that he could in anticipating each move. "There are many of whom we are unsure, and we know not what offices they may hold in any rebellion. We need to ensure that our plan is followed through, and we capture all those who are treasonous."

"And Jamie?"

"He will receive word in due course, and upon redemption shall receive full and complete exoneration."

"Ha! Should he live that long and not die of gaol fever ere he is free," Cristoforo replied scornfully.

"Fear not, I shall ensure that does not happen. He will be kept safe as far as is within my power."

Cristoforo remained impassive for a few moments, seeking any sign of treachery within Whittington's visage. Seeing none, he said: "Very well. I shall treat you at your word and leave you to your slumbers." Then he remembered John's words: "I should also beg your pardon for such an unseemly intrusion and ask your forgiveness on Jamie's behalf." The words were wrung from him as blood of a stone, yet he wished to keep his friend safe.

"Just so. Loyalty is a rare and stalwart currency, and as such, should be valued and recognised," Whittington responded, then as though it had just occurred to him, "one small matter?"

"*Si*?"

"How did you gain access to my house that was so securely barred against the night?"

There was a blur of movement as steel reflected upon the candlelight in a sudden flash of light. Then the candle's wick was crushed, and darkness reigned. Whittington suddenly realised that he was alone with only the smell of a smoking candle and the tiny trickle of dried blood upon his neck to assure him that these last few moments had not been a dream.

"Hell's teeth, I shall dream of demons this night," he muttered, crossing himself and letting out a sigh of relief, the sweat now cold upon his brow.

Chapter Thirty-Two

The Tower of London

It was now three days since Jamie's arrest, and he had already learned that the Tower was far from what he expected it to be from the perspective of a prisoner. It didn't just serve as a prison, and the windows of his cell in the Salt Tower within which one of the main prisons was set opened out onto the inner bailey. The building served many functions, all working separately yet linked within an intricate collection of towers and precincts supporting a variety of purposes and trades.

The Bowyer Tower stood in the centre of the north wall and here, he was to learn, Nicholas Frost, Master and Provider of the Kings Bows, fletchers, bowstring makers and all their residencies lived and worked. The whole setup took in his mind the form of a small yet industrious village within the confines of London. The Royal mint and armouries, together with storehouses, all these resided within its severe and formidable walls. Jamie paced the dingy cell, smelling the raw odour of the river and was glad that he was at least high up, away from the pervading damp and the rotting slime that invaded the lower quarters. For it was this that all said encouraged gaol fever, bringing ill humours to stalk the body.

It would be freezing in here come winter, he thought, if he lasted that long, and his mind turned again to his arrest and what the reasons for it might be. Had Whittington and indeed the king himself betrayed him, turning all that had been achieved in his name against him? He could not give such thoughts credence. He paced to and fro, and then in an effort to turn his humour from the depths of despair he went through a series of exercises and stretches that he performed daily to keep himself supple and maintain his strength for swordplay. He ran on the spot, picking his knees up high, pushing himself until he puffed and his lungs roared, craving fresh air. Stopping to catch his breath, he heard a commotion and shouts from the main gates above the general activity in the bailey. Jamie could not see well from his position in the southeast corner, as his view was blocked by the White Tower. He heard horses and the jingle of harness and supposed it to be a delivery of armaments or materials for storage.

Then he heard footsteps approach his level as the grating of leather against the stone steps of the tower echoed upwards, heralding the arrival of a guard.

Jamie heard the clank of bolts as the metal was drawn back. The door squeaked on its dry hinges and a hard faced guard appeared at the open door, with another man-at-arms staying out of reach on the landing, a dagger drawn in readiness. Clearly, they were wary of their prisoner.

"Come, you have visitors without. Another two men wait ready at the foot of the tower. They are alert for any sign of trouble," the guard warned gruffly.

Jamie nodded in acknowledgement and moved out of the room, curious to know who had come to see him, whether it was an official or a friend. He moved steadily down the steps to find a doorway leading out into the sunny, grassed area of the bailey, guarded on each side by extra men-at-arms as he had been told. Blinking in the bright light and shielding his eyes he saw a vision that melted his heart even as it soared at the sight.

"Alice!" he cried.

He was caught up in a flurry of blonde hair and sweet perfume that was immediately so familiar to him. She hugged him hard then pushed back to see him more clearly.

"Dear heart, what have they done to you?" she cried, wrinkling her nose in disgust at the smell of him and noting his hirsute appearance.

"'Tis nothing untoward, but the rot of a gaol and the lack of a bath for which I must apologise, as I am hardly the best company for a lady," he offered, making a small attempt at humour.

Then, from the off side of the carriage, Alessandria, Cristoforo and Mark appeared. All came forward and embraced Jamie, ignoring the unwashed clothes and the gaol smell that hung about him. After a few moments of embarrassed conversation, Cristoforo broke quickly into a recounting of all that had occurred between him and Sir Richard Whittington.

"So whilst I rot in a Tower cell, Whittington sends his apologies wrapped up in courtly intrigue?" Jamie spat, shaking his head in disgust. "Truth to tell I would rather fight the double-dealing French or the Scots than fight the smoke and mists of court." Then, considering all he knew of his friend, he smiled humourlessly. "I expect poor Sir Richard nigh on died of fright when you appeared as a wraith in the night right there in his bedchamber, of all places"

"Just so, Jamie. He shook with fright and I had to steady him afore he could give discourse. Yet I left him in good humour I believe, upon John's command. Sir Richard informed me that you will be moved to a better place at Rochester Castle, where you will remain under house arrest, he assures me."

"Rochester, you say? Why I do take the place so recently quit by none other than the royal traitor Mortimer. It seems I am in good company, yet I wouldst pray that my stay is not as long as was his."

"Whittington says that you shall be held while the problems arising in France act as a lack of evidence against trial, and should it necessitate the need, why then you will be close to Cooling Castle and the den of Lord Cobham."

"So why the Tower first?"

"To give more credence to your suit and present ignominy of station that would appeal to any who would wish a strong right arm on their side if and when all comes to war within the kingdom."

"Aye," Mark intoned with a greater knowledge of the castle where he had been staying. "Oldcastle is well set up there and attends to all manner of fortifications, securing the keep and walls with provision against all comers. I think Sir Richard – though it pains me to say, given your sorry state – has the right of it, and will not surrender lightly to any Royal or ecclesiastical demands."

"So the old rogue wouldst play chess with me as his white knight to jump and prance at his command over walls and into camps where no normal man could go with ease. Damn his eyes and damn his dark soul." Jamie cursed. "Well, I have but little choice, and would gladly trade a sword against the crown's foes if I were released from this hell hole in which I now abide."

Alice stood next to him, her hands by her sides and her gaze downcast, shaking in anger and dismay. "And yet all will be arrayed against you as before. Your good name so hardly won will be besmirched once again upon the altar of the crown's ambition and Whittington's games of politics and gain. It is so unjust and is a scourge against all that you represent in honour." She shook her head, unshed tears forming in her eyes.

"Be not faint of heart, my love. Stay steadfast with me, for we shall weather this storm and come about, fear not." Speaking softly close to her now, Jamie reached out to take her hand.

She made to say something then stopped herself, looking to the ground and blushing slightly, whether in rage or sadness he could not tell, for her eyes were masked to him. Not letting go of her hand, Jamie began to walk about the keep, closely followed by the guards. The procession made for stilted conversation, despite Mark and Cristoforo giving them as much time to be alone as they could. But in the end it became untenable to them both, and reluctantly Lady Alice made to leave.

"Take good care of her both as you may, for something is amiss and I cannot breach her wall of secrecy here in this place and under such circumstances."

Mark and Cristoforo nodded and so too did Alessandria, who was now comforting Alice as she made to say a final farewell. Cristoforo too looked slightly puzzled at his wife's demeanour, but in the end he shrugged and afforded it to the eternal mystery of women.

Once back in the carriage the two women held hands: "You did not tell him?" Alessandria asked.

At which Alice shook her head, her eyes again tearful: "No I could not, he is so stoic and brave and in such a place under such circumstances, it would sap his courage I'm bound, and he needs must exercise all his mind upon the moment." She sighed.

Inside the carriage Alessandria's maid Francesca, who had not dared leave its safe confines, looked on frowning, her mind working hard to ensure that she had grasped all that had been said in the language that she'd been struggling to master since her arrival in England. She too had made a decision that might change her life.

×✼× —

Westminster Palace

"Majesty it has now been a sennight since we incarcerated Sir James de Grispere in the Tower, and his arrest has done all that it might, and has disgraced him thus to our ends," Sir Richard Whittington opined. "Yet I fear that to lose him as our pawn forever may be the end result. To wit is there any news from Archbishop Arundel and his case against Sir John Oldcastle?"

The king looked out, his eyes cast at mid distance that saw all and nothing, for the next action pained him, and here he mentally gathered himself as to what needed to be done. "Indeed, and the news is grave. Archbishop Arundel posted a summons and citations at the doors of Rochester cathedral for Sir John to attend a hearing, and these were torn down. He is now denounced and condemned, and has been excommunicated *in absentia*, and seeks attendance upon us to confess all that we must eventually grant, for I'll wager that he will not attend any or all courts and no good shall come of it. We also hear that he makes preparations to defend and strengthen Cooling Castle against any attack, and this too bodes ill. For a civil war beckons if these smoking embers of dissent are not smothered at the earliest instant. So in that regard release our knight who is a pawn in all respects, and let him insert himself within the ranks of Cobham's traitors. I shall leave the detail to you and Sir Thomas and will have our Lord Chief Justice sign a warrant to release him under house arrest at Rochester Castle, where no doubt he shall learn more of their plans."

Whittington smiled, inwardly pleased at the release of his godson from the oppression of the Tower.

"By your leave Sire, I shall attend upon Sir William, and with a warrant arrange for Sir James's transfer to Rochester Castle. He will enjoy easier lodgings there, I'm bound." With which he bowed and moved quietly out of the chamber to leave his king to greater matters of state, the crown weighing so heavy upon his head.

Chapter Thirty-Three

The guards came for Jamie the following day, and he was taken downriver by barge before disembarking on the southern shore and riding south towards Rochester Castle. Set on the north bank of the Medway River, the castle's mighty keep rose above a long and meandering curtain wall that dominated all – including the spire of the nearby cathedral.

Jamie knew as he spied his destination that the castle was under the custodianship of Earl Thomas Arundel, and he hoped that he was not in residence. Jamie had crossed him in the Nottingham plot against King Henry Fourth, and despite those fences having now been mended and an outward demeanour of civility at court, he did not know how he would be received in his current disadvantaged position.

The group made for the river bridge and crossed the wide moat, passing under the main tower gateway into the huge inner bailey. The castle walls rose high, in good repair now after a chequered history of sieges and capture under different kings. Close to, the keep was even more impressive. Rising to well over a hundred feet, it was said to be the tallest in the whole of England. The captain of the guard was called out, and Jamie was escorted up a long flight of stone steps to the main doors and through into the great hall that was, in keeping with many such structures, set on the first floor.

He was expecting a rudimentary dwelling set up for war and defence, but found instead a great hall graced with wondrous tapestries, strong wooden floors and hangings of delicate design and intricacy. His thoughts were disturbed as a figure approached, flanked by two knights. The features bore a certain resemblance to the Earl of Arundel, as this was Sir Richard Arundel, cousin to the earl. The captain of the guard bowed his head and introduced Jamie.

"My lord, I have here Sir James de Grispere, who has been brought under house arrest to remain here under your charge by order of his majesty King Henry Five." He presented the official papers consigning Jamie into his care, and Sir Richard said nothing as he read the document twice. "It says that you are charged with high treason, is this true?"

"No, my lord. 'Tis a pack of lies and a slander against my good name. I serve the crown loyally and would dispute at arms any man who says otherwise."

The constable snorted in response. "Well, you shall see yourself kept tightly secured here, and my rules are simple," he replied. "You are under house arrest, to be given freedom within the keep, bailey and inner grounds. You may amuse yourself as you wish, and we shall accept your word of honour as a knight of the realm that you will adhere to these rules whilst you are in my castle. Do you agree?"

"E'er it please you my lord," Jamie answered non-commitally, bowing his head sufficiently to offer respect to the constable.

"Very well, you will be treated civilly until we are told otherwise, and shall be afforded all the comfort and as much freedom as we may offer that befits your rank. Hugh," he motioned to a servant, "show Sir James to his quarters and then instruct him to wait upon me in my private chamber afore vespers." The servant nodded and unbound Jamie's hands. Rubbing his chaffed wrists, he followed the servant to a private chamber high up in the keep affording views from a small window across the rolling Kent countryside.

"By the good Lord I am trapped as close to heaven on earth, and yet still I am in hell," Jamie muttered to himself. He noticed that the door to his chamber was not barred against him – although it would be impossible to affect an escape unless he grew wings like Daedalus and flew to freedom. Yet escape he must when the right time came to serve his part well against all the odds.

×✤× —

Cooling Castle.

Jamie's release had not gone unnoticed, and forces on both sides had recorded his journey to Rochester.

"You say, my lord Chaworth, that he now resides at Rochester Castle under arrest pending his trial?" Oldcastle asked.

"I do, Sir John, for all who are treasonous would seem to spend their days there, and his is a crime against the state for aiding the French, I hear, as well as rumours of sedition against the crown."

Oldcastle was suspicious and wily and sought an answer to the obvious question that was uppermost in his mind. "Then why, prithee, has he not been brought to trial before now? For if such evidence exists he should receive swift justice under King Henry's new regime of bringing law and order to the land. It seems the king wishes to supplant his father's heritage and not let any who fall foul of the law stay above its wrath by virtue of status or friendship or past deeds of loyalty as did his father, who was at best lenient to those he loved," he finished rather bitterly.

"My lord, the cause lies much farther afield, in that the witnesses to bring forth are within France. Paris is still in chaos after the rising and Burgundy has fled to his lands in the Low Countries, there pursued by the king's men and those of the Armagnac camp. A bloody revenge is being sought, and none think of bringing witnesses to England with all at home in disarray. From what I have heard in parliament all they have are documents drawn up and signed, and these are not sufficient in themselves without witnesses to uphold the statements as true."

Sir John did not answer at once, but ran his fingers through his hair and tilted his head in thought. "This weight of conscience that lies so heavily upon me I doubt will be solved unless by friendship. To this end I have written at length to my friend the king and he has finally granted me an audience with him to put my case and confess all, pleading to his mercy.

"Yet should this fail and I am taken before a court it will be with dark arrest, and we shall need men of Sir James de Grispere's stamp if he could be brought to our side. He is a fierce and loyal fighter and is spoken well of by Sir Robert de Umfraville, with whom I fought in France. He likens him to a young devil, the quality of which he has never seen in combat. He would aid our cause most well if he could be brought about."

"My lord, think on't, there is more to his ceding to our suit than prosecution. His father, Thomas de Grispere, is one of the leading guild members, and many within the guilds are already flocking to our cause. To add more persuasion, if pressure were brought to bear there," here he paused, stressing the word, "it would cement him to our cause more strongly. To wit do you recall the wrestler Mark of Cornwall who, distressed at court upon the match failed to win his bout?"

"I do, the man is a fine wrestler of great strength."

"Just so. He wins nearly all his bouts, but the reason for his failure that day was that he heard the news of Sir James's arrest, for they are great companions, and it was they who managed the journey to Italy to carry the papal remit for the crown this year past. I also hear from spies within the Tower that he and the Italian Cristoforo Corio, who was in France upon a royal fiat, attended Sir James upon a visit to the Tower."

"You think they could all be brought unto our fold?"

"Mark, certes yes. As to the Italian, I know not – yet he appears most loyal to Sir James and mayhap will come aboard."

"If I am taken after I visit the king, then set all in motion and bring as many as you can to our banner. The Scots are canny, and will aid us only if they see might is on our side. If that happens, the shires of Hereford and Gloucester together with others will all rise in our cause and indeed some of the guilds within London. If we can do this we shall but take the head that leads the realm."

"Amen to that my lord, for we shall prevail as God is my witness, and he is on our side."

Chapter Thirty-Four

Sir Thomas Chaworth waited outside the Chapter House. He had secured himself a discreet position in the gallery above for the meeting between Sir John Oldcastle and the king, where by virtue of the acoustics he could hear all that was said and reported. Knowing well the wiles of the court, he could see the path the questioning was taking and predicted the outcome. He held little hope of Sir John being released, and suspected that a death sentence would be conferred upon him. He made his way from the building, where he awaited the exit of the senior clerics and the royal party, but the voice that hailed him belonged to a man he had hoped to avoid.

"Sir Thomas!" Bishop Beaufort called. "Wait upon me, please do, for I desire to speak with you this instant."

Chaworth turned with a smile upon his lips that was fixed in place. "Your grace, I was expecting you without the building."

"Fear not, for all is aboard now as you will see. Oldcastle

has lost his case unless he recants, which I doubt he will by his performance this day. He is to be returned to the Tower pending further interrogation and a sentence upon the findings. Now, where shall you travel upon this news?"

"Your grace, e'er it please you, I ride for Cooling Castle to warn all there of what has occurred so that we may see who else can be drawn and caught within our net."

"T'will do well, for I would catch all who seek to besmirch the name of the church and foment heresy throughout the kingdom. Go to and report the names of all you find caught up in that nest of heretics."

Chaworth nodded, bowed and left the bishop's presence. Yet once mounted, he did not ride for Cooling Castle. Instead he made his way to Smithfield and the shop and premises of a parchment maker, William Fisher, who was a Lollard and one of the leading captains of the movement within London. It was he who had orchestrated the infiltration of the guilds and trades to seek out new members and bring them to secret meetings. Leaving his horse at the rear stables, Sir Thomas entered from the trades door at the rear, meeting a servant who bade him wait upon fetching his master.

A scholarly looking man appeared at length, around thirty years old and well dressed in good quality clothes. He had the healthy pallor of one who ate and lived comfortably. There was no preamble, as the two men knew each other well, bonded by the same cause that was close to their hearts and souls. The man looked about carefully to see if it might be a trap or if Chaworth had been followed, such was the precarious nature of their circumstances.

"Sir Thomas, why this is unexpected, and does not bode well I fear. What news do you bring?"

"The gravest tidings, for an ill wind dost blow across our cause. Sir John was heard this day before the court, and it bodes not well for him. He is to be arraigned on the next Monday, yet having spoken with Bishop Beaufort I fear that unless he recants all and signs a confession – which he will not do whilst breath is in his body – then he is doomed to be found guilty and a terrible death will follow."

Fisher shook his head in disgust and anger: "I knew that this would be the outcome. No court would treat with him fairly, and his faith will remain steadfast 'til the end. What shall we do?"

"Remain here and rally all that you can to our cause. Have those who can travel meet at Cooling Castle. Those of the guilds and trades that are stapled to their work in London, let them stay here and bring all to bear, marking out those whom we would bring down when the hour comes."

"Just so. Our ranks grow daily and the apprentices who are young and strong seem keen to aid us as they can. Their masters will be brought into the fold, and all will rise up when the moment is propitious."

"Certes yes. Now I must away to Cooling and there put in place plans that will aid us even more in Sir John's cause. I will have word sent to you again."

With that Sir Thomas strode out to his waiting horse and rode down to the riverside quay where he boarded a barge, loading his palfrey aboard with him. From there he sailed downstream to Gravesend, where he disembarked and rode the remaining distance to Cooling Castle. He passed under the gate tower to enter the inner bailey tired and hungry just as vespers were ringing, yet he knew that he could not rest until plans that would aid Sir John had been put in place.

He was greeted by Joan, Lady Cobham, who was Oldcastle's wife and from whom Sir John had inherited Cooling castle through estates of her father, whose niece Chaworth himself had married. Sir John was Lady Cobham's fourth husband, and she had benefited financially from each marriage. She was at best a handsome woman now in her thirties, yet she still retained the good bone structure that would stay with her all her life. Her dark, deep-set eyes studied Sir Thomas as he bowed to her, and on seeing his harried and untidy appearance she knew that he had needs greater than rest and there was much to do concerning her husband. Sir John had bidden her stay safe at Cooling, with loyal knights about her who would defend the lady unto death.

"My lord, I shall send for refreshment, for you look in need of such. Prithee rest here and tell me all that has occurred, for I perceive that there is much to tell."

Sir Thomas agreed, drank a goblet of wine clear down and proceeded to inform Lady Joan of all that had occurred. She remained impassive throughout, knowing and agreeing with all of her husband's spiritual leanings. She was fearless and would, like her husband, die for her beliefs.

"Now what would you have us do to aid my husband?" She asked calmly.

"Are Sir Roger Acton and Sir Thomas Talbot within these walls?"

"They are, my lord, and I shall have them fetched." At which she beckoned a servant to bring the two knights to an audience with her.

A few moments later the servant returned with the two knights, who were already known to each other. Sir Thomas was a bluff northern knight and he had had dealings with Chaworth in the Stanhope rebellion two years earlier. He now resided in Kent, and was one of the chief orchestrators and paymasters for the Lollard group of the shire and in London itself.

Sir Roger Acton had been constable of Ludlow on the Marches and was raising factions all along the borders to link up with Lollard supporters in Oldcastle's native Herefordshire.

They were both dedicated men, wedded to Oldcastle's cause. "Sirs, I bid you good morrow and thank you for coming thus to our aid," Chaworth began, "for we have grave news concerning Sir John and the fate which we fear is to come upon him."

He told them of Sir John's predicament and at length, after some mutterings and oaths, Sir Roger spoke. "We needs must make plans to free Sir John before they pass sentence upon him and carry out the punishment – which will almost certainly be death."

"I wholeheartedly agree," Chaworth replied. "Now Sir John left instructions should he be incarcerated, to wit we need someone who is lately conversant with the Tower of London and its workings. Someone who can lead a group of stout-hearted men with knowledge of what they must face and spring Lord Cobham from the clutches of the Tower.

"Where are we to find such a paragon?" Sir Thomas asked. "My brother Henry was imprisoned there years past when he served the old king, yet now he serves to the north, gaining support from those who would aid our cause under the banner of Richard Second aided by the Scots. He cannot avail us of his experience from such a remove."

"No. The answer lies much closer to our presence here," Chaworth said, an expression of cunning upon his face, "We must first spring free a felon, then use him to our own ends. Such a felon has two abilities that are worth their weight in gold: a knowledge that we must utilise and an ability with arms and cunning that is second to none. I know of such a man, and though I like him not, he is perfect unto our needs."

Chapter Thirty-Five

Rochester Castle

"Sir James, it is your move – yet I relish not the occasion," Sir Thomas said. "For I fear I am about to be taught a lesson in tactics that will offer me little hope of redemption."

Jamie snorted in response, well aware of the flattery the constable used as a weapon to goad and encourage, and inveigle his way into the mind of people close to him. "You wouldst seek to distract me from my work with honeyed words and hope that I fail to see that you draw me into a labyrinth of options of which only one will win me this game," he said. Jamie stroked his chin, and having considered all options he moved carefully, hopping his knight up and across to place it within striking distance of his opponent's king.

"Checkmate, I do believe," he commented, carefully looking and assessing all aspects of the board before him. Sir Robert had been keen in the training of all the squires in his charge, and had insisted that they should learn and practice chess. 'It is the foundation for all combat: whether by strategy or by direct route of arms upon the field of battle,' he would say again and again to his charges, playing each man in turn through numerous games at one sitting.

"Bravo, Sir James. You win the day again. You study well and were clearly well taught."

"Indeed, Sir Robert was an able tutor and taught me well."

"And what of other matters aside from use of arms and battle tactics?" Sir Thomas asked.

Sensing that there was more to this than idle janglery, Jamie answered courteously: "Of arts, manners, Latin and other things that a squire should know to carry himself well at court and serve with honour."

"And did this include a knowledge of history?"

"Indeed it did, yet my father's man-at-arms and bodyguard did also serve me well in this regard, having attended royalty and nobles in their careers, including the old king and others of note. We looked hard at all those since the Conqueror, and studied the government of such nobles and lords that made their mark upon our realm."

"The Conqueror, you say? So you would be au fait with the great great grandsire of King Henry, Longshanks, and all the stories attributed to him."

"The Hammer of the Scots? I have read of him. To what do you allude, my lord?" Jamie asked, tired of the game.

"The story is well known that when he was held captive by Simon de Montfort he escaped upon horseback after racing horses to and fro."

"I know this well, and it was a fine and brave stratagem

aided by loyal household knights. How is this relevant to my present circumstances?"

"I have received word this day that Sir John Oldcastle has been taken to the Tower to be interrogated by the Ecclesiastical See. It has not gone well for him, and his case looks likely to fail. At which juncture he will be held at the Tower pending sentencing."

"Prithee how dost this affect my station here?" Jamie asked again.

"The Lollard movement grows in influence, and none it would seem are immune to its tendrils of heresy. There are those across all counties, in particular Kent, where Sir Thomas Talbot – a knight of this shire – is suspected of supporting Lord Cobham and lodges even now at Cooling Castle, I am told." Sir Thomas watched Jamie's reaction, seeing a fierce intelligence behind the warrior's guise. He continued. "I am informed by one of my loyal captains that he was approached to be bribed and others too, some of which have succumbed. I gave orders that none were to be betrayed but instead watched carefully. Silver it seems is a greater attraction than a lord – or mayhap it is faith that breeds such loyalty. I know not.

"Either way, upon the morrow we shall be testing and trying horses upon the common fields outside the castle. This will now be regular exercise as the weather is clement and new destriers must be proved and trained. I am persuaded that you will readily participate in such a welcome diversion."

Jamie smiled. He realised what he thought that the earl was alluding too, yet was still puzzled, but clearly saw the way in which the stratagem had been offered. "As you please, my lord, I would relish the opportunity to ride free, and such would be to my liking." Jamie set a slight emphasis on the words "ride free", but Sir Thomas's face gave nothing away.

"Just so, then shall we hone our skills of tactics some more and engage in another game of chess?"

×✟× —

25th September, Dominican Friary, Ludgate

A greater presence had gathered for the second hearing of Sir John Oldcastle, comprising eleven doctors of divinity, Archbishop Arundel, the bishops of London, Winchester and Bangor together with priests, monks, canons, friars, parish clerks, bell ringers and pardoners. All had been gathered to add gravity and audience to the momentous occasion of the trial, so there could be no room for ambiguity and an accurate record could be kept of all that occurred.

All clerics wore their official robes, the bishops in formal attire including mitres and crosiers making a grave and distinctive procession as they entered last to the proceedings. A friar strode before them, swinging the thurible of incense which was burning to ward off the evil of heresy that all felt pervaded the court of inquisition. At length all the senior clerics and lords took their appointed places and the prisoner was brought before them under an armed guard, his wrists in manacles rattling as he walked and a man-at-arms to each side of him. He was shown to a hard wooden seat before all to hear the addresses of the court.

Archbishop Arundel, as the senior cleric, rose and began to address Sir John Oldcastle: "Lord Cobham, do you now, having had time to reflect, seek absolution for your blasphemous words and behaviour, recanting all your heresies?"

Oldcastle stood to respond: "My lord archbishop, I would reiterate, I believe fully and faithfully in the universal laws of God; I believe that all is true which is contained in the holy sacred scriptures of the Bible: finally I believe all that my Lord God would I should believe."

This, as all before him knew, was a direct quotation from the Bible relating to the terms of the Sacrament, and thus avoided providing a direct answer to Arundel's question. He was pushed further under direct questioning, and eventually condemned himself with his final words, playing into the hands of the clergy present, by summing up his view.

"So, in the sacrament of the altar is Christs very body and blood, also I believe. However, the bread is the thing that we see with our eyes; the body of Christ, which is his flesh and his blood, is thereunder hid, not seen but in faith."

This confirmed that Sir John saw the whole process of the sacrament as spiritual, rather than a miraculous transformation, which was a foul heresy in the eyes of the gathered clergy. More questioning followed, and he was finally committed to speak against the church by answering a direct question from King Henry's own confessor, a Carmelite friar called Thomas Netter. Here in frustration, Oldcastle lost his temper, saying: "The Pope and you together make up a great Antichrist, of whom he is the head!" There were gasps of outrage at this, before Oldcastle continued: "You bishops, priests, prelates, and monks are the body, and the begging friars the tail, for they cover the filthiness of you both with their equal sophistry..."

At this there was uproar amongst the congregation. Arundel called for silence. "By your own words you have condemned yourself," he continued, facing Lord Cobham in a silence that was suddenly absolute, "and I would in all honour and humility ask once more: Do you agree to submit to the church? For if not, you leave yourself in great danger."

"I know not to what purpose I should otherwise submit. Much more have you offended me than ever I offended you, in thus troubling me before this multitude...Do with me what you will!" Oldcastle responded defiantly.

"Then Sir John, you leave me no choice," Arundel rejoined, at which he stood up and read out a bill. "It is the decision of this court that you are condemned as a heretic, and within a secular jurisdiction empowered in me, I hereby sentence you to be put to death."

There were gasps, jeers and a stamping of feet amongst the congregation. Fists were raised and shaken at the heretic Sir John Oldcastle. His fate had been sealed.

He was taken away by officers of the court under armed guard and removed to the Tower for his sentence to be carried out.

Chapter Thirty-Six

Archbishop Arundel departed the court and left to attend King Henry directly. He found the king in his private chambers, in conference with Sir William Hankford, Whittington and Sir Thomas Burton. He entered the chamber, bowed to the king and came forward.

"A good morrow to you, your grace – or mayhap it is not so," the king said. "For your face predicts the worst by the gravity of its demeanour."

"Majesty, I fear that you are as prescient as ever, and justly so. For this day we sentenced Sir John Oldcastle to death, and your majesty's signed warrant is required to proceed with the punishment."

"Prithee inform us of all that occurred so that we may have intelligence as to the facts of the case, for this is a sad day that so great a knight should be brought so low."

Archbishop Arundel proceeded to inform the king of all that had occurred during the hearing that led to the judgement upon Sir John Oldcastle. "Majesty, it therefore remains only for you to authorise the warrant for his execution."

The king looked sorrowfully at the distasteful document that had been hurriedly drawn up for him to sign. Yet even as he was reaching for his quill to sign the document, he was offered an alternative course of action by Sir Richard Whittington.

"Majesty, may I be so bold as to offer a suggestion that would mayhap show you in good light and also play into our hands by helping us to find others of the plot, who by any delay might show themselves as supporters of the Lollard faction?"

"We would prithee continue, Sir Richard, for any solution or means may aid us in this decision."

Archbishop Arundel scowled at the interruption, and while Whittington bowed to him in acknowledgement, he continued to air his thoughts. "May it please your majesty, yet mayhap you should consider granting a temporary reprieve to Lord Cobham." Arundel sucked air in between his teeth in annoyance and surprise, and Whittington held up a respectful hand to him. "Sire, such a move would serve two causes. With such benevolence you would be seen as just and considerate to offer him time to recant and give consideration with a stay of execution." Here the king raised an eyebrow in interest.

"Continue, Sir Richard." He encouraged.

"I would also add that with the head of the Lollards in such obvious peril, others may seek to aid him in his time of need and thus reveal their hand. We know that many are deep set against us and merely bide their time to act, yet we are uncertain of who such people are."

Arundel finally managed to interrupt Sir Richard's reasoning. "Majesty, I must protest. We need to make an example of this heretic at all costs. For if he flourishes and is seen to escape with his life, it will bring others to believe that there is no justice nor need to fear the mother church but to treat her with contempt, raising others to the banner of heresy. He should be punished forthwith, and the Lollard faith stamped out and put to the sword and fire. And should others rise up then they too will be dealt with summarily," He finished, his anger at Whittington's suggestion of leniency rising to the surface.

"My lord Archbishop, we as always welcome your strong desire for justice, and we appreciate full well the dangers of allowing such a sect to prosper," the king replied. "Yet here we see how two birds may well be brought down with one stone.

"Fear not, for we shall be ruthless in the end, and if reconciliation is not given by Sir John he shall burn in earthly fire and in the fires of hell for his heresy, be assured. Yet Sir Richard's plan also has much merit, for we know not how many lurk in shadows and seek to revolt against us. So let us use Sir John as a staked goat to bring more cowards and heretics forth. This is our judgement, and we will this day sign no warrant for execution. We shall write to Sir John offering him forty days to reconsider his position and faith. Upon the expiration of that term, and if he has not recanted, he shall be executed forthwith. This is our final word."

Archbishop Arundel bowed in obeisance, "As your

majesty pleases."

"We heartily thank you for all your service in this matter, your grace, and we now bid you leave us to discuss other matters of finance with Sir Richard."

Once the archbishop had left the chamber the king turned to Whittington and the other two men. "What news, Sir Richard?"

"It is as we feared, your majesty. The guilds are being suborned from within, and even I have been approached, albeit obliquely, to side with the Lollards. I have spoken with the heads of all guilds, and it seems that others within their ranks are also being approached. There appears to be great dissension that is being coordinated by those who hold sway over the guilds, and it is those men whom we should be watching."

"And of Sir John?"

"We are certain," here he gestured to Sir Thomas Burton by his side, "that an attempt will be made to free him once his fate is heard. In leaving more time for them to plan by delaying his execution you have achieved much, your majesty, and despite Archbishop Arundel's reluctance it was a wise move. I should be interested to see the reactions of the other senior clergy – in especial Bishop Beaufort."

The king frowned, unable to fathom the depth of Whittington's concern, yet did not seek at this point to delve any deeper. "An escape? How will this be achieved, for he is securely locked in the Tower?"

"Others have achieved the impossible and escaped its clutches, majesty, including Sir Roger Mortimer in years gone by under King Edward Second."

"Just so. And should we seek to aid or hinder them in their attempts?"

"Majesty, we should do neither. Already I hear that moves are in hand to aid the heretic in his escape, so we shall not bring to bear any force, nor ease the matter directly, but put in place men who may seem friendly to their cause, yet will play them false at their own game upon the board of chance.

"Sir Thomas and I shall push the pawns in their direction – and even now the gambit is being taken up, so we know what they shall do before they make the move."

×⚜× —

Mark and Emma's new abode was adjacent to the workshop and home of his mother-in-law, which suited Mark well. It had taken him a little time to adjust, but a year later he found that they were not disturbed by constant intrusion and he and Emma had settled easily into married life. Emma had known when she married Mark that any man associated with the crown and all its intrigue would never lead a normal life of routine and boredom. Sometimes it palled, and sometimes she worried for the fate of her husband, who was often gone for long periods. Now they were seated after a fine supper and were recounting the day's events both in the trade and at the news that Oldcastle had been sentenced to death, which had been cried at every major street in London.

Their thoughts and conversation were disturbed by a thump upon the door. They looked at each other in dismay, realising that their evening together would now be disturbed at this late hour. Not troubling his servant, Mark raised himself and went to the door. Upon opening it he was surprised to see one of his Cornish brethren there, the wrestler whom he fought at the display before the king.

"Branok? What brings you here at this hour? Is there aught amiss?" he asked in concern.

"Mark, I bid you a good evening. May I step inside, for there is much to tell and I would impart all away from the street?" Mark beckoned him into the hall and shut the door. "I should apologise for disturbing you and your good wife upon this hour, yet I am one of many abroad this eve, all seeking to bring together supporters of Sir John Oldcastle, who has this day been sentenced to death, as no doubt you have heard."

"Aye, for it seems right catching to sentence good men to the gallows these days," Mark responded cryptically in reference to the arrest of Jamie.

"Certes yes, none it seems are safe upon the new reign who would be honest and keep their faith. To wit for those of us who remain faithful to Sir John we are bidden to come to the tavern of The Wrasteleyre on the Hope in Smythefeld this eve, there to hear what may be done to aid him. Are you with us Mark, for there is much that we could do?"

Mark made a thoughtful face and said that he would need to speak with Emma. "Rest assured I shall attend upon the hour, yet I must discuss this with my wife afore I go jaunting abroad, for her safety is paramount to me." At this he ushered a disappointed Branok out of the door, knowing the man had hoped Mark would accompany him then and there to attend the meeting. Once the door closed, he stood deep in thought, sighed and went in to face his wife, who would be both curious and worried.

"Mark? What vexes you so, for I see in your face that all is not well?" She asked, fearing the worst.

"I must attend upon a meeting this night at the Wrasteleyre Tavern upon the Hope in Smythefeld. I wouldst ask that you write a missive on my behalf and have it delivered to Sir Thomas Burton at court, for your hand is quicker and fairer than mine."

"Mark, my heart," she said rising and grasping his huge, callused hand in her own. "Is this into danger that you venture again? I worry so."

"Hush my love, I know. Yet this is to aid Jamie as much as the crown, and I would have Sir Thomas Burton aware of all that has occurred, for he suspected that I would be called upon again to further the Lollard cause. Yet there is more; Cristo too must be informed, for him I trust more than any other to save my skin if I am in peril. Now let me instruct you in the words that I would use, and then I shall venture to this meeting and see what all is about."

It was an hour later that Mark found The Wrasteleyre on the Hope. It was near his old house in Chikenelane that he had bought with the first bounty money he had received from the prince for his part in defeating Glyndower. He had passed through the minor northern gate at St Nicholas and rode on towards the common ground of Smythefeld where stood the Elms, and within that row the inn. He rode past and left his horse at his old property that had been let to a local farrier. The man was still up and abroad, seeing to his forge for the night. He readily agreed to stable Mark's horse, and from there Mark walked the short distance to the inn, taking with him his quarterstaff, for if this was a trap he would take men with him, he knew.

The door was guarded by two men, daggers and swords at the ready, who turned towards the door as it opened, tense with expectation. This was not just an inn, it served also as a fortress and hideout for wrongdoers and malaperts, Mark thought. He was taken back to Edinburgh when he and Jamie had first breached the castle there to find all around him were enemies ready to slit his throat. The room was huge, with beams and divisions of wattle and daub forming small booths where groups of men sat at ease in each other's company. Various groups were identifiable by their trades, dressed in appropriate garb, some = with fingers stained from their occupations. They were divided into groups, and to Mark's dismay he saw two apprentices there from Emma's own workshop. The rot went deep indeed, he thought.

Others were sat at a table being given coin by a man who appeared to be a knight, and at his side was one he instantly recognised: Sir Thomas Chaworth. Mark forced himself to calm his nerves and relax, he had after all been invited to attend, and should be here as of right.

Branok, upon seeing him, came forward with a smile upon his face, "Come Mark, for you are most welcome here."

At which, with Branok's arm of friendship around his broad shoulders, Mark was escorted through the throng. On seeing his approach, Chaworth smiled in greeting. "Ah, Mark of Cornwall. You are well met sir, and we thank you for joining our gathering this eve, for there is much that we would discuss in private with you."

Mark accepted the welcome with good grace, and at this both he and Chaworth were joined in a separate back parlour by the knight who had been handing out coin to the queue of men.

"This is Sir Thomas Talbot, a knight of the shire of Kent and loyal to our cause," Chaworth said. "Sir Thomas, this is Mark of Cornwall who formed the party of wrestlers before King Henry and was companion to Sir James de Grispere, who now languishes at Rochester castle at his majesty's pleasure awaiting trial and no doubt death for supposed high treason," he finished, painting as grim a picture as he could of Jamie's plight.

"I bid you good eve, Mark of Cornwall, and admit to having seen you wrestle, for which part I was much impressed. I am most sorry to hear of your companion's plight, as from his reputation Sir James has served the crown well and 'tis a great shent that he should be of so ill usance. For the glossers that now surround the new king urge him to strange ways and are intemperate in their actions."

"Aye, and more's the pity," Mark replied vehemently, "for Jamie is a good man and loyal too. Yet he is now betrayed, and I will aid him where I can."

"Just so, then we wouldst not striddle the fence here, but lay out a plan to you that will aid your companion in arms. You shall be at the heart of the matter, for it needs your part if it is to succeed."

Chapter Thirty-Seven

Rochester Castle.

The seasons had begun to change over the last few days, and autumn was starting to show its golds and russets as the winds began to pluck the leaves from the trees around the castle. The broad wooded areas that lined the routes to and from the fortress took on more vivid hues, creating vast canopies of colour that swung and waved in the breezes that heralded a change from the lazy summer of blanched grasses and ripened fruits. Stooks were now stacked at attention in ragged regiments awaiting collection where not long before had stood waves of yellowed corn.

The smells that wafted in upon the air too had changed, sweet with the fragrance of plums unpicked as wasps buzzed around the fermenting juice. Blackberries hung ripe and shiny, and to Jamie's amusement his horse seemed to find them every time they stopped, its agile lips sorting, selecting and munching as his great jaws moved with amazing dexterity, tugging at the sweet black jewels.

"Come Costner, enough." He chided gently, vibrating back on the reins to stopping the horse munching. "For we are next, and you shall slow us down with a full stomach of berries."

They were part of a group of horsemen who when called would divide into twos or threes to race along a loosely defined track that stretched out to the trees for half a league or so, forming an area where they raced and put the horses through their paces. All were stallions and fit from training that had matched their strength with the energy needed for the field of battle. The training had gone well, yet as the horses gained in fitness with such exercises, there came a build-up of tension within the animals that cried out for sudden and explosive release. After a warm-up consisting of a gentle walk and steady canter for some three leagues in each direction the party, which was made up of knights, squires and grooms, reassembled beneath the walls of the castle. The racing back and forth had drained all the pent up energy and aided the wind of the mounts. It was moving towards the middle of the day, and this was to be the last race before the bells of sext were rung and a repast set.

A groom sidled up to Jamie and asked: "May I ensure that your girth is secure, my lord?"

Jamie nodded, knowing that there was more here than appeared. The man was of medium height, thin and gnarled in the fashion of many grooms, unremarkable in his appearance with rough features and the thickened fingers of his calling. Once close, he looked up at Jamie and spoke more quietly than before.

"On this last race, my lord, there will be but you and the squire of Earl Thomas. If you value your freedom and wish to escape, then the time is now nigh, for there are those at the end of yonder land who will aid you in your bid for freedom. You have merely to ride out of sight into the woods and they shall guard your flight and lead you to safety."

"Against so many? How will that be fashioned, with knights and squires here to prevent it, and crossbowmen without the walls of the castle?" He motioned to four men with bows who stood at the castle gates.

"You shall be beyond their range when you make the turn. It is half a league thus, and too far for a quarrel. As to those waiting, they are well prepared, and you are but two and the squire Simon will not hinder you. 'Tis your choice to be a free man or linger here to be tried and hung for a traitor. What say you, sir knight?"

Jamie made to consider the matter, knowing that he would agree come what may, for his future lay in the venture before him. "So be it, yet how will they know I am for them?"

The groom produced a red sash from under his jupon. "Tie this round your waist. They'll know you by it," he muttered.

Jamie took the bright sash and knotted it on top of his jupon in full view. The head groom then called out. "Sir James and Simon de Lattral. 'Tis the final race this day upon the track and back, then we retire to the castle for rest and a repast."

All watched expectantly and some made a few ribald comments as Jamie had become popular within the garrison during his time there despite his situation and the terms upon which he was held. Small wagers had been cast all day and this was no exception. "Five marks upon Simon to win." Called Earl Thomas loudly, causing Jamie's head to turn in his direction, at which he saw a nod and a wink from the earl. Some took the bet, and all stood expectantly as the last pair were to be raced and put through their paces.

The head groom called them to their marks and shouted "Off!" at which both horses sprang as if loosed from a bow. Their haunches compressed and flexed with a surge of power as both riders leant forward, feeling the thrill of the animals surging to full gallop within five strides. On their second run the horses were not quite as fresh, yet still the trees flew by in a blur of motion, hooves pounding as each rider, hollow cheeked from the buffeting, felt their eyes watering with the speed of the chase. Ahead stood a lone oak tree that acted as the far marker, proud of the wood and showing the start of a route through the trees. Each man was to circle the tree and return.

Both men urged their mounts to greater effort, lowering their profile against the wind. Simon pulled ahead with Jamie cleverly keeping Costner on the bit and holding with his legs. It was difficult, as the stallion was powerful and wanted to run and it took all Jamie's skill and strength of seat to rein him in. The oak tree drew closer, and he watched as Simon collected his own stallion, fighting its urge to run on and on, using every fibre of his thews to restrain him.

Jamie had started early, anticipating a reception at the

entrance to the woods and the turning point, but now lagged nearly a hundred feet behind Simon. Fighting the horse as it bucked and humped against the bit, Simon finally brought it under control and took one quick look over his shoulder. Seeing Jamie behind, he grinned with satisfaction and took the stallion into a wide curve that would circumnavigate the tree and send him back on a route towards the castle.

To those watching from the start of the race, it seemed as though Jamie lost direction and was struggling to control Costner as he veered wide of the oak tree towards the forest road.

Jamie's heart leapt for the first time since his incarceration, for he had spotted a familiar face, and there was the hulking figure of Mark waving at him to come to the forest opening. At the last moment he swerved away from the tree and rode towards Mark, whom he saw was surrounded by six men in full harness and more at the rear armed with crossbows and mailled, their swords at the ready.

"Jamie, here to me, for we shall ensure your safety and passage to a clear escape." Mark called out to him. Jamie did not hesitate, although he thought in a fleeting moment, *how did Mark become involved in this escape?*

The horse responded well, suddenly lost to view from the watchers at the castle as it was enveloped by the trees, offering cover and a road to escape. Simon de Lattral heard a voice on the wind and turned to see Jamie disappear from view. He made to rein in his stallion from a full gallop, dismayed at what saw. There were cries from those gathered in front of the castle awaiting their return, as many made to mount and give chase. At which point the gathering from the wood came forward, their armour glinting in the sun, backed by men-at-arms, crossbows and a handful of archers with war bows. In all some twenty men now waited, forming a line of steel and threatening death to any who might venture forth against them.

At the castle foreground Earl Thomas shouted at the reckless few who were about to launch themselves to their deaths. "My lords, look you, they are well armed and mailled or in full harness expectant of our arrival. War bows are ready and we with no swords to our name nor armour shall be cut down afore we get within distance. Come, let us return and remount, for our horses too are done to death and flagging. With arms and thus supported we shall track them down and arrest the traitor who has broken his promise of honour."

The others snarled curses, yet they saw the sense of it. They had been duped by a clever trick, and those who knew the famous story thought back to Edward Longshanks' escape from Simon de Montfort the Younger in similar circumstances.

"Damn his eyes," cursed one of the knights. "The whoreson breaks his word and makes us look fools for it." At which he wheeled his stallion to the castle, calling for his squire to fetch a new horse and his armour.

At the entrance to the forest road the party of armed men saw this, and Sir Roger Acton laughed mirthlessly. "The ploy worked right well. Come, let us away afore they reequip themselves and give chase."

By this point Jamie was remounted on a fresh horse, cantering through the forest road to the Medway lower downstream than the usual crossing, where ferries awaited their arrival.

"Mark, I was never more glad to see a face than yours upon this day. How came you to be so equipped to aid me?" he asked as they rode side by side.

"'Tis a long story and one that I will gladly tell. For now we make for the safety of Cooling Castle and ferries wait to make a crossing away from the main road. The route to Cooling by road be long and twisty, but this way we cut the distance and shall be there within the hour."

It was a matter of minutes to the waiting ferries, flat bedded with a single sail each. The jetty afforded easy boarding, and all were soon loaded. Yet they did not sail across the river as Jamie had supposed, but downstream to Upnor Beach opposite St Mary's Island on the south bank of the river. While they were sailing Jamie went to thank his rescuers, Sir Thomas Talbot and Sir Roger Acton. Both knights stood by the mast of the vessel looking back to ensure that no party followed their hasty retreat.

"Good sirs, allow me to thank you most earnestly for my escape. Yet still I confess to being confounded as to your actions, for I know you not, having seen you both but a little at court."

"A good morrow to you, Sir James, and we rejoice that you are hale and well. As to our aiding you, there is much to tell upon this matter, and we would in return ask your support in due course," Sir Roger replied with caution. "We shall be at Upnor Beach soon, and from there we make for Cooling Castle. Once we are within the safety of its walls all shall be disclosed." The words were said with a finality that brooked no further discourse and Jamie remained silent and returned to Mark's side.

The ferries bumped up onto the shallow beach at Upnor, and the horses jumped ashore to be held waiting until all were disembarked and ready. Now rested and having regained their wind, they set off at a slow gallop for Cooling Castle across country again, passing along tracks and backways known to the local men.

The imposing semi-circular turrets of the gatehouse came into view. Above, on the ramparts linking the two towers, a guard kept watch and shouted down for the gates to be opened upon seeing their arrival on the road. He called the alarm as preparations were made for any attack, yet no pursuit seemed to be in evidence.

The troop of men rode under the archway into the outer bailey. Jamie looked up and saw the presence of murderous machicolations, and more surprisingly ten x-arket holes for the firing of arquebuses, for he had heard of such things yet never before seen them in England. He was amazed, having heard much about the extraordinary defences here. The castle enclosed an area of some eight acres, and unlike any other fortification there was not one but two baileys, each with a keep set on separate mounds surrounded by a figure of eight moat and ditch system. Each turret and vantage point could be crossed with arrows and bolts, giving no quarter to any invader who would be exposed to death on all sides even if they succeeded in gaining the bailey. It was clever, he thought, a soldier's castle and well suited to what he knew of Sir John.

The horses were taken by grooms and the gates barred

behind them, the drawbridge ready to be drawn upwards at the first sign of pursuit, leaving the wide moat fed by the Thames as the first line of defence. The company was led through to the inner ward of the larger keep that was surrounded not just by a moat, but also by a dry ditch some twenty feet deep. A causeway was in place joining the two keeps that could be easily destroyed once crossed. It was an incredible system, Jamie thought, built with every effort and thought for defence. He looked up at the forbidding keep and wondered what awaited him within.

Chapter Thirty-Eight

Jamie and Mark were shown through the main gate and up a steep flight of steps to a garderobe, where they washed away the stain of travel before being escorted to the main hall. Seated there was Lady Cobham, who was rarely present at court, and flanking her were Sir Roger Acton, Sir Thomas Talbot and Sir Thomas Chaworth. Jamie and Mark moved forward and bowed respectfully before Lady Cobham, who was reputed to be nearly as fierce and strong-willed as her husband and as straight and direct as the flight of an arrow, brooking no dullards or janglery.

"My lady, I am your most obedient servant Sir James de Grispere, and I thank you for interceding in my fate."

"I know who you are, and I bid you welcome to my castle, albeit under strange circumstances. Refreshments are upon the table and I prithee avail yourself of them, for there is much to discuss and time presses as ever upon us, giving little leave for civility."

They each retrieved a goblet of watered wine and helped themselves to sweetmeats from a salver. Thus replenished, they returned to Lady Cobham's audience. "Now I shall be compact in my discourse," she said. "For my husband languishes as you yourself recently did, not only imprisoned but falsely charged and sentenced to death. His stay of execution has been brought about at the behest of the king, who realises that it suits his needs to be benevolent in this regard. To wit, we now have less than forty days in which to secure his release from the Tower."

"My lady, I have sympathy for his plight and so to yours. Yet what would you have me do, and how may I be of service? For my situation is not that far wide of Lord Cobham's. Though he be incarcerated I am not myself at full liberty, trapped against my name that is in itself imprisoned."

"Your imprisonment, such as it is, could be annulled upon full liberty if a different power lay behind the throne," Lady Cobham answered. "My Lord Cobham has prepared a great uprising that will take all power from the crown and supplant it with a joyous and righteous religion that will offer freedom to all. And with such improvements, the power of the crown shall fall to him and those within his meiny. For this to take place we must have Lord Cobham freed so that he may lead the troops and forces at his disposal in person, all of whom are loyal and represent all manner of society from apprentices strong in thews to knights of the realm in many shires who shall rise up. The Scots too are pledged to our banner if we can rise and take all, as is our due."

Jamie was astounded at the directness of her words, having little inkling of the full power and magnitude of the forces that would be arrayed against the king. He continued as he knew Whittington would wish, in a way that was designed to gain as much knowledge as he could. "My lady, I am unsure as to how I may aid you in this venture, for I am but one man and you appear to have many in your army. Would my sword aid you much more?"

He realised that the hesitation he showed, which would have been natural in his position, may have been in error. "Sir, you seem reluctant and less than grateful for your freedom. Do you not hate the forces that have been false to you, and which have brought charges against your good name?"

"I do, my lady," Jamie recovered, "yet too I am wary of becoming entangled still deeper, and I wish to clear my name or flee to safer shores."

Lady Cobham arched an eyebrow at this and drove straight to the point, wishing to see how he would respond. "We require you to aid us in Lord Cobham's escape, and wouldst charge you with the task. You have intimate knowledge of the Tower and its workings. You are a reputed fighter and blade whose courage has never been in doubt, and rumour has it that you are resourceful and cautelous. You are, in short, perfect unto our needs and will be well rewarded in the new order once Sir John is at liberty, when you will receive full clemency."

"You wish me to rescue him from the Tower?" Jamie asked, apparently incredulous yet suspecting all along that this would be the task set for him.

"Just so. Will you aid us in our cause?" she asked directly, seeming to become irritated with his lack of commitment.

"My lady, you place great responsibility upon me, and I must own to being discomposed despite my state of disworship and would ask that you grant me time to consider the matter. For what you ask of me will need planning and careful consideration."

"Think not long upon it," Sir Thomas Chaworth interceded, "for we have much riding upon Lord Cobham's release, and we needs must know if you are for or against our cause."

It was now Jamie's turn to frown as though annoyed at the inference of threat. "And should I not aid you?" he asked provocatively, wishing to see what line they would take. He could not have foreseen the response that he received, and was shocked to the core of his being at what he heard.

Sir Thomas's lips quirked in what may have been a smile as he imparted news that would change Jamie's life. "Sir James, you have been shut off from the outside world now for more than two sennights. I would assume you have received little correspondence." Jamie had received letters from Lady Alice, but they had been opened and read, and the intimacy was lost between them. In her last letter she had indicated that she would make the journey to Rochester to visit him, yet all had now changed. "The Lady Alice, your wife, is watched – and so is your unborn child that she carries."

The words hit as would the blow of a mace. Jamie's eyes widened, and his face lost all colour. Yet before he could form words to respond upon the shock he was struck again, in a different way. "We have talked of the guilds and all those who would there come to our cause, and I must tell you that these include your father Thomas de Grispere's guild. Should your loyalty be ever tested and found wanting, it shall not solely be your fate that hangs so by a thread, but those of whom you are asotted and hold most dear." Sir Thomas looked pointedly at Mark. "Now, I shall ask you again, shall you be for us or against?"

The final words burned Jamie terribly, and it was all he could do to control his temper. His fists clenched and he involuntarily reached for his sword that usually hung at his side. Seeing the action Sir Thomas blenched, and his hand went for his own weapon.

When he spoke Jamie's words came out in white hot anger: "Aye, you recoil, sir, and if what you say is true then you needs must look to yourself, for there will come a day of reckoning and as the light dies from your eyes with my sword run deep into your body, then shall you remember this time and beg me for forgiveness." He snarled. "Yet so be it. I shall not gamble upon the lives of those whom I hold dear. I am your man, yet I wouldst say to you with the advent of such news that I would have aided you afore the threat, given time to consider, for I hold liberty and honour above all. Yet now am bound in new shackles of your design, and I am fain to proceed."

"That is understood, Sir James." Lady Cobham responded. She had been silent and impassive throughout the discourse, studying carefully the manner of man before her. She broke her own spell. "Consider all now carefully.

You will be shown to your new quarters, and then we shall make plans for Sir John's escape."

Jamie was glad of the respite and followed the servant who guided him and Mark from the great hall to a room two stories above. Once the door was closed Jamie rounded on Mark in anger: "Did you know aught of this? How they wouldst procure me to their demands?"

"No Jamie, I followed the fiat placed upon me by Sir Richard and played the dupe right well, for they asked me to aid you to escape and be there as a friendly face that you wouldst recognise upon the instant. This I did, yet I heard no threats before this moment. All I heard were their mad plans. I did all that was asked of me, and Sir Richard knows all, for I left word and a letter that Emma should take to him and Sir Thomas Burton. We shall be watched, I'm bound." Mark offered quietly, hurt by his friend's rounding upon him in such a manner.

"And of Alice? Did you know she was with child?"

Here Mark looked shamefaced: "I did, for women talk. Emma and Alessandria agreed that it should aid you not to know, and that it would affect your judgement. That be the reason she'd not leave Lunnon, for she now begins to show the child and you would see all."

"By God's holy breath, am I the only man in England not to know my wife is with child? I'faith for how many months has she carried it?"

"I believe it is now but four months past. Yet what be a mystery is how they below us here knew, for only upon intimacy of Lady Alice and seeing her close to would anyone know that aught was different."

Jamie looked aghast at his friend: "You did not tell them of her condition?"

"I? Nay, for by God I am faithful as ever to you and was as stunned by the news of their knowing this day as ever you were. I was bound by Lady Alice to keep the secret for her," Mark responded, pained at the accusation.

"Then who? Hell's teeth what a coil we find ourselves in. 'Tis deeper than Whittington could ever have imagined. Yet I must play their game and seek a way to provide what they wish and secure the safety of my family. To wit we must plan above their games and seek our own to counter their moves."

×✤× —

Cristoforo had been away from London now for a week. Upon Mark's missive to Sir Richard Whittington he had been summoned to the knight's house and there briefed as to what he must now do to aid his friend. He had bidden Alessandria farewell and left London for Cooling Castle, there to watch for whatever movement there might be. For three days he had resided in a tavern within Cooling itself, a village that boasted but two inns. One was favoured with a view of the castle, which lay at the west end of the village. Here one morning he saw a party of knights and men-at-arms leave, and spied Mark within their company. He left his room, saddled his horse and followed at a distance. They were easy to track, and he was almost certain that they would be riding to Rochester Castle. He arrived sometime after and watched Jamie's escape, going ahead of the party for the nearer river crossing, and was just in time to see the party enter through the gates of the castle, returning with Jamie in its midst.

He returned to the inn and waited one more day, certain that Mark would be allowed to return to London and supposedly aid the Lollards there however he could. Upon the second day he was rewarded when he saw Mark and one of the knights from the castle leave and make for the river together with a squire and man-at-arms, presumably to travel upstream to London. He knew Sir Thomas Chaworth by sight and saw that it was not him. He came late to the ferry just as it was about to depart with the tide and a favourable wind to aid its journey to London.

Cristoforo boarded just before the gangplank was raised and secured himself a place amidships without any acknowledgement or recognition of Mark. He barely nodded at anyone and ignored the glances of curiosity that came from the knight and his squire. With his darker olive skin he often caused comment, and here, after a passage of time the squire approached him.

"Who are you sir, and where do you travel?"

Cristoforo frowned, and feigning poor English he replied in French, at which more questions were fired at him. He answered them with alacrity and satisfied the squire, who returned to the knight.

"Well?"

"He is but an Italian oaf, on a fiat for his master who lives with all of his countrymen in Langburnestrate. He is here to secure a passage of silk from his homeland and to make payment for collection." The squire shrugged and the knight gave Cristoforo one more glance and then ignored him for the rest of the voyage. The cog sailed upstream and only once, unseen by anyone, did Mark manage to wink at Cristoforo.

Chapter Thirty-Nine

Cooling Castle, October

Jamie spent the days after Mark's departure practicing scaling walls and lifting rocks to recoup his strength from the period of inaction during his capture. He increased his sword practice to two hours daily in readiness for his attempt to spring Sir John from the Tower. He had drawn plans showing the layout of the prison upon parchment in charcoal, with walls, moats, the inner enceinte and a more detailed study of how the towers were arranged on the inside. Each tower was different, and at least two were being used as gaols and cells for prisoners.

"Do we yet know in which tower Sir John is housed?" Jamie asked Lady Cobham. "For this shall be crucial to how we effect his release."

"I have received letters from him, and he posts them abroad for the guard is lax and easily bribed," she replied.

"Then let me impart this: Sir John I know both by reputation and sight. He is without peer as a warrior, yet with that comes a disposition that will not endear him to his captors. For I'll warrant he serves his gaolers ill and is not well disposed towards them, being obdurate and redeless in his manner. They in turn will have little ruth for him, and this will not serve our purpose.

"Among the letters smuggled in, I prithee adjure him to a compromise in his position, saying that he is reconsidering and may now recant, making him more seemly to his captors. At this they will remove his shackles, for if he be so bound in iron it will make his escape impossible. I took this route myself and was unchained once they knew I should accord them no trouble."

Lady Cobham snorted. "I know my husband, and he will find such a thing most difficult to achieve."

"Then the choice between freedom or death lies entirely in his court, my lady," Jamie replied tersely.

Sir Thomas Chaworth interceded, as the main instigator of all connections to Sir John. "I will have instructions given to William Fisher, and we shall make certain that he achieves this aim." Jamie registered the name and locked it away for future use. *Another of the conspirators,* he thought.

"That will be well done, and once we are certes sure of this I can embark upon my devoir to secure his freedom," Jamie said.

"Just so," Chaworth confirmed, "I shall speak with Fisher and ensure that Sir John complies."

×✦× —

St Lawrence Lane in Jewry

Those assembled around the table in Thomas de Grispere's house looked on with a mixture of anger, surprise and trepidation. Mark had met them there and had been careful, going first to exercise his horse at Smythefeld, then heading west along Forestrete that bordered open country and marshes where no one could follow with ease. He returned by a small gate that lay equidistant between Crepelgate and Bishopsgate that was used mainly by farm traffic. He then walked back into the city via the huge churchyard of St Stephen de Colemenstrate and by back lanes to Thomas's house.

"This is what was imparted to my son? That there are those within my own guild who wouldst take my life if he does not obey their commands? Then I would sooner he ignore them than to touch such a state of disworship!" he cried angrily.

"Father, no," began Jeanette. "We shall ensure that you are well protected until these scullions are all dealt with."

"Amen to that," John snarled, his scarred face creasing in anger.

"This too is of great concern, yet there is another matter upon which *sono molto curioso.*" The statement was almost a musing to himself, as Cristoforo often did in moments of stress or introspection. All eyes turned to him, and Alessandria asked in response: "*Dimmi tutti.*"

He caught himself; "I wonder how the Lollard *bastardi* knew of Lady Alice's condition. This causes me worry."

Alessandria frowned and Lady Alice blushed at the acknowledgement.

"Aye, Jamie thought to my shent that I had broken my vow to you, Lady Alice," Mark said. "Yet I was at pains to tell him otherwise for fear of Emma turning termagant against me, of which I be feared above all." His laconic words eased the tension and the others smiled at the thought of his petite wife berating him in such a manner.

"Who now of my household knows?" Thomas asked rhetorically. "Why none, for we have kept it secret from all, so the guilds if they be foul would not have known. That leaves households of others. Come, this cannot be so for I cannot doubt those whom we trust and hold dear. Where else may this have been spoken?"

"The first time I knew aught was after the journey we took to the Tower," Mark said. "And that was at home when Emma told me after a visit with Lady Alice. Since then no word has been spoke that I know." Mark said.

Alice looked up at this, seeing that they were all making sure they were guarding her as best they could from future harm. "Of mine own household, only my most intimate maid Nesta is cognisant of my condition, and my mother and father lately returned from the north, both of whom wouldst keep a secret. So where could this have been slipped out? No tavern talk or janglery would bring it forth."

"Aye, and yet I am assured that it unmanned Jamie to hear it so spoken aloud and from such malaperts," Mark opined.

Cristoforo, with his mind ever attuned to secrets and double dealing, turned his thoughts to the problem, wondering who might have known and may have liked to cause harm or mischief. "This hole must be found and stopped, for with this, other intelligence may too leak to their cause, mayhap to our detriment."

Kit, who had been listening and who had remained silent throughout the discourse now commented: "Even now these Lollard heretics are posting bills about the town, causing disaffection and urging all not to believe the sentence upon Oldcastle as so much lies and slanders. I know not where it will end, for such insurrections are dangerous."

"I have seen where such things end, and the result is hell upon this earth, for we saw it in Paris and never should I wish to see its like again." Cristoforo said, shaking his head in disgust. Turning to Thomas de Grispere he offered: "Master Thomas, you have been like a father to me in many ways and have suffered me when I was a burden. Now I should repay the debt and be your guardian with John, and seek to ensure your and Lady Alice's safety. Just say the word and I shall be at your side."

"'Tis well said Cristoforo, yet I have my protection here with John. If any be in need it is Lady Alice, as you say, so I prithee look to her if you will."

"Cristo you are a dear friend and one whom I wouldst call brother, yet I have my father's men-at-arms, squires and knights upon whom to call. Fear not in my regard." Lady Alice replied bravely, at which the Italian bowed slightly, yet in his heart knew that he would guard them both. For as he knew so well, it was one thing to be protected from an apparent threat and another to be plagued and set upon by assassins of his own ilk.

"As you please my lady, Master Thomas." He replied obliquely, yet even as he spoke his mind was turning to other things. "Come my dear, let us away, for I have matters to which I must attend ere vespers is rung and supper is set."

The pair made their excuses and ventured forth into the evening that was now laden with far less oppression than the summer months, as Autumn stretched its reach and new winds blew colder breezes from the nearby Thames. Alessandria pulled her cloak tighter around her at the chill, and Cristoforo handed his wife into the carriage, as on this occasion they had travelled the short distance without her maid. He bade the groom drive on. Normally they would have walked, yet after the news of the threats against Alice and Thomas, Cristoforo had taken more care as to how exposed any member of his family might be, and with that his mind turned to considering everything once more – and he liked not the conclusion that he came to.

"What ails you, my heart?" Alessandria asked him.

"I am considering what viper that we must have in our midst, who smiles whilst it strikes and spreads poison as it goes," he answered cryptically.

"You feel someone betrays us? In particular someone who is close to us?"

"I do, and I fear the answer yet cannot plumb the cause, but for certes I worry that the debit lies at our door, not elsewhere."

Alessandria frowned at this: "You believe that we have been at fault? How so?"

"*Cara mia*, I shall say no more until I have looked more closely at the matter seeking a reason for my thinking."

The carriage took little time to make its passage through London in the evening and they arrived shortly at Langburnestrate. The carriage swept to the rear stables, where they alighted. Cristoforo bowed to his wife politely and offered her through the doorway first. He heard her call out: "Francesca? Francesca!" Then curse in Italian asking where the wretched girl was to be found. Her uncle's steward answered, stating that she had gone out on an errand and would return shortly. Cristoforo raised an eyebrow and stated that as the hour was becoming late he would go into the street himself and see her safely home. Alessandria made to protest but he had slid quietly out almost upon the thought of such action. He did not tarry long and knew exactly where he needed to be stationed.

The houses of the two Albizzi families, who also provided funds to the English merchants and others who would trade abroad, were bitter rivals of the Alberti clan and occupied properties further along Langburnestrate. It was they who had alerted *routiers* and planned the capture and possible assassination of Cristoforo and his party when they bore the payment to the Pope the previous year. They also supported the Avignon pope, and as such sided more often with the French and indeed any who would aid them in their endeavours to rule the financial world. Cristoforo had considered all avenues, and his conclusions led him here as the only possible source to have betrayed their faith and secrets. He secreted himself in Rookesie's Inn opposite their houses, where he procured for a small amount of coin an upper floor window casement facing the street, where he could watch contentedly in comfort and stealth with a small stoup of beer at his hand.

He did not have to wait long. A small, cloaked figure emerged from the side entrance of the opposite building, looking furtively to her left and right before stepping out into the street and hurrying along with urgency in her step towards Uncle Filippo's house. Cristoforo had seen enough, and rising swiftly he flipped another coin to the landlord and hurried out to follow the departing girl. He entered just behind her, with her unaware of his presence or that she had been followed. As she entered she made to scurry to her mistress, untying her cloak as she went. As she dropped the garment from one arm her wrist was grasped, and she gasped in surprise and horror. A voiced hissed in Italian: "I wouldst speak with you, Francesca."

"Ow! You hurt me sir," she mewled.

"And you *signorina*, you wound both me and your mistress by your betrayal."

"I know not what you mean."

"Do you not? Your lies mean nothing and were my sister here she would take a dagger to your eye until you squealed the truth of your deceit. Whereas I shall merely twist your arm until it snaps like your honour and treachery." Francesca made to cry out and Cristoforo put his hand across her mouth and forced her into a garderobe, slamming the door. "Now I shall have the truth, or with two broken arms you shall find it hard to swim when I throw your useless body into the river." The look on his face told her that he would carry out his threat without a qualm.

"No! please, mercy, what would you know?"

"Why did you visit the Albizzi and why did you betray us there with secrets of a most intimate nature concerning Lady Alice? Deny it not, for I know all." He bluffed, breathing hard before her.

"I, I told them nothing, I..." then she burst into tears, deflating before him, the fight and defiance gone from her. Cristoforo softened, still angry at the knowledge that her treachery could cost the lives of his friends. The door behind him swung open and there was Alessandria in a state of agitation and shock. At the sight of her crying maid and Cristoforo before her, clearly angry and upset, she asked in fast Italian. "*Cosa ci fai qui?*"

"This creature has betrayed us to the Albizzi. It was she who gave away the fact that Lady Alice was *incinta*."

Alessandria's expression reflected a gamut of emotions. "What? Why? No you must be mistaken."

"I saw with my own eyes, not moments past," he raged, "her leaving the Albizzi house, furtive and sly."

Alessandria's ayes narrowed to slits. "Yet why should you suspect her?"

"Think on't. Who else, apart from those present at the visit to the Tower, could possibly know of Alice's condition? We have discounted Alice's maid. No, the answer lies here. Francesca, your faithful maid whom you brought from Italy, was in the carriage and heard all, and I'll wager you discussed this with Lady Alice in her presence, thinking yourselves safe and secure from deceit and betrayal. Yet what I am curious about is why. Why did you betray us?"

Alessandria lost her temper, ranting at her disconsolate servant, casting aspersions upon her family and her heritage and demanding why, when she had treated her well all this time, she had been so disloyal. Then to her surprise Francesca smirked in a sad and evil way.

"My parentage you question? Pah, that is all you know, that is the..." here she tried and failed to find the English word for irony. "*questa è l'ironia*. Think back, Contessa, to when we fled Bologna and you asked after my parents and how I came to be at your father's house. My mother died, I told you, and I was raised by an aunt. Well, when your father was widowed he took his comfort where he could and that comfort was my mother, who died in childbirth bearing me," Francesca spat.

"No, it cannot be. You are my half-sister?" Alessandria said, torn between emotions.

"*Si!*" She shouted proudly, her head raised high.

"But why betray us?" Cristoforo asked puzzled.

"I was treated as a servant. I who was of noble blood, never acknowledged, but my task was to fetch, carry and serve. I could never tell you that he was my father too, and I lost all hope when you trapped me here in this evil, cold, wet country," she shivered, then continued. "Vincenzo Albizzi befriended me, coveted me, pleased me. I was respected as more than a servant, and he has promised he will marry me when I am free and the new order of Lollardy reigns."

Cristoforo snorted in disgust. "*Ma non credo*! And you, foolish child, you believed an Albizzi?" he shook his head in disbelief, slapping the walls with the flat of his hand "*Porca miseria!*" he swore. "He will slit your throat and throw your body in the river the minute your usefulness to him is ended."

There were then more tears as Francesca's defiance deflated into regret and sorrow. Alessandria realised that she had a half-sister, her only living sibling left in this world, and in a moment of passion she embraced her maid as an equal.

"Now we must stop this madness and make amends to Lady Alice whom we have endangered, and the hurt caused to Jamie." Cristoforo sighed.

Chapter Forty

London, 18th October

St Katharine's Hospital of the Augustinian Canons lay to the east of the Tower and outside the walls of London. Land had been sequestered in earlier days to provide for the New Moat, which had been dug during the reign of Edward I. The hospital was situated outside this on the road running east to west known as Estsmethefeld, and south of a long unnamed lane. At the top of the lane, where the road met the main highway a settlement of cottages and houses had grown up for those unable to live within the city walls, forming a small village in its own right, some of which faced towards the moat and the Tower. More houses and warehouses fronted the river; including the factories of the tanners, who plied their noxious trade close to the river. St Katharine's Mill was actually located on the New Moat, in the lee of the river, with a secondary mill further in from the riverbank.

At the end of the terrace of houses lived Rouland the Miller. His warehouse was located at the rear, away from the immediate vicinity of the Thames, giving the flour some protection from the damp air of the river. Carts were being brought into Rouland's courtyard, with two carters on the bench above guiding and coaxing the oxen that lumbered along pulling the heavy borel sacks of wheat. Once inside, the gates to the enclosure were closed and the carters jumped down from their perches. Dusk was falling and the bells for Vespers rang out from the local church. The two men who had ridden as mate to each drover pulled back their cowls to reveal themselves as Jamie and Mark.

William Fisher came out of the miller's house to greet them.

"I bid you a good eve, sirs. You are most welcome here and we thank 'ee for your aid in this most pressing venture. I am William Fisher and this stout fellow here," he motioned to the round figure at his side, coated in a white dust from his day's labour, who was nodding in concern at the two newcomers. "is Rouland the Miller. Fear not, for he is of sound persuasion and will aid us in our venture on the morrow."

Fisher looked less like a parchment maker this evening, dressed in stout doublet and hose, with only his stained fingers betraying his profession.

"A good eve to you, sir. I am Sir James de Grispere and this is my companion, Mark of Cornwall." He introduced himself with little warmth to his voice, aware of what he had been pressed to do. Mark had willingly offered to aid Jamie and with Sir Thomas Talbot and Sir Thomas Chaworth's blessing had returned to Cooling castle to help prepare for the planned escape of Sir John Oldcastle. Emma had been against it, but he had brooked no argument on the matter and left with her in tears, fearing for his safety. Sir Thomas Burton had met him clandestinely at his home, where he explained all that was to take place. A final note had been left for Cristoforo, then Mark had ridden down to the river and taken passage to Cooling.

Jamie had welcomed the presence of his friend, and together with Jamie's knowledge of the Tower and all its weaknesses they planned how they would free Sir John from gaol.

"Come, let us inside, for the night air is no friend here and who knows what ears may catch our business upon the currents of rumour."

They followed Fisher into the miller's home. The inside was warm and tidy and well set up, with good furniture in place. A feeling of affluence abounded. Fresh rushes were on the floor and the night was barred with the shutters firmly closed. A wonderful aroma of baking bread filled the air, overriding the fragrances given off by the crackling fire and the sweet smoke of burning applewood.

"My wife is seeing to a repast as no doubt ye'll be hungry after your journey from Cooling," the miller offered.

Mark was always eager to eat and agreed heartily that he would welcome food. Jamie smiled, and for a short moment relaxed enough to quip: "Now you shall pay mightily for this venture, not in coin but in victuals, for my companion has an appetite that will render your larder bare."

The others chuckled at this, and Jamie's words settled

the tension in the air as Mark played up to the well-worn jest. "I know not what you mean, I just need a morsel to stop me fadin' away," he said.

Two men wedded to the Lollard cause appeared; Thomas Kempford and John de Burgh, a carpenter. They were senior members of their guilds and brought with them a pledge of many apprentices and others of good station who would all flock to the banner, they assured the company. As they sat at the long refectory table with wine in front of them, Jamie raised a point that had concerned him all along once the introductions had been made. He knew only too well Sir John's reputation for being bluff and full of courage, often to his own detriment.

"There is much I would know of Sir John's position. Did he abide by my advice and supplicate himself before his gaolers, advancing his position to be unfettered? For without this I cannot attempt to free him," Jamie stated categorically.

"Indeed." Fisher confirmed. "We have been able to smuggle out notes and other pieces of information concerning not only his state, but also his position in the Tower. We have also sown further dissent at his direction, posting bills in all prominent places within the town, much to the anger of the government.

"He is now housed in Salt Tower – as were you, Sir James. They that are without manacles are placed here as it is more secure accommodation that lies farther from the inner walls of the tower."

Jamie nodded in satisfaction, his mind turning over the new information. "And the guards, are any sided with us?"

"Yes, for certes. They have been bribed to our cause. There may be more against us, but nothing that a draft of dwale will not annul."

They set the final plans in place for the night of the following day. Thus satisfied with all that could be encountered they made to sleep in the miller's house that night on hard pallets, from where they would steal quietly into the mill early the following morning.

The dawn came gently in from the east, bringing with it cold, damp serpents of mist that tongued inland as a new day began. The smell of the river, muted by the onset of Autumn was less oppressive than when Jamie himself had languished in the Salt Tower. Mixed with this was the eyewatering stench that emanated from the tanners some way downstream from the mill – a mix of urine, rotting offal, hides and animal dung, all necessary for the foul process. The cloying stench stung Jamie and Mark's nostrils, urging them to greater speed to escape the noisome smell and move into the workings of the mill, which was ready to have its sluices opened for the huge grinding wheels to begin their daily chant of stone scraping upon stone. Once inside, they removed their cowls, de Burgh and Kempford showed their nervousness at the upcoming actions.

"Now show me what you have prepared so that I may ensure it accords to my needs," Jamie demanded, hoping only to ensure that all was in accordance with his orders. The miller was slightly taken aback by his brusque tone, yet bade him follow further into the mill. There, in another section away from the workings of the huge wooden cogs, sat two coracles of leather hide bound to a light frame of willow basketwork. Each would comfortably hold two men, and yet be easily manhandled from one moat to the other.

"And what of the siege ladder?" Jamie asked.

"'Tis in the other mill building, from where we can go directly onto the inner moat, each coracle bearing the end of the ladder." The miller confirmed with a satisfied smile. The secondary mill building was of later construction, built upon the original ground that had been left in place and broached almost the entire width of the New Moat.

"Come then, let us try these craft," Jamie urged, for he was keen to see how the coracles handled on the water and practice with the paddles before attempting it in the dark that night. The second mill could be reached via a small bridge from the outer bank of the New Moat, but at night this was raised, rendering the mill a fortified island joined only by a *chemins de rondes* that linked the Develin guard Tower to the mill above at the battlement level. The coracles were awkward to sit in initially and had a strange balance upon the water for those who were not used to them. As they set off gamely trying to right themselves and avoid being sucked into the Thames, they were hailed by a bemused guard from the ramparts above, who called out, mocking them.

"What it this, master Rouland, new ducklings to be taken abroad for the first time?"

"Aye," Rouland called back in hearty response, inwardly scared that their true purpose should be revealed. "Carpenters and joiners checking the sluices. I pray that their knowledge of wood is greater than water!"

More rough laughter sounded from above as another guard came to see the fun and games. It was all in good spirits, yet Jamie was more concerned than ever that he might be recognised. They paddled furiously to put distance between them and the guards, and with their two passengers they finally made it to the inner mill. The joiner, John de Burgh, made a play of looking at the wooden sluices that were currently closed, seeking to add credence to their mission. Seemingly satisfied, they pulled up to the low lying wooden jetty that gave off to landing platforms and steps up to the bridge above.

"I like this not Mark, we are terribly exposed, and I pray that it be a dark night this eve."

"Amen to that – and let us be glad that Cristo be not a passenger in these frail craft, for that would not auger well."

Even with the fear of discovery close and their nerves fraught, the two men could not help but laugh at Cristoforo's discomfort had he been a passenger upon the craft. Clapping his giant friend upon the shoulder, Jamie made his way towards the mill door. "Come, let us see how good a carpenter you are, de Burgh, for our life shall depend upon your skill this night."

They looked at the huge paddle wheel that would drive the mill once the sluices had been opened, and saw the corkscrew gears that raised the gates.

"You would not wish to get caught in that wheel," Jamie commented.

"Indeed not, for no amount o' swimmin' would free you from its clutches," Mark agreed. They went through into the far tower of the mill that was built adjacent to the outer bailey wall of the Tower. Here, leaning up almost vertically, was the long siege ladder that de Burgh had crafted for their use. It was, Jamie saw, well built, the rungs jointed and glued, not roped in place. He expressed approval and flexed the ladder.

"As good as any I have seen or tried in war." he proclaimed. "Then all is set, and we must now wait for night."

In one of the chambers above them they heard the start of activity as feet stamped and padded about on the boards, accompanied by thumps as the heavy sacks were lifted by the jetty arm, swung inwards and dumped one sack at a time onto the floor. The sluice gates were opened, and the bags of wheat undone. Both men looked on with interest, never having been in a large commercial working water mill before.

"We 'ave one at 'ome like, powered by wind and sails drivin' straight off'n the sea. But here is the first I've seen close to, and so large." Mark commented.

Above they heard grunts and the squeak of hemp ropes as the sacks were hoisted, untied and the grain emptied into the collecting hod above them. Then one of the miller's boys cranked a handle to lift the sluice gates and the rush of water was followed by the creak and groan of the water wheel that was exposed before them. Slowly and inexorably, like some waking giant, it trembled and then started to turn with a creaking sound at first and a slosh of water before the power of the falling water powered it to full speed. The top mill stone started to rotate in its turn, then a wooden gate opened above, letting grain swish down the hopper to the waiting funnel and the stones below.

A Knight and a Spy 1413

The four men looked on with fascination as man and machine worked in harmony, and as they watched the grist started to appear, spewing out into the collecting box by the side of the lower stone. Dust rose along with it, and a fine white powder permeated the air.

"Come, let us away," Mark urged as he knew of old how this dust would coat them as the powder worked itself into even the finest nooks and crannies of the building and their clothing. "This flour dust will do us no good, and we'll be coughing and such afore long, mark my word," he warned.

They retired to an upper level and a small office that was far enough away from the dust and noise of the wooden machinery. Here they would wait out the day and prepare for the evening.

As Vespers rang at the end of the day, William Fisher brought them more food as darkness fell with the promise of a cloudy and opaque night.

"We have brought a third coracle in under darkness, and now we shall all be able to paddle across the inner moat leaving a space for Sir John. We can all scale the walls and wait within to aid you in his escape."

"That was not my plan, nor shall it be," Jamie replied. "Have you two ever practised with a siege ladder and scaled walls in daylight, let alone at night?" he asked de Burgh and Kempford, who looked sheepishly at him, shaking their heads.

"And you, Master Fisher. You wield a pen right well, I'm bound, but have you ever been up against an armed man who is trying to gut you with a sword?"

"No sir, I have not," Fisher answered.

"Just so. I pray there will be no bloodshed and garboil, but should they learn of our presence we needs must have men waiting for our speedy departure, and with Mark at my back on the walls I shall have all the aid I need."

"Now let me look to my needs. Mark, you have the rope and grappling hook. Tie it fast now, for I should not like to fall." Mark raised a querying eyebrow, shaking his head in disgust. Jamie smiled at his poor jest and then produced a small costrel that had been filled with oil. Placing this at his belt, he secured it in place with a buckle.

"You take no swords?" Fisher asked, seeing Jamie's borrowed weapon discarded upon a bench.

"No, it would hinder me, and if I need a sword then I have failed, for all shall be known and we shall be captured. No, this shall be quiet work in part, and I wish to God I had another with me this night, yet it is not to be. Mark and I shall suffice."

Fisher was surprised and puzzled, but asked no more questions. They waited through the evening, and as the hour approached midnight they carefully made their way down to the coracles and the water. De Burgh and Kempford lowered the ladder down from an upper window to waiting hands below, and in their nervousness nearly dropped it.

"Have a care, goky!" Jamie cursed, but his words were too quiet for them to hear above. Then all was made ready with final checks. One end of the ladder was secured to Fisher's coracle while Jamie and Mark seated themselves in the other as Mark's great arms forced the wooden paddle to cut deeply into the water, driving the coracle across the inner moat to the looming dark wall in front of them. The Salt Tower was easily recognised, lying as it did at the corner of the north and west walls. The walls to its north were some thirty feet high, and Jamie prayed that the calculations as to the length of the ladder had been carried out correctly.

The craft made hardly any sound, and they need not have worried, for Fisher seemed competent enough for his part and secured as they were by the ladder they made safe crossing in near perfect darkness. The gentle sloshing sounds of the paddles were lost in the noise of the river and lapping of the current against the walls, and they were enveloped by the omnipresent mist as it rose upwards. They reached the small, narrow ledge of rock at the base of the inner curtain wall, and using tie ropes they secured both craft to the narrow shore and began untying the ladder. Mark hopped out and stood with his back to the wall. They were, Jamie judged, some twenty feet along from the Salt Tower, setting the ladder along the narrow stone bank with Jamie and Fisher at one end and Mark at the other.

"How do we raise the ladder?" Fisher asked in alarm, "for we have not sufficient angle to stand in the water and the shelf of stone falls off most sharply I am advised. It is impossible." he pointed out. "We cannot traverse the shore, for the width will not permit it."

Jamie said nothing, but tapped the ladder gently with the hilt of his drawn dagger. It was the vibrations as much as the sound that Mark caught, and with that, he tapped back and placed his left foot against the base, with his arms raised as high as he could to grasp the rungs.

At the other end Jamie got under the ladder and started to walk it hand over hand towards Mark, who heaved and pulled for all he was worth. When Jamie was but a third of the way along, it seemed to lift of its own volition like a drawbridge raised by invisible chains arcing up into the night. Mark's arms bulged and writhed within his gambeson as the ladder continued to rise, powered by his massive strength. The higher he raised it, the easier it became to manoeuvre, and Jamie moved forward across the rocky shore to aid Mark in stabilising it at the base.

Now it was vertical, and carefully pushing and pulling in dynamic tension, steadying the heavy ladder as Mark went, Jamie gently allowed it to rest against the wall. He looked up, seeing that it almost made the top, stopping about a foot short of the crenulations.

"It's a sharp angle Mark, can you do it?"

"Aye, that I shall. Climb up the inside first and twist over halfway up. I'll keep 'er steady ne'er you mind," he whispered, and winked in the darkness. "Don't forget the rope at my feet." Jamie nodded and began wrapping it around his own waist, then squatted between Mark's torso and the wall, climbing up through the gap of Mark's arms, all his weight pulling the ladder inwards. When he was halfway up and the walls got so close that they restricted his movements, he pulled himself around to the outside of the ladder, Mark fighting the outward momentum, bracing himself against the strain. Now it became easier for both men, as the higher Jamie climbed the more his weight pulled the ladder inwards. When he reached the top Jamie paused, listening for any approaching sentry.

Satisfied that no shapes lurked waiting to kill him, he placed his hands on either side of the crenulations and vaulted up and forward, to land quietly on the rampart behind. He was in!

Chapter Forty-One

Jamie strained his ears as he crouched down to present no outline against whatever ambient light there might be. There was silence, then a voice floated across to him in the darkness from the top of the tower, making him start.

"All well?" came the cry, and Jamie heard an affirmative response from the turret to his left. No one had seen or heard him, and he realised he had been holding his breath, which he gently released. He moved on silent feet towards the turret before him, and as he did so he heard footsteps move away along the rampart and up the steps to the flat roof of the tower. He stood now, and was just able to make out the departing figure of the guard. He knew that the roof was not completely flat, but sloped a little to allow rain to run off. To one side was a large chimney which would act as the test for their plan. If it was warm to touch it would mean that fires had been lit below, and his mission would have failed. Jamie moved cautiously forward and laid the flat of his hand against the brickwork of the chimney. He smiled with relief and allowed the tension to relax from his shoulders when he found that it was cold to the touch.

He looked around once more, then carefully unwound the rope from his waist and set the grappling hook in place over the wall at the top of the huge chimney. Levering himself up off the stone collars surrounding the stack he climbed up, and spreading his legs he wedged his feet against the inside before grasping the rope and belaying himself downwards, hand over hand. He knew from Fisher's intelligence that Oldcastle was being held on the upper floor, supposedly making it harder to escape despite the window openings being larger the higher up the tower they were set. Jamie had been locked away on the same level, and took a moment to remind himself of the internal geography.

After descending for a few feet, the chimney split into two channels, and he saw a pale light coming from the first level. Jamie dropped down towards it, pulling the tail of the rope with him. He emerged at the entrance of the first fireplace, covered in soot and grime from the chimney, a fall of dust and detritus heralding his arrival. He stifled a dry cough that rose in his throat brought on by the dusty air, forcing the dirty sleeve of his gambeson to his mouth to deaden the noise. When he was satisfied that the coughing fit had passed, he orientated himself, standing quietly to see if his arrival had been noticed. No steps and no sound of alarm could be heard, although he could hear a voice from further down the stairwell floating up on the strange acoustics of the turret.

Jamie ducked and crouched down, still nervous of being caught. Then he stood erect, his senses stretched taut in the gloom, the only light coming from a single torch lodged in the sconce at the top of the stairwell. The landing was large, with four cells leading off it, each with a small, barred grate that offered a view into the dungeon beyond. In the centre stood a rough table graced by an unlit candle secured in an iron holder, with a stool at either side. Walking on the balls of his feet, Jamie crept from one cell to the next. At the third, facing out over the moat, he saw a figure who was sitting awake and alert, clearly ready for escape at the earliest instant.

"Sir John?" Jamie whispered, his voice sounding harsh and loud to his own ears.

"Aye, 'tis me. Get me from this hell hole, for the guard will return soon upon his rounds." Oldcastle ordered, his voice arrogant and used to command.

"Await me a moment." Jamie replied. Pulling the costrel from his waist and removing the stopper, he began to pour a trickle of oil onto each of the two long bolts that kept the door fastened securely shut. Satisfied, he then turned his attention to the hinges. Making sure that they were well coated, he rubbed the oil in with his fingers.

"Come now, hurry," Oldcastle urged.

"Wait!" Jamie snapped, "for if this door squeaks we shall both be caught."

Realising he had done all he could to prevent any sound emerging from the iron locks and hinges he started to pull back the top bolt, which caught at first, and then began to slide more easily as the oil penetrated it and aided the movement was aided. The bottom bolt proved easier, and seeing its release, Oldcastle pushed the door outwards in his impatience. A small squeak sounded, sounding like a banshee howl in the silence.

"You fool!" Jamie hissed. Both men paused, holding their breath as the muted conversation below stopped, and the sound of leather rasping upon stone came to them as a guard began ascending the steps to investigate. "Get back in and hold the door shut." Jamie ordered. Seeing this done, he grabbed one of the oak stools in his left hand and drew his dagger with his right, moving into the shadows to the left-hand side of the spot at which the steps entered the landing. The footsteps were getting closer, and Jamie's pulse raced at their urgency.

A torch proceeded the guard, who appeared with his sword drawn upon the level. As he emerged into the space, Jamie allowed him to pass and to take two more steps forwards before stepping quickly behind him. The guard sensed a presence to his rear, but before he could raise the alarm Jamie brought the stool down heavily upon his head and he collapsed to the floor as though poleaxed. Oldcastle cried out a warning from the door, and Jamie turned to find a more menacing and determined foe. The second guard, whom he had not heard, had taken time to don a helmet, and like his companion wore a habergeon of maille under a tabard bearing the king's livery. His sword was drawn, and he held it at the middle guard, advancing carefully, clearly knowing his business.

"So, two for the price of one," he crowed through broken teeth. "Surrender, for more will be here shortly and there will be no escape except at the sword's edge."

Jamie said nothing, measuring the distance, the stool still

in his hand and his dagger in the other. If he went to swing and slash, he would have chance to slide inside his opponent's guard, he knew, closing the distance and gaining the advantage. But if the guard's sword-point licked out, all he had to offset the advantage of the guard's length was a stool for a shield.

He feinted with the stool, seeming to raise it and strike at the blade before him, leaving a gap. Instantly the guard flicked his point forward, seeking to skewer Jamie's torso. Jamie took a step back and to the left, moving off the centre line, barely in time as the point nicked the padding of his gambeson. Jamie knew what was coming for it was what he would have done himself, and the blade slashed in a vicious backhand to follow his step, and then the dance began as the guard chased him with three quick thrusts and parries across the floor.

Such was their position that Oldcastle had no opportunity to gain the other stool for fear of being killed. Each time he went to move the guard slashed around widely and then came back on guard before Jamie could gain the advantage. He raised the stool again, and the sword came up into the gap from a low guard. This time Jamie was ready. As the point came in, he didn't block it, but moved inwards towards his opponent, closing the distance between them and nullifying the advantage of the guard's sword and the extra reach it gave him. Jamie dropped the stool and pinned the man's sword arm, driving his dagger hilt up under the exposed throat. The guard rasped as he struggled to breathe, eyes wide in pain and his brain refusing to register the fact that there was no air to be gained. The guard sank to the floor unconscious, his hand clutched to his throat.

"Twas well done," Oldcastle said. "Yet why did you not kill the whoreson and be done with him, for he will come to and raise the alarm."

Jamie sheathed his dagger. "By which time we will be long gone," he replied. "Now let us not daddle." Oldcastle frowned but made to follow Jamie's lead as he moved to the huge fireplace and ducked inside, standing on the iron grate.

"A rope, by the Good Lord." Oldcastle exclaimed.

"Go, Sir John, and I will follow," Jamie urged, and with that the knight began to haul himself hand over hand up the chimney, using his legs braced against the wall to aid his progress. Jamie moved back and quickly dragged both guards into the empty cell and bolted the doors. He stood the stool upright again at the table and ran for the fireplace and escape. It would only aid them for a while but hopefully it would add to the confusion. Oldcastle had made good work of his ascent and Jamie felt the rope go slack as he reached the stack above. Jamie wasted no time in grabbing the rope – having first attached the end to his belt so it would not dangle in plain sight as he climbed. He reached the top once more covered in a new layer of grime and soot, glad of the clean air and the open sky above him.

"Come, this way," Jamie whispered, motioning to the parapet a few feet away. Oldcastle followed his lead, ever wary of a trap and looked over to see the ladder still in place.

"We go down that?" he asked incredulously.

"No it will not do, and we should be exposed. We shall use the rope and belay down." He secured the grappling hook to the crenulation, tested it and slipped over, starting to abseil down the wall. The rope was strong enough to take both men, and they arrived in short order at the tiny shore of rocks at the base of the wall. No hue and cry had been raised as yet to their relief. Mark and Fisher each sat in a coracle awaiting their arrival, the paddles at the ready. The two coracles were now roped closely together as they had left the ladder in place.

Oldcastle gave one final look upwards, still unable to believe that he was free from his prison as he eased himself gratefully into the waiting craft. They made little noise and remained silent as each man paddled towards the welcoming embrace of the waiting mill building that joined the bridge above to the outer wall of the Tower. The two coracles floated silently, until the gentle current began to pull them towards the river. The craft were riding close together, and Fisher risked a few words: "Let us press our luck and make directly for the river where the lighter awaits us moored nearby."

Each man looked to the other, and as one they nodded. Jamie for his part was aware that Oldcastle's escape could be discovered at any moment, and the full guard would be called out.

They took a risk, allowing the current to take them under the arch of the bridge above. To their relief two wherries passed along the river as they did so just ahead of them, the bargemen steering and causing ripples of passage that masked any noise their shallow craft made. Then they were under the arch and the current caught them as they paddled for their lives, fighting to stay close to the shore. Their only advantage was that the shoreline extended out much further once they were into the river, impeding the flow of the current as would a groyne upon a beach.

Ahead of them, tied some twenty feet away, was the lighter they were seeking. The captain, who was watching out for their arrival, was surprised to see them exit from further upstream and immediately produced a rope to throw in their direction, saving them from being swept quickly by.

"Belay there," he hissed at his mate. "Cast off, for we must catch our fish right quick."

The mate slipped the stern line just as the coracles came parallel, and the lighter gained speed to match the smaller vessels, one of which had been snagged by Jamie, who caught the line as Mark paddled furiously, no longer heeding what noise he might make. At that point they all heard the clanging of a bell and a call to arms from the Tower. "Prisoner loose, prisoner loose! Call out the guard!"

With both coracles securely strapped to the side of the low lying boat, they scrambled aboard just as the lighter caught the current. Oldcastle could not help himself, he laughed out loud as the vision of the Tower faded into the darkness.

"By the Good Lord, I am free, God be praised," he cried.

"For the love of God, hush man," Jamie admonished him. "We can still be caught, for faster boats than this one may be launched. I wish to put leagues between us and your prison, and the water carries sound, even in the mist that cloaks us."

Despite their efforts at secrecy, other ears had heard Oldcastle's outburst, and a sharp pair of eyes watched their progress as the lighter disappeared into the mist. Cloaked in black, the hidden observer nodded and made for his horse further downstream.

"Scappano!" He muttered under his breath, with a nod of his head and a wry smile.

×✙× —

King Henry's private Chamber, Westminster Palace.

"You say that Oldcastle managed his escape yester eve, and was not discovered until all were away?"

"Yes sire," Whittington answered. "It was well executed. Sir John and his accomplices are believed to have climbed up the chimney to the roof of Salt Tower. They descended on ropes and then escaped via the river, my lord king."

"By the rood, 'twas a good plan – and whose hand, we wonder, was behind it? And no guards were killed in this exploit, you say?"

"No sire, some have headaches from being bludgeoned, and others were perhaps bribed to stay away, leaving but two guards to watch the prisoner at the time of the escape," Whittington shrugged, leaving ambiguity hanging in the air. The king, who was no fool, caught the implication and raised an eyebrow in ire.

"Then we should like to interview master Robert de Morley at his convenience, once we are aware of all that occurred, for we are persuaded that Oldcastle's escape could not have been contrived without aid from within the Tower's walls."

"All shall be revealed majesty, my inquiries will leave no stone unturned."

"As well they should. Now to other matters. What news of France, Sir Henry?"

The king's Chamberlain, Sir Henry, Lord Fitzhugh, offered the king a brief bow. "Majesty, e'er it please you, a courier has lately arrived from his Grace the Duke of Burgundy, begging you to grant an audience with his embassy as a matter of some urgency."

"So John the Fearless still lives, despite his crimes in Paris. He should be renamed John the Fox, for he is wily and cautelous enough to escape any trap or ploy that is set to catch him. Where is the fox's lair now?"

"Majesty, I understand that he fled with many of his retinue to the Low Countries, and fights there against the united might of the Armagnacs and the crown of France, supported by your cousin King Charles and the dauphin." Lord Fitzhugh finished with a hint of satisfaction in his voice.

The king and Whittington welcomed the news, sharing a small but meaningful smile of satisfaction: "A divided France? Praise God!" The king said

"Indeed, majesty." Whittington inclined his head.

Chapter Forty-Two

Cooling Castle: November

The escape by river was a success, and with no pursuit Jamie's party travelled several miles downstream to disembark in the misty light of an autumn dawn at the southern pier of a river crossing. There they were met by men-at-arms to welcome Sir John to his castle once more. John de Burgh and Thomas Kempford had returned to their trades, and were even now recruiting more men to the Lollard cause in London, which was awash with rumour and distrust as all manner of men from every rank looked over their shoulders, aware of a change and a sense of expectancy that settled over the whole town. Uncertainty was everywhere, and rumours of all sorts spread like the plague with each new posting of sheets and notices on street corners and boards throughout the town.

"All against us are worried and none feel safe and secure," Oldcastle opined, "and into this cauldron of rumour and uncertainty we shall strike this Christmastide to bring down this reign so shortly begun. Any man who goes against the wishes of the good Lord shall perish."

The gathered company of knights and commoners in front of him responded with cheers and applause. An experienced orator, Sir John went on to encourage and inspire them with tales of uprisings planned in the shires as their cause gathered momentum.

Jamie was alone as Mark had returned weeks ago to his home in London to protect his name against any attachment with the escape. Jamie looked around at the madness of a zealous mob being whipped into a fervour, and saw again the bloody horrors of Paris but a few months past that were about to be visited upon his beloved land. He was now a wanted man, with a bounty upon his head for his capture dead or alive. As such he had remained within the confines of Cooling Castle, which was as yet unassailed by royal forces. Once the fervour had died down and most of the crowd had moved away to trestles laden with food that had been set up in the great hall, Jamie was left with lords Chaworth, Acton and Talbot, who all stood close to Sir John together with other knights who were hanging upon his words.

"Now, good sirs, we come to the nub of this matter. Yet first I must give thanks to Sir James de Grispere, who has aided us most bravely in our service, not least myself, who without his help would still be languishing in the Tower."

Jamie nodded his acceptance of the compliment. He felt almost as if he was in a trance, for he could not believe how deeply he had become embroiled in their plotting.

Oldcastle continued. "This is the first time our company

has been so collected in one place, and I must tell you all how much we have achieved and instruct you in what is now to be done."

Jamie listened in horror as the strategy unfolded before him, never believing that Oldcastle would go this far. *By God*, he thought. *Will I ever see my family again and see my unborn child ere I am hung and gutted like a roasted fowl?*

When Oldcastle's plans had been revealed in full, the other knights slipped away to the waiting tables of food, but Oldcastle beckoned Jamie to stay with him a moment longer.

"You will see that our plans are both strong and complete in their imaginings. I see that the scope of them gives you pause for thought," Oldcastle said as Jamie remained impassive. "Yet think on't, you are now fully wedded to us and our cause, whether you believe in Wycliffe's teachings or not. The only way forward for you is to support us to the hilt."

"Certes yes, you have the right of it. I know that if I do not comply and throw myself on the mercy of the king, you would kill my family."

Oldcastle shrugged his broad shoulders and showed another side to his character, grinning without any hint of mirth. "It is regrettable, yet I needs must have your complete support. Once we are through, you have my word of honour that you will be recomposed and have complete discharge from any wrongdoing, for with me in power as Regent my word will carry all before it."

"'Twould seem that I have little choice, Sir John, and as you say, my way forward is with you in completeness." At this Jamie broke away and settled down to eat at the table with the others.

Once the meal had ended, Sir John nodded to Sir Thomas Chaworth, indicating that he wished to speak to him in private conference. "I have spoken with de Grispere," he said, "and I trust him not, for all that he is within our coils. If he could spring and leap clear of us I doubt not that he would, and the Devil take the hindmost."

"I concur, so what would you have me do?"

"Double the men who watch his family, in particular his father, who is less well guarded. The Baron Macclesfield's daughter is better protected just now, for her father is returned from the north with all his mesnie, I am informed. And upon my honour I would not arrange for the death of a woman in child."

"Nor shall you need to. The father shall be the target. A merchant guarded by servants and by one old soldier, he is surrounded by members of his guild, many of whom, Fisher informs me, are loyal to us. He should be easy to take and hold – and if not, well, his life will be well spent securing our faith. and 'twill stop Sir James from making rash moves lest his wife be next."

 —

King's Council Chamber, Westminster: November

The gathering of immediate intimates of the king was

this day very sombre. The kingdom – and in particular London – was as all knew on the brink of anarchy the like of which had been seen earlier in the year in Paris. Full reports had now been made of all that had happened in France, and having heard about the aftermath from witnessed accounts, events that would have been thought unimaginable previously now held more credence, bringing with it the fear of a repetition at home in England.

"Majesty," Lord Chief Justice Sir William Hankford began, "we cannot permit a rising to occur in England again. The Peasants' Revolt that nearly unseated your uncle is still too fresh in everyone's mind. The people of England are tired of constant warring with Glyndower and the Scots, and your Majesty knows too well how hard it is to hold together a kingdom that is fractious and disparate."

"You give wise counsel, Sir William, and we heed your words well. And for this reason we have not summoned troops to lay siege to Cooling Castle. If we were to do so, it would mark an outbreak of civil war, and such an event must be snuffed out afore it begins. We shall keep the fowl penned, for with such actions we know at least where they are. If we should approach Cooling, we are persuaded that our bird would fly the coop and all efforts would be wasted. With nothing to counter, Lord Cobham must dictate his own actions, and we may deploy while these plans remain unhatched.

"With this in mind, Sir Thomas, would you inform the Council of all you have learned."

Sir Thomas Burton nodded with a slight bow of his head. "Majesty, e'er it please you, Lord Cobham has sent out dispatches throughout the entire kingdom to foment unrest and encourage civil risings in counties and shires from Kent to Wales and the north. I have warrants ready for your signature, my king, to warn sheriffs around the kingdom and give them free rein for the arrest of all who may be complicit in such actions."

"We shall sign these as a just measure and prevent the rising as we may. We expect this month the arrival of an embassy from Duke John of Burgundy, and would not upon their visit wish to present them with a kingdom aflame and in revolt, for this will be reported back and make us seem weak and subject to easy submission to our French cousins. We are certain that as we spy upon them, they do return the favour likewise. What say you, Sir Richard?"

Sir Richard Whittington inclined his head to one side and tugged at one ear as he nodded in agreement.

"As your majesty is aware, the Albizzi bankers have been colluding with the Lollards and sending messages not only between Lollard factions but also to France. They are deeply involved and aid any cause that might bring down the Alberti family and supplant them in their stead. I am certain that we are spied upon by them also, and yet we have some measure of what is returned to France in that regard. But as your majesty wisely opines, no open conflict should pollute these shores while the ducal envoy is here."

"Then we are in agreement," the king said. "Send out these warrants, and may God help us to weed out these traitors and secure knowledge of their plans before they can be actioned. For we have men within their ranks who even now inform upon the traitor."

At this, Bishop Beaufort's eyes narrowed in interest, wondering who might be informing upon his own man and on Oldcastle. *Could they be alluding to de Grispere?* he wondered. *Was all a ploy here?* He would need to confirm all, and mayhap seal the knight's fate in so doing.

"And for you, Archbishop Arundel, is all concluded?"

"Indeed so, my lord king. Lord Cobham Sir John Oldcastle is now formally excommunicated, may his soul find eternal damnation."

All nodded, and mutters of agreement were heard around the council table. Other matters were then discussed, and the company broke eventually with all business concluded.

Bishop Beaufort bustled away as quickly as he could, and sent a messenger to fetch Sir Thomas Chaworth to his palace south of the river away from prying eyes.

When he finally arrived, Chaworth was nervous, unsure of what his summons premeditated. He forced himself to remain calm as he was ushered into the bishop's private chamber.

"My lord Chaworth." Beaufort's honeyed words offered Sir Thomas no clue as to what may have precipitated such an urgent summons. "Thank you for attending upon me at such short notice."

"Your Grace, it is ever my pleasure to aid you in whatever manner that I may."

"Mmm, just so. Intelligence has reached me that there is a traitor to the Lollard cause that serves within it, and this traitor seeks to unbalance their position. Dost thou think this may be a reference to yourself? Are you in the employ of any other lord who instructs you? Or do they suspect another who may have been inserted as an *insidiore*? Speak now, for I would have the truth of it," Beaufort demanded.

"Your Grace, if such a thing is true I have no knowledge of it. Sir John continues to confide in me, and his plans are as yet undecided – other than that he intends to raise the shires at some point against the king," Chaworth declared, knowing that this was a general matter with little substance that was likely common knowledge or indirect rumour in abstract form. He played the fool, seeking to find out what he could by subtly interrogating the bishop in his turn. "The only member who is suspected is Sir James de Grispere, for he had been pressed to our suit, and the threat of reprisal hangs above his head like the sword of Damocles."

"Reprisal? In what form? I thought that by your last report he was complicit in Oldcastle's escape and is now firmly bound by both his own treason and his actions to free Lord Cobham."

"Aye indeed, Your Grace, yet still he wavers, and his heart appears not true to our cause despite all the actions in his favour. I know that Sir John watches him closely, along with his family, who will serve the deficit should he break and try to unite with the crown and seek his freedom in return."

The bishop narrowed his eyes at this intelligence, wondering how he could use it to his advantage, mayhap by bringing his brother to the fore with force of arms, taking both Oldcastle and the king. In so doing he would bring the crown within his reach, all the while pretending to aid the king, who would be caught in the maelstrom that followed any attempted coup for the crown.

"And you, do you suspect de Grispere despite all that is weighed against his character? Would he still seek to aid the crown when all is cast against him?"

"I think, my lord bishop, that I wouldst trust him as much as I would a fox within a hen house. For if he had free rein, a good sword in his hand and half a chance, both Sir John's and my life would not be worth their weight upon the scales."

"Thank you for your words, I shall mull upon them and look forward to your next report. Depart now, ere you are seen, and have care when you leave."

Chapter Forty-Three

During the first few days of December, Jamie and Sir John Oldcastle slipped down to the river on an incoming tide with a chill breeze blowing from the east. The skiff took them upstream to within a few feet of where they had escaped only weeks before. They disembarked at the tannery in the early dawn, easily drawn to the location by the terrible stench that emanated from the works that were already in full swing, with foul waters being ejected into the Thames. The nightly soaking of hides had been completed, and the soiled water was gushing into the giant swirling sewer of the river.

They entered by the water gate leading to the yard, where they met with William Fisher, who had once more facilitated their entry and movement across the city. "Good day, sirs," he welcomed them merrily, the look of a zealot sparkling in his eyes as he saw Oldcastle once more,. "We are ready for you now, and I must apologise for the manner of your next transport, for it will serve you ill as a conveyance, yet well as a means of arriving in safety."

With these perplexing words he ushered them forward to the side of two waiting carts, each harnessed to oxen. Roughly tanned hides were laid upon the bed of each, forming a tentative cushion for what would be their mode of transport for this leg of their journey. The pervading stench that surrounded them was eyewatering, making both men want to vomit, and they knew that close to, layered within the hides, it would be worse. Even though the hides had been dried and cured, the cod liver oil used in the final suppling process was slimy and stank of rotting fish. More hides were laid upon the bed until the carts were about two thirds full. Any more and they would be crushed, unable to breathe under the pressure of the heavy hides. Wrapped in old cloaks with the cowls pulled up, they were told to lie down as further layers of hides were placed on top of them.

Eventually the carts lumbered out of the yard and travelled the short distance up the lane to join the main road of Estsmethefeld. When it forked, they made for the small gate of St Botolph without Alegate, just a few hundred feet from the dauting structure of the Tower from which both men had so recently escaped.

The cart approached the gates to join the queue of farm traffic and flocks of sheep being driven into the town. As it was market day, few were stopped by the guards, and small herds of cattle were prodded and poked to enter the unfamiliar environment. When it came to the turn of the hide carts, they were waved through as a regular occurrence to the guards, who wrinkled their noses at the smell of animal dung splattering the cobbles and sheep droppings that would cause the unwary to slip and slide and fall to the fouled roads beneath them.

The carters gave a nod and a friendly greeting, and with a cracking of whips above the oxen's backs the carts lumbered through the gates into the city, turning immediately right up Woderouelane, running parallel at first, then turning left to be lost in the main streets of the town. It was not unusual for the hide carts to call at William Fisher's premises, and this day they pulled into the courtyard at the rear, where in the privacy of its confines the hides were pulled off to reveal the rough and oily figures of Jamie and Oldcastle.

Jumping down and coughing, Jamie cried: "Ye gods, never again. I should rather be taken and charged with treason than make that journey thus bound a second time. Rather a dung cart than a tanner's, for that is good honest shit, whereas this is surely the spawn of Satan!"

Oldcastle coughed too, agreeing with Jamie. "'Tis good to breathe clean air once more, and never shall I take for granted my boots and belts again."

Fisher, who had arrived before them on horseback, came from the house to greet them. "All is well, I see, and fear not for I have arranged for hot baths to take away the stench and oily slime, and you soon shall be returned to a civilised state."

Two hours later, when they were bathed and dressed in clean clothes, a visitor arrived for Oldcastle. Jamie was excluded from the meeting, yet asked of a servant who had been admitted to the house. The man replied that it was Sir Thomas Chaworth.

The meeting took place in Fisher's private office that was

attached to his place of work to one side of his spacious house.

"Sir John, why 'tis good to see you free of your shackles and looking so hale," Chaworth began. "You received all my letters to Cooling Castle?"

"I am very well, thank you. I did indeed receive all correspondence and they gave me cause for concern. You say that the rogue Bishop Beaufort instructed you in this matter, and he with intelligence direct from the Court?"

"Aye, Sir John. He was suspicious that it would be me that they had latched upon, yet I think not. There could be many, yet one name did spring to mind, and he most close to your situation."

Oldcastle rose up to his full height, considering Chaworth's words carefully. Ever a suspicious man, he had remained at large for so long by his wits and an innate animal cunning. "Thank you for this valuable intelligence, Sir Thomas," he said finally. "I shall act upon it and ensure that de Grispere does not betray us. He shall be so caught up with our cause that when the time comes to take account he will have no choice but to remain at our side in the final conflict. We will ensure that hostages are taken, and it will be made clear to him that their lives shall be forfeit should he attempt to betray us."

"Will you inform de Grispere when they are taken?"

"No, I shall keep it to myself and use the intelligence when it is most appropriate," Oldcastle replied.

When Chaworth had left the meeting, Oldcastle summoned Jamie to join Fisher and himself. "Sir James, we shall now reside here until the time is nigh to strike against the king," he said. "Is there aught that you would wish for that may aid you in our endeavours?"

Jamie considered the matter and was curious to see the response to his next question. "You have told me of all that is to occur, namely a rising in armed conflict and the taking of power. There will I understand be risings not just in the shires, but here in London town. To wit you say you would value my right arm, yet I have no sword to call my own nor armour to protect me, and for certes there will be a battle between our forces and those of the crown. Even with the element of surprise the conflict will be bloody, and needs must I should be able to protect myself and your cause, for I am sure that you will be mailled and in harness. Therefore, I beg your leave to fetch my own harness and ready myself for the fray."

Oldcastle considered the request, seeing the merit in it. Yet the danger of having a skilled and well-armed knight within his lair also gave him cause for concern. "Very well, it shall be so. Where is your harness now?"

"It is in my new home in Le Straunde. I removed it from my father's house ere I departed for France these months past. I fear discovery as much as do you, mayhap a messenger could be sent to Mark of Cornwall, and he could fetch the harness for me. 'Twould do well, as he has in the past acted as my arming squire," Jamie suggested, hoping that he would be believed.

"Very well, a messenger will be sent to the wrestler's house and he shall bear the harness here." Jamie was about to breathe a sigh of relief when Oldcastle added a warning. "Yet if there should be any misstep or treachery, you know what will be the consequences."

"Sir John, I have proved my worth now a hundredfold and bound myself securely to your mast, yet still you doubt me when if naught else all I see as my redemption from a charge of treason is that you should succeed and grant me clemency. I can do no more," Jamie dissembled, shaking his head sadly as he made to leave.

Once he had left the room Oldcastle said to William Fisher, "I trust him not in full. Have a messenger sent by the back lanes to Mark of Cornwall, but have him watched by another to see if he is followed."

As the servant made to leave, the second man lingered to see if any should spy his companion's departure. He looked up and down the street behind Fisher's premises, secure in the knowledge that he would not be spotted – but he was wrong. At Whittington's behest, Sir Thomas Burton and Cristoforo had joined forces to spy upon William Fisher's home, based upon Mark's intelligence following Oldcastle's escape.

Cristoforo had secured an upper room in a tavern to the front and near the side entrance, while Burton had rented another room with the crown's coin. From these vantage points, Burton and Cristoforo could see each other as well as the two streets outside Fisher's house, and here they waited for any sign of movement. The first servant left Fisher's house, and Cristoforo motioned to Burton who nodded from his casement at the front and made to slip down the stairs to the street. As he was leaving, Cristoforo waved him back, seeing a second man slip into the street behind the first.

He smiled grimly. *Va bene*, he thought, *we shall play your game*.

Cristoforo dropped down the stairs, went out of the back entrance of the tavern and into a street that ran parallel to St Martin's Lane. He moved north up St Vaste's Lane, dodging in and out of cursing pedestrians and horses, jumping the rivers of sewage as he went. He emerged onto Pope's Lane to see the servant head east then south to the district of the cloth guilds, and by that time Cristoforo was almost certain of his destination. He slipped down a side lane, gambling on his ability to understand his prey, and was rewarded: *Ah, and so the scullion appears*. He nodded in satisfaction, lodged himself in a shop opposite Mark's house and waited.

Minutes later, Mark emerged from the rear on horseback and leading a second pack horse, the same servant following some feet behind. In the packed streets it was almost as easy for a man on foot to make progress as on horseback. People cursed, pushed and dodged the horses, carts and animals that thronged the busy streets.

Cristoforo positioned himself on the offside of the servant messenger, and when he was close enough he looked up at Mark and winked. The giant caught on immediately and made to bend as if to check some piece of harness that had become loose on the leather breast plate strap of the horse. Breseler was calmer under Mark's influence than he had been, yet still shook his head in disgust at the transfer of weight and at being kept to a snail's pace despite people making way for the huge horse and rider. The movement brought him level with Cristoforo's head, and he whispered, "Jamie's house, retrieve his harness."

It was enough, and Cristoforo slipped away with the servant none the wiser. Unencumbered by a pack animal he arrived at le Straunde well ahead of Mark and quickly apprised Lady Alice of all that had occurred awaiting Mark's arrival.

On Mark's approach, the servant was made to wait in the rear yard while the wrestler went to Lady Alice, where he found his Italian companion. "Cristo, by the Good Lord you are well met. I have a little to tell and must do so quickly. The request for his harness tells me Jamie must expect a battle and soon. I am to take it to the house of William Fisher, where I believe Jamie is hiding. I know no more than this, for what little use it may be."

"It is more of the riddle that shrouds this uprising, for that is what it shall be. I followed the two men who aided you in Oldcastle's escape and know where they live."

"Aye, those two be not sure of their position for all their pledges to the Lollards, I'm bound. Were you to stick a knife to their throat they would bleat like sheep to save themselves, I reckon, for they had no stomach for raiding or swords. Like many of this rising they are not trained to it and are no more than lads with money to gain and some adventure. Though have a care, for there are many of the knighthood who firmly believe in Oldcastle and his cause, and they are well set about. Now I must be on my way so as not to cause suspicion."

"Fare thee well, Marco. Leave your gate unbarred this

night and wait for me in the courtyard behind your house, for I should learn more once you have seen Jamie."

"Nay, Cristo, for two of Emma's apprentices were attendant at the meeting in the Wrasteleyre on the Hope and I durst trust none of 'em. Let us meet at the Palace this eve, at Whittington's quarters, for he spends much time there and often stays overnight."

"Mark," came Lady Alice's plaintive cry, breaking the discourse. "See well to Jamie and send my heart to his for I do miss him so, and would wish him to be in his home for Christmastide."

"My lady, I shall, fear not, and please God that this shall be over soon, for it is building so fast that the dam must soon burst and no mistake," he said, gently clasping her tiny hand in his huge, calloused palm and giving it a gentle squeeze.

She compressed her lips into a sad smile and nodded in agreement with his words.

"Now I must return to that scullion without and meet Jamie."

"I will follow at a distance and see what I may," Cristoforo said. "For I too am assured that he resides there since the cart came early this morning. Yet none of the watchers nor Sir Thomas have seen him. Mayhap with you distracting the company we shall see some sign."

Yet it was not to be, for when Mark arrived at Fisher's home he was shown into the rear yard. The harness was unloaded from the packhorse, and he was met in the yard by Sir John himself, with no sign of Jamie.

"Sir John, I bid you good morrow on this chill winter's

day, and I am most glad to see you hale and free of your shackles once more," Mark said, greeting the knight amiably.

"We thank you, Mark of Cornwall, and this shall be passed to your companion at Cooling Castle, for he will be in sore need of it soon. As to my freedom, I shall remember you well when the time is nigh for power to be allotted in this new reign. It behoves me to say that I am in your debt, for you did me great service that night at the Tower."

"'Twas my pleasure, my lord, and am reet glad that you are returned to Lunnon, where you will do most good," Mark answered, hoping more information would follow. Little was gleaned other than he would be needed soon and that he was to be ready and watchful as should all his brethren of wrestlers who would side with the Lollard cause.

Mark took his leave and promised to await the call to arms. Once he was gone. Oldcastle called to his servant. "Well, did aught occur that should be reported?"

"Nay, my lord. We were not followed, and he saw no one save Lady Alice for moments, and then we came back. Wilbur says that I was not followed in either direction, so all is well as I did not inform the wrestler of our destination until after we had left Lady Alice. None will know, and the wrestler seems sound."

"Just so, but follow him back to his abode," Sir John ordered.

The servant left the yard too late to witness the exchange that occurred between Jamie and Cristoforo. Arriving ahead of Mark, Cristoforo had secreted himself opposite the main house and waited, watching. Jamie had been locked in an upper room at the front away from the yard with a guard upon his door, despite protesting his loyalty. He looked out upon the street and saw Cristoforo waiting in an opposite alley. Cristoforo looked up and a smile broke out upon Jamie's face. He had in the servant's absence busied himself writing a brief account of all that he knew, realising that he would never be allowed to speak with Mark alone and hoping at some point to be able to pass the missive on. All his hopes were dashed when he was imprisoned in the bedroom. But now, reaching for a small candle, he tied the missive around it. Beckoning Cristoforo to wait beneath the casement, he dropped the parchment down to him. Cristoforo saluted with a wave and was gone out of sight in time for Mark to leave, followed by the servant.

Chapter Forty-Four

As ever, the atmosphere in Whittington's quarters was warm to the point of being stuffy, with a roaring fire warding off the December frost and snows that had heralded the Christmas that seemed to be bearing down upon them so quickly. Divested of their cloaks, Cristoforo and Mark waited expectantly, standing before the fire each with a goblet of wine in his hands.

Whittington held before him the missive that Jamie had written and flung down to Cristoforo. Both men had read and re-read its contents, still finding it hard to believe the audacity of the plot that was described in the words inked upon the parchment.

Whittington's eyes widened as he read more, the short sentences stripped to brevity by Jamie's shortness of time. Sir Richard shook his head and re-read the text.

"You have both read this?" he asked, disbelieving.

"Indeed, my lord," Cristoforo answered.

"They plan to await the king's sojourn at Eltham,

favouring as he does the palace over Christmastide as did his father before him, and there while in the company of the royal princes and their families to kill them all and seize the crown? This upon the pretext of mummers entertaining at Twelfth Night. By the Good Lord, he lures James away using history as his guide and now seeks to emulate the attempt upon the old king's life, God rest his soul!"

At which the other two men crossed themselves.

"Indeed, my lord," Cristoforo said. "'Tis a bold plan for Oldcastle to seize the crown upon the charge of Regent and to take London and the shires by force, ceding all to himself and in doing so gaining absolute power."

Whittington nodded: "God bless James for this, as it has put us upon our mettle and ensures that this plot shall fail. The gathering that is to take place upon the tenth of January will be without the walls at St Giles Fields and Smythefeld, roped in from the shires, and amongst the company will be knights and men-at-arms, all well set up and ready for the fray. If Oldcastle took the day it would be as you described Paris, reincarnated as an abomination, as God is my witness. We must prevent this at all costs.

"And more worryingly, Sir James describes the infraction and sedition of the guilds – including mine own and his father's. This is worrying news indeed, and he fears for the life of his father and family."

"Fear not, my lord, for I shall now look to them as all is known of the hideout at Fisher's abode, and Sir Thomas Burton and his *insidiores* will aid the intelligence," Cristoforo responded.

"Then I wish you Godspeed in that regard and pray for

your safety and that of Sir James' family, too. And of Lady Alice, is she too well provided for?"

"She is, my lord. Her father has latterly returned to London and does not now intend to travel north as is his usual custom, looking instead to the safety of his daughter above all else. He has around him a full meiny of knights and men-at-arms, whilst Lady Alice ventures out little in her condition, and always with a full quotient of armed men around her."

"Then gentle sirs, it remains for me to bid you goodnight. For I must bustle to seek an immediate audience with his majesty, despite the late hour. I trust that you shall liaise with Sir Thomas, Cristoforo?"

"As you say, my lord, consider it done."

The two men left Whittington pacing his chamber, then with a decision made, he strode out, calling to his clerk and an armed servant to follow him. Even within the confines of the Palace he went nowhere without an escort, so worried was he at the rapid turn of events. He knew full well how dark and dangerous these passageways could be late at night. Even with guards placed at intervals on corridors and in doorways, death could come quickly, and the murderer could be gone before aid could be brought. Cristoforo had demonstrated to Whittington how vulnerable he was, and he had taken the lesson to heart.

Arriving at the outer door of King Henry's private chambers he begged an audience with the king.

The king's personal body servant appeared at the door, his eyes tired, disgruntled yet still fully clothed, indicating that the king was not yet asleep.

"My lord, are you aware of the hour? Our lord the king is at prayers!" he said.

"Then mayhap they have been answered, for I have news of great import. And to this end have the goodness to also summon the Lord Chief Justice and Richard Lord Grey of Codnor."

Servants were raised and messages sent, and within minutes all were present in the king's private chamber. The king had in his hand the letter penned by Jamie, and was as aghast as Whittington had been. Henry read it aloud that the others might hear the contents. The faces present expressed a mixture of anger and concern, verging upon disbelief.

"In truth I find it most difficult to give credence to such an outlandish plan," Lord Richard concluded.

"Such was the attitude of the French court not many months ago, yet consider what occurred in the civilisation of Paris, with only the town itself in arms," Whittington warned. "Here, Lord Cobham seeks to raise a national uprising converging upon London, with the city beset from both within and without. It would be cataclysmic, and its results should not be underestimated."

"As always, we defer to your thoughts and perspective, Sir Richard," the king said, looking at Whittington. "We shall take steps and ensure that the two forces do not join, for that way lies disaster."

"And of your sojourn to Eltham?" Sir William questioned.

"We shall keep our promise of a festive time at Eltham Palace and not be dissuaded by the dissolute forces that are cast against us." Sir William made to protest, but the king silenced him with an upraised hand. "It is our will, and it shall also ensure that Sir John does not suspect that his surprise has been spoiled. Plans will be made and the mummers – such as they be – shall never reach Eltham.

"Sir Richard, it seems we are once more in Sir James de Grispere's debt, for without him we should be in desperate stakes. We pray that he survives this debacle, and if he does we wish to reward him most richly for all that he has endured."

"Amen, Majesty, him and his two companions, who as ever are an integral part of the whole."

"Just so, just so. Now we shall cogitate upon all we have learned and in the morning warrants and forces shall be mustered to divide this force that is weighed against us. We bid you good night, my lords."

Chapter Forty-Five

Jamie sat at a bench in a ground floor workroom, polishing his armour and seeing to its maintenance as a father would cherish a beloved child. He rubbed sand and vinegar into the metal, erasing the lanolin that had protected it from rust these past months, and as he did so the armour began to shine to a perfect reflective surface. Having the harness and his own sword back again was of great comfort to him. He took up his shield, his eyes slightly unfocused and thought of Richard, memories of his horse brought back by the badge of arms now before him, and of Forest, his loyal wolfhound, whom he had not laid eyes on in many months. He had gained hope from seeing Cristoforo yesterday and managing to alert his companion to the dangers that were pressed against all, and looked forward to an end to the uprising.

It was, he realised, the first opportunity he had been given for direct contact with the outside world in weeks, and it pained him to not be able to see his wife at Christmas. It also gave him great cause for concern as to the safety of his family, in particular his father, who seemed at the mercy of Sir John's reach. Anger was steadily building within him now as the time for action seemed to draw ever nearer. He dared not show his true feelings and still denied any thoughts against Oldcastle. He knew that he would have his reckoning with the knight and Sir Thomas Chaworth when the moment was propitious.

His thoughts were disturbed by the sound of shod hooves reverberating into the courtyard and the sound of many voices calling for grooms. A figure appeared at the doorway of the work room, a knight by his dress and hauteur, seemingly a few years older than Jamie.

Seeing him at his labours cleaning armour, he addressed Jamie: "Hoi. Step to, squire, for we have need of service without to care for our horses and more besides. Long we have travelled this day and we wish refreshment."

Jamie looked up insolently and raked his eyes up and down the knight as though he had only just become cognisant of his existence. "Do you address me, churl? I shall take no orders from you. Find a lackey more suited to your station and your needs."

"On your feet and obey me." The knight snarled, his face suffusing with anger at Jamie's response. He took a step forward as if to grab Jamie and heave him to his feet, as more knights stood at the doorway, tired, impatient and keen to see what was amiss.

Egged on by his peers the knight shouted, "Up, dolt," as he moved towards Jamie.

Jamie was still one instant and in full motion the next, flying into a spin and rising as he did so, his newly reacquired dagger drawn and at the knight's throat in an instant, point under his chin, as the man's mail coif was down. The knight froze.

"I too am of the knighthood. I am Sir James de Grispere at your service. I am reduced to the penury of cleaning my own harness for my faith and service, so do not tempt me, or your life will be forfeit to my raw temper, sir knight," Jamie spat, his face inches from the newcomer's.

Then a familiar voice broke the impasse. "Hold, both. Sir Richard, this is indeed Sir James, whom I hold in high esteem, for it was he who rescued me from the Tower. Now put up your weapon and unite in friendship, for we need no animosity here in our camp and all must be as one to our cause. There will be time enough for fighting in the days to come after Christmastide."

The two knights broke apart warily upon Sir John's command.

"De Grispere, this is Sir Richard Compton from the Welsh Marches and his companions in arms, Sir Roger Duckton and Sir Lewis Clifford. They bring their squires and men-at-arms to swell our ranks, Sir James, and more await us without the town walls."

This was a full army he was assembling, Jamie realised in horror. If they should meet with all those promised from within the town it would be civil war. *Please God that the king and Whittington heed my warning to greater effect than did the French*, he thought. Jamie nodded in a more civilised fashion and asked, "Where shall they all be billeted, Sir John, for we become right full here?"

"Fear not, other inns about the town are at our

command and these new men, together with the mummers now present, shall reside at the Sign of The Axe in Bishopesgatestrete," Oldcastle assured him. At this, Jamie ventured outside into the courtyard to see the whole company. To one side, clearly a group within themselves, were the supposed mummers. They were a motley group of some twenty players, both men and women. Yet to his eyes, which had seen many such travelling players, they appeared of mixed appearance. He heard a familiar language – Italian!

Jamie moved closer to test his ability and see if he could understand what they were saying. He made to stand by a horse as though a groom and heard all. The women were from Genoa, and having seen Cristoforo's sister he was not surprised that they should be amongst the ranks of assassins, for that is what they were, with plans to murder the king, his brothers and their families.

At this moment another rider entered, and Jamie saw it was Sir Thomas Chaworth. He moved away from the horse and greeted the knight, making himself amiable and friendly with all the while holding the red mist of murder in his heart. "Sir Thomas, I bid you a good day and trust you are hale."

"I am indeed, Sir James, thank you. New arrivals, I see, and ready for the fray I'm bound," he answered heartily.

"They are, though no doubt sad to be away from hearth and home at Christmas which presses down upon us now with its blessings in but a few days. I fear that is the worst part of being lodged here and away from my family, for I do miss them so."

Sir Thomas was slightly taken aback at Jamie's amiable demeanour, and could not help but respond in kind. "Aye, I do feel for your position. Please God that all will soon be resolved, and you shall return to their embraces. After Twelfth Night all will be ours to hold, and you shall be a free man to carry your head high again."

"For certes yes, and I do most assuredly count the days," Jamie agreed, now certain that the uprising was to take place on the ninth of January by his reckoning.

All repaired to Fisher's house where both John de Burgh and Thomas Kempford were present. *So the two are still at large – and hopefully watched,* Jamie thought.

London, Christmas Eve

The Guilds were breaking for a day's rest to celebrate Christmas, and all were in a festive mood, although Thomas de Grispere was suspicious and felt an oppressive air to the proceedings that had not been apparent in previous years. John had accompanied him on the short journey by foot to Basingeshawe Street, the home of the Weavers Guild. The building was a fine three storey hall set back from the main thoroughfare with a railed courtyard to the front and access granted via a wooden lych gate, at which stood a liveried servant. The streets were still crowded as they departed, turning right out of the property. With Thomas was John and two more servants in stout jupons and armed with long knives. John had ignored the edict and wore a sword, despite not being a knight. The weapon was partially hidden beneath his cloak, which he wore now over a maille habergeon that came down to his knees. Not for him pattens, but rough soled boots studded and ribbed with leather to better grip the slippery street.

Dusk had driven the light from the day early, and heavy grey clouds had converged with the promise of more snow to come. It was bitterly cold, and breathing hurt the lungs as clouds of vapour billowed out before the pedestrians hurriedly making their way upon errands or retiring early for the day to celebrate Christmas. The church bells of St Mary in the Jewry rang out Vespers as they passed, and others echoed across London as the churches began the celebration of the birth of Christ.

"By the rood 'tis cold this eve, John," Thomas de Grispere commented as they left Basingeshawe and turned left in Cattestrate, exposing them to the lazy easterly wind that did not trouble to blow round them but speared their clothes instead as if passing through a sieve.

A group of four men appeared from a lane to the north, and more joined behind them from Ismongerelane. John, his instincts alert, let his right hand fall to his sword, while his left went beneath his cloak to the buckler at his waist. He unhooked it and slipped his hand through the leather straps, still unaware of the presence behind them of another four men. If he had looked, he would have seen that one bore the marks of a knight, with the broad and unbalanced shoulders brought on by use of arms.

"Ware ahead, lads, this is trouble or I am a Southwark whore. Master Thomas, draw your dagger now and no argument, and if I go down stab everything in reach and shout like the very Devil. Your house is so close, run for there if you get the chance."

At this, the two servants and Thomas drew their weapons. They were alert and frightened, but prepared to sell their lives dearly. As they drew closer to the alley, the crowds around them somehow sensed a change in the way of town dwellers, as a different atmosphere pervaded the air. They melted away for the most part into the background, leaving the street eerily deserted but for the combatants.

John made the first move, drawing his sword, knowing that the threat must be dealt with as no bluff would suffice. "Hold there, make way," he called striding forward to meet the four men with no slowing of his steps.

Surprised at his direct command, the leader of the four took a pace backwards and drew his own sword. "You will yield, for we wish to have words with your master on matters pertaining to the guilds."

"On that, you needs must–" John thrust with his sword before he had finished the sentence, aiming for the element of surprise. It was a long strike and he stamped forward to close the distance that the leader would have sworn no sword could have achieved, even as the tip lanced into his torso. John knew that he was over-committed and prayed that he would strike home, for if not he would be horribly exposed to a counter. Yet with the lunge he bent his knee, and felt the sharp point press deep, cutting through the jupon of his opponent. He ripped the blade up and around causing the maximum damage, and as he withdrew his sword crimson liquid poured forth from the gaping wound as the leader failed to staunch the flow with a hand pressed to the cut.

The others were shocked at first, but were soon upon him. John's buckler came up to fend off the first attacker, giving him a sense of feel and distance that he used well, driving into his upraised arm as his opponent's long knife shot out from a high guard. John's sword stabbed overarm down into the man's neck, resulting in a satisfying spurt of blood. But John's move exposed him to the side and felt a sharp blow to his ribs from another man. The mail absorbed the impact, the links holding, but the strike caused him to flinch and arc over. He smashed the pommel of his sword into the attacker's face and saw his nose explode into a red mush as he fell back to his knees. At his left, Thomas' two servants set upon the fourth attacker, one receiving a knife to the ribs for his pains.

John heard Thomas' cry for help and turned to see him being attacked by four men, one of whom was a knight who stood guard as the others surrounded Thomas, seeking to take him prisoner. The knight advanced, his sword menacing. "Stay back, old man, for we have your master, and you will not win through."

The words and the arrogance drove John into a battle madness, seeing his master so beset. He launched himself forward and thrust three blows in quick succession. The knight caught one, which glanced up to be halted by the stop rib of his breastplate, at which John closed the distance following the blade to begin half-swording, seeking to drive the pommel into the knight's open helmet as his visor was up. It was a fast move brought on by anger, and so nearly succeeded, but the knight turned his head at the last instant, taking the blow to the side of his helm. It rocked his head back, but he grasped John's blade and pulled, throwing an arm around his neck. The two of them fell to the ground, with the knight landing on top, knocking the wind out of John as he did so. He fell astride John's supine figure, his armoured elbow smashing into John's chest as he landed. The remaining servant turned to see him raise his sword two handed, preparing to drive it down into John's exposed face, and knew that he would not be able to aid him in time.

"No!" he cried, beginning strides that he knew would not get him there in time to save John.

"Too bad, old man, you're game," the knight hissed as the sword tip began descending.

The stroke was never finished, and a soft whistle was barely audible above the cries of the onlookers as a quarrel sloughed through the air, striking the knight with a thud, piercing the joint between pauldron and breastplate and slamming through the mail to drive the knight backwards, the bolt lodging in his upper body. He screamed in agony as he toppled, and the three remaining attackers looked on in disbelief at seeing their leader so disabled.

John looked up, seeing his imminent death prevented. He sought to rise as the twitching armoured knight fell back across his legs. As he did so, a stabbing pain lanced through his left side, causing him to hiss in agony. The servant was torn as to what to do.

"Aid Master Thomas!" John shouted. At this, the servant leapt forward to face the leading man in front of Thomas, who was now securely held by the remaining two attackers, one with an arm around his neck holding him immobile. The second attacker stood ready, his rondel dagger out to take on Thomas' servant as soon as an opening arose. Then there was another whistle of air, and he was thrown sideways with a quarrel in his neck, dead before he hit the ground.

The third man, thoroughly alarmed now, dragged Thomas closer, using him as a shield and moving steadily backwards towards the alley to seek shelter from the deadly crossbow bolts, offering as small a target as possible, his dagger held high close to Thomas' neck. The remaining spectators ran for shelter away from the melee, none of them wishing to find themselves at the mercy of another crossbow bolt.

In the noise, the assailant holding Thomas heard no sound as a black-clad figure slid noiselessly up behind him. His first knowledge of the man's presence was a blinding white pain in his kidneys as a dagger point slid home and ripped sideways. His back arched in agony as dark, almost black blood oozed out to stain his jupon. All thoughts of harming Thomas de Grispere faded with his vision as he slid to the ground, groaning in his death throes. The dark figure dried his dagger on the man's cloak and slipped it back into his boot. He gently came forward to aid the older man.

"Come, Master Thomas, we must away afore more come to aid these *bastardi*." Cristoforo urged the merchant forward into the street, close to where the servant and last attacker were still fighting with daggers, the blood flowing. Cristoforo did not hesitate; he pulled out his falchion and slashed the attacker's neck, dropping him dead to the cobbles.

John had managed to rise to his knees, and was helped up by Cristoforo as he advised the other two to run.

"Get back to your home, Master Thomas. Make haste. More will follow, it is not safe here," he adjured.

The servant, who was bleeding freely and limping, pulled his master with him as they scuttled away. It was but a short distance of some thirty feet or so and they turned left into St Laurence Lane in Jewry and Thomas de Grispere's home. Seeing them safely away, Cristoforo, his eyes ever vigilant, helped John to his feet. John winced in pain again from his damaged side, and the two of them hurried away.

The man who was holding the horses in the alley from which the attackers had emerged looked on in horror and disbelief. He went forward and found the knight alive with only a little blood showing from the wound, the quarrel still protruding from his armpit.

"Fetch a horse and aid me to mount," he rasped weakly. With great difficulty and nearly fainting with pain, the knight finally mounted his horse and the two left before the constable could be fetched and questions asked about the bloody scene in the street.

Chapter Forty-Six

The banging of a fist sounded upon the barred wood, and the doors of William Fisher's premises were opened. The two men had made the short journey across the town, and the surviving fighter now stood before Fisher with the knight slumped in the saddle behind him. Servants came to his aid and helped slide Sir Roger Duckton from his mount. He could barely stand, so weak was he, seemingly from loss of blood, yet they were puzzled for there was little evidence of bleeding. Many came out to the courtyard to see the cause of the uproar as the knight was carefully helped through to the back of the house.

Jamie smiled inwardly at the sight before him as he saw and instantly recognised the small quarrel lodged in the knight's body. He could guess who had loosed the bolt. Yet for Cristoforo to be involved, the attack must have struck someone close to him, and he remained in attendance to assure himself that all was well with those he loved.

"Why didst thou bring him here?" Fisher demanded, appearing from the inner hall.

"It was closer than the Axe, master, and we did not wish to draw attention to the blooding with others around at the inn. A surgeon has been sent for and we await him. 'Twill not be long now afore he arrives and all will be well," he offered with more confidence than he felt, for the knight before him was dying, unless he was much mistaken.

At this point Sir John Oldcastle appeared, taking in the scene before him.

"And the others who accompanied you?" he demanded.

"All dead, my lord," he answered.

"What? Eight of you, including an armoured knight, against two servants, an old man-at-arms and a weaver?"

"The soldier fought like the Devil, was armoured and in maille, seemingly expectant of our ambush. One servant lies dead and the other wounded. Yet there was another; a black clad wraith, who sent bolts scudding forth from the shadows and killed Bart, who held the merchant to secure him. He gutted him like a fish, so he did. Then 'e leaves 'im to bleed out and takes the master with him and the old soldier."

"The Italian, I'm bound. So de Grispere is free, and we'll not have the opportunity again."

Jamie, who had been lurking in the shadows of the rear antechamber, stepped back into the hall and made himself scarce, returning to his dormer on the upper levels.

With a sudden feeling of wariness, Oldcastle looked around but did not see him depart. Before him the wounded Sir Roger Duckton heaved and sighed, blood frothing from his lips as he died with a series of shuddering spasms. All present crossed themselves at the knight's passing.

"Have the body removed – and not a word of this is to reach any outside these men present on pain of death, in particular Sir James. Have Sir Richard and Sir Lewis sent for as I would have discourse with them forthwith."

The servants hurried off. In his rooms above, Jamie smiled wickedly to himself. *So the ploy failed and now I am free to kill whomever I wish when the time arises.*

St Laurence Lane in Jewry

The home of Thomas de Grispere was frantic with activity. Jeanette boiled water and went to fetch cloths. The one remaining servant left alive had been stabbed in the shoulder and about the arm that he had used to defend himself.

Cristoforo fetched herbs, which he added to the bowl of boiling water along with a needle and thread. With care he cleaned the wound with alcohol as he had been taught, then with the servant fainting away he sewed up the main cut to the shoulder and bound the others. This done he turned his attention to John.

"Have that habergeon off him as easy as you can, for his ribs are broken if I am not mistaken," Cristoforo urged. "Gently now, as I wish them not to puncture the skin, for if that is done, foul humours are released from within the bones that spoil the blood, causing death."

The leather straps that held the mail coat in place were undone, and with each movement John winced, yet said nothing save cursing under his breath at each painful movement. When bare of torso, Cristoforo gently probed the skin that was already purple with bruising from the blade. He saw where the sharp point had been turned by the mail, but damage had still been done as it was rammed home.

He bathed the skin with hot water and felt the bones under his fingers.

"Curse you for a Saracen heathen, you damned Italian, are you trying to finish what that other man started?" John roared.

Cristoforo ignored his shouting, used to men in pain being loud and insulting during treatment. "They are broken. Two I think, but not grating and still part joined. All will be well, yet they will be very sore. I shall bind them for support, but there is naught else I can do. No swordplay for a while, *va bene*?" He grinned at how irritated the old soldier was. John growled at him in response as he bound the ribs as tightly as he dared.

"I shall prepare a poultice and paste of *consolida* that you must eat, but not too much, only as I prescribe you, you curmudgeonly old goat." He laughed at the old soldier.

"What heathen sorcery is this?" John growled. "I should have skewered you in Paris and none would be the wiser, you heathen necromancer!"

"Talk not of more lives lost, for I owe you all much for this day's work and am most obliged," said Master Thomas, "and of Paris, why 'twas a good day's work we did that day in taking you unto our fold, Cristoforo, and we are all most grateful for your service since that day."

"Think nothing of it, I am as always in your debt for those days," he replied. "Yet I must depart upon another errand this eve."

As quickly as he had arrived, he departed with little more than a bow, picking up his cloak and the small deadly crossbow that was laid upon the table. He slipped this on first by its shoulder strap, then threw his cloak about his shoulders and was gone, disappearing into the darkness of the night.

It was not long before he found himself at Mark's door, nor seconds until it was opened by the giant, who bade him welcome.

"Cristo, why I bid you a most merry Christmas Eve this night. Come in, I bid you, for there is hot wine mulling and sweetmeats." As Cristoforo entered he became more serious. "Yet I see from your visage that all is not well – and is that blood, still sticky upon your gambeson?"

"Aye, yet the blood is not mine. It belongs to whoresons who shall no longer trouble anyone but the Devil. An attempt was made this eve to take Thomas de Grispere on his way home from the guild meeting. I knew of his plans from Jeanette for she tells me each time that he ventures forth far abroad, and I was in time to save him from a terrible fate."

"Tell me all," Mark asked. When Cristoforo finished explaining everything, he asked very simply: "What would thee ask of me?"

"To accompany me now to catch two scullions who even

now rest in their lair expecting a peaceful Christmastide. Let us show them what seasonal greetings they have brought down upon themselves."

Emma was in her workshop next door, and rather than face her, Mark left word with his servant to inform her that he would be back in time for church that evening. He and Cristoforo made their way through streets that were now nearly empty of people and were turning white as flakes of snow fell to garnish the world. They arrived at John de Burgh's house, where Cristoforo had followed him after Oldcastle's escape from the Tower. With Cristoforo hidden, Mark banged upon the door, which was answered by a wary de Burgh. Upon seeing Mark he fretted even more.

"Greetings, master de Burgh," Mark said. "I bring you Sir John's compliments, and he asks you to attend him now at the Wrasteleyre on the Hope, for there is news and plans have changed."

"It is Christmas Eve, man. You ask me to leave my family on this of all nights?"

"I do only as Sir John bids. Is your faith so challenged that you would fail us all at this late time? Come, we ask but a few moments of you, and you will return for Mass this eve."

The carpenter sighed and moved inwards to speak with an unseen figure before returning dressed in a cloak and cowl.

"We must attend upon Thomas Kempford, for he too is to be party this night, as are all to our cause," Mark said as they trudged through the snow.

"This way, then," de Burgh mumbled, turning to the left

up another street. It was a similar story with Kempford, who was a little more heartened at seeing his companion in Mark's company. He too left and with Mark between them they headed northwest in the direction of Smythefeld. Within a few paces, Mark placed his hands upon the shoulders of the two men and suddenly stepped back, smashing their heads together with a hard crack. The force of the collision was such that Kempford fell to the ground, semi-conscious. De Burgh, the stronger of the two, made to punch at Mark, his arm flailing outwards. It was a futile gesture as Mark swatted away the blow with ease, punching him hard in the stomach, at which he doubled over in agony and collapsed to the snowy street.

A passer-by appeared, puzzled at the semi-comatose pair on the street, but Mark jovially assured him. "They been 'avin too much ale this eve, and now they're payin' the price."

The man moved on, smiling at the antics of the drunken men. Cristoforo appeared and helped drag and push the two of them into an alley.

"Now, good sirs. We wish you well this eve, and would that you return to your families whole and hale," Mark began, holding de Burgh in a crushing grip upon his shoulder. The man was strong from his work as a carpenter, yet he had never experienced strength like Mark's before. It felt to him as though the joint was being gripped in one of the wooden vices that he used in his trade. The pain was intense, adding to his headache as the fingers bored down into the nerves surrounding his shoulder.

"We are here as emissaries of the crown who wish to

suborn you to their needs. All is known of the Lollard plots brought on by the traitor Sir John Oldcastle and others, yet we needs must have further details to stem this tide of treason. Therefore our question to you is simple: Where do the mummers meet to leave for Eltham Palace and assassinate the king, and which day and hour do they depart?"

Both men made to speak, yet Mark stayed them in their tracks. "Now, think hard afore you answer me and be true. We seek but confirmation for we know all, and if you lie we may cut your lying tongues from your mouths to stop you prattling more treason. My companion here is most adapt at such sport."

He motioned to Cristoforo, who removed a dagger from his boot and held it to Thomas Kempford's throat. "If you comply with all we ask," Cristoforo said, "the crown in its clemency will grant you an annuity of ten marks a year each and full pardons. I shall leave you to guess your fate if you do not comply."

The men's eyes opened wide at Cristoforo's promise, for it was a vast sum of money and would keep them comfortable for years to come. It was evident to both Mark and Cristoforo that both men were already very nervous, and with clear doubts about Oldcastle's plans and how successful they would be in the uprising, all the fight had gone from them.

"We do not wish to be tried for treason," de Burgh spluttered, trying in vain to remove the grip from his shoulder. "If we had our way we would wish nothing more than to leave in peace and never see Sir John again. It was more to do than we thought, and now we seem trapped in the coils of the plan, as there are many in our guilds, and others are flocking to his banner in their thousands," he continued.

Cristoforo looked at Mark, surprised at the numbers believed to be involved.

"Then tell all, churl, or you shall find yourself swinging from a gallows with your guts spilling from you before your eyes along with many other thousands." Cristoforo snarled menacingly.

It was Kempford who broke first. "You promise upon your word that we shall receive a pardon and ten marks a year?" he mewled.

"I do, as God is my witness this Christmas Eve," Mark answered.

"Then it shall be as you say. They currently stay at the Sign of the Axe in Bisshopesgatestrete and will leave on the eve of Twelfth Night to travel to Eltham Palace, where they will take or kill the king and his brothers. That is all I know, I swear by almighty God."

"Aye, 'tis true, and that is all we know by the Good Lord I do also swear," de Burgh added.

Mark released his hold and Cristoforo withdrew his dagger.

"Well, good sirs, we bid you good night and a merry Christmas Eve, and pray to God that you speak truthfully or your lives will be forfeit," Mark threatened.

"And our annuity?" de Burgh asked.

"When – and only when – all proves true, then come to the Palace and you will receive your reward. If aught else occurs and we find that you have played us false you will be cursed as traitor and shown no mercy. We shall be at the

White Horse on the night of the fourth of January as the bells strike Vespers. Attend us there and bring any further intelligence that you may have," Cristoforo ordered them.

With nods and mumbles of agreement they complied, keen to be away and back in the safety of their homes. They hurried off into the night with wary backward glances at their two interrogators. Cristoforo and Mark looked at each other with mirthless grins.

"I shall now report to Whittington and with him Sir Thomas Burton, and will see you at Mass later this Christmas Eve. Fare thee well, Mark, and soon, praise God, this coil of madness shall be but a bitter memory."

"Amen to that, and I long for the day that Jamie shall be free, for that would be the greatest Christmas gift of all."

Chapter Forty-Seven

Westminster Palace, 5th January 1414

"Majesty, I bid you a most welcome return to the Palace, and wish you a prosperous New Year. Praise God that you enjoyed a safe sojourn at Eltham for Christmas." Whittington addressed the king, who in the middle of the night had packed away his entire meiny, including his brothers and his family, and re-deployed to Westminster Palace. The king had left it until the last possible moment to secure the strategy of deceit and hopefully continue with the plotters unaware of the subterfuge and his immediate movements.

"We did indeed, thank you. Your message to us was timely, and we have now removed all our family within the confines of the Palace both for safety and so that we may conduct the forthcoming campaign against these heretics directly. And of these heretics what news? Are we any clearer as to their intent upon the Epiphany of this month?"

"Sire, Cristoforo Corio and Mark of Cornwall do meet with the two Judases this eve to learn all they may in that regard, yet we must assume that the mummers leave for Eltham as your presence there is still unchallenged. Do you have anything to add, Sir Thomas?" Whittington deferred to Sir Thomas Burton, one of the many within the room as this was a council of war that included King Henry's most loyal war lords the Earls of Warwick and Arundel.

"No, Sir Richard, no further intelligence has reached my ears," Sir Thomas replied. "We wait and watch the Sign of the Axe as directed by de Burgh through the good offices of signor Corio and Mark of Cornwall. The hostelry is owned by another traitor, a carpenter in the same guild as de Burgh by the name of John Burgate. He too is watched most carefully, and has led us to other guild members who collude and plot for the uprising upon St Giles Fields. Yet still we remain uncertain as to the exact date. We pray that the events of this evening will furnish us with details upon which to act."

"Just so," replied the king. "And you, my faithful lords, are you and your captains ready for this fray?"

"We are, my lord," Sir William Hankford answered. "Captains have been assigned to take control of all gates to the north of the town, securing them against any exit whether by force or subterfuge. They attend upon your orders upon the hour, Majesty."

The king nodded in response, pleased with the answers he had received. "Then we await the latest intelligence and pray that it is good news. In all this we would advise most strongly here and now to all – and let this be alerted to all captains and men-at-arms – that our household knight Sir James de Grispere is no traitor and has these past months suffered great deprivations and hardships in our service. He is not to be harmed."

At this the king cast a steely glance around the assembled company, meeting every man's eye to ensure that all understood his words. "His coat of arms is well known to you, and he will bear them in clear sight. Any man, of whatever rank, who brings him down shall answer to us and no mercy will be shown. He remains our most loyal servant and is even now at peril on our behalf."

Again the whole war Council was met face to face with the king, including the Chancellor Bishop Beaufort, yet he would not meet his sovereign's gaze for long before bowing his head in obeisance. "Very well, send a message to Sir William Cromer, the Mayor of London, and have him on alert with troops in readiness. Do this on the morrow, as he is of the Drapers' Guild and we trust him not to mayhap inadvertently advise those whom he should not and spoil our plans." The king adjured his clerk and spy Sir Thomas Burton. "Then, my lords, go to and await my command, for we shall once and for all eviscerate this madness that lurks with foul humours within the body of our government."

Various members of the meeting left, leaving only battle commanders who would review the final instructions and plans of strategy for sealing the town.

Bishop Beaufort made himself scarce, seeking a meeting with Sir Thomas Chaworth with the utmost expediency.

×✟× —

The White Horse Inn at Vespers

The booths of the White Horse were full as labourers finished their day and made for ale or hot spiced wine according to their taste. The noise of conversation drowned out any fear of being overheard, and as the door opened to a winter's eve, de Burgh and Kempford made their way inside to seek out Cristoforo and Mark who had arrived before the hour of Vespers was struck by the nearby church bells.

The two newcomers hesitated, searching the tables carefully as they made their way to the rough bar and taps. They spotted the two men in a nearby booth and with stoops of ale made their way over to the table.

"Sit and join us," Mark offered amiably to any who may be listening above the hubbub of the inn.

The two men did so and looked furtively around. "So let us to business. What intelligence do you bring that may aid us and you in your turn?" Cristoforo demanded, in no mood for civility and eager to be gone and put all arrangements in place.

"We have been told to be expectant of a gathering at St Giles-in-the-Field upon the night of ninth. We are to assemble there and meet with those within the town who will rise up in their thousands, breaking through the gates against the Watch and unifying against all to take the Crown. The king is to be killed this night at Eltham, as we advised on Christmas Eve.

"There will be a void, they say, when all is paralysed and none will know which way to turn. This is when Sir John will strike, and master Fisher is most excited at the prospect. All is coming to plan, he says."

"What will happen to the king? Will all be well with him?" Kempford asked timorously, worried now whether by lack of coin or of being found out, neither Cristoforo nor Mark could tell.

"Worry not, plans are afoot to take care of all, and now we know the time of the uprising to ensue. We needs must leave and act upon your plans," Mark finished tersely.

"And what of our annuity? You promised to confirm the terms should we comply and meet with your demands."

"You will get your thirty pieces of silver, the both of you. You have the word of the crown upon it. So pray that the king survives, for I fear that Oldcastle would not honour our agreement in the regent's stead," Mark scoffed, at which he and Cristoforo rose and left the inn.

"Mark, attend Sir Richard and apprise him of the dates for action. I am for Sir Thomas Burton and a post opposite Jamie's window, for I needs must inform him of all so that he may be ready."

Mark nodded and clapped his friend upon the shoulder, wishing him well and moving off into the cold evening, his breath billowing before him as he strode forth with his quarterstaff at his side.

Cristoforo arrived at the building where Sir Thomas Burton and his confederates occupied a room overlooking the street opposite Fisher's home and premises. He arrived by the rear door from the yard, bade a good evening to another lodger and made his way up the creaking staircase to the single room above. He knocked three times to ensure that he did not receive a dagger in the ribs for his trouble when he entered, for Sir Thomas was this night on watch himself. Despite the coded knock, he entered slowly to see Sir Thomas, sword and dagger drawn off to one side in readiness, trusting no one.

When he saw the Italian the tension left his shoulders and he walked forward into the light. "Ah, Cristoforo, you are well met upon this frosty eve," he said. "Come, I have a small fire thus, tho' all that it does heat is the spirit, it seems, for this frozen garret is not all that it could be. Tell me all that you have learned."

Cristoforo did not baulk, or remark upon Burton's precautions, for if the positions were reversed he would have done the same thing himself. Instead, he bade the spy good evening, carefully placed his leather satchel upon the single table and moved to the fireplace, where he warmed his hands in front of the small blaze, that brought some small amount of heat to the room. He explained what the two men had told him in the White Horse.

"And is Sir Richard and therefore the king aware of this intelligence?" Burton inquired.

"He is, or should be so shortly, for even now Mark ventures to the Palace to seek an audience with him."

Burton nodded in satisfaction. "Then all should be well, except for poor Sir James, who is still caged and held captive."

"Has aught stirred?" Cristoforo asked in response.

"No, but it is at this hour that Sir James normally shows himself, albeit briefly, and we exchange three flashes of a candle to show all is well. Any more and we risk discovery. How do we inform him of all that has occurred?"

"Fear not. Do you have a quill and parchment?"

"I do." Sir Thomas went to produce the writing materials from his own bag and returned with them to Cristoforo.

"Now keep watch, for I would wish him to know all this eve," Cristoforo instructed as he began writing a short and direct note explaining all to Jamie.

With this done, he opened his satchel and removed, to Burton's great interest, his small crossbow that was in two parts. He clicked them together as the spring catch dropped home. Cristoforo then freed one of the three quarrels from under the tiller and began to carefully and tightly wrap the note around it.

"Your finger, Sir Thomas, if you please," he asked a fascinated Burton, who obliged, keeping the parchment tightly wrapped as Cristoforo wound it first with a fine cord and added a seal of wax all along the joint to hold the note in place.

"By the rood, it was you! You were the one who killed the men who ambushed Thomas de Grispere before Christmastide. What a wicked weapon this is, and deadly I'm bound. What is the range?"

"She will kill at sixty yards and is highly accurate to that distance if there is no wind, as this night." Cristoforo's teeth glowed white in the dim light. The wax cooled quickly, and he tested it with a single finger. "*Va bene*, now we wait."

It was not long before a figure appeared in the gloom at the opposite window above street level at the usual hour.

Burton moved the shutter wide three times, at which an answering light shone and faded three times from the room across the street. Bracing the mechanism against his stomach muscles, Cristoforo drew and cocked the bow, carefully placing the quarrel with the wax uppermost so that it would not get caught on the tiller groove. Satisfied that it would not foul the groove, he moved to the window to see Jamie's rough outline against the dim light and one closed shutter.

Squinting down the weapon, Cristoforo breathed in and out as he squeezed the trigger. There was a twang as the quarrel loosed, a familiar soughing whistle and then a thud that sounded like a crack of thunder to the two men. The figure on the other side disappeared and they heard a curse shouted out in alarm.

Jamie heard the crossbow bolt but would have been too late to avoid its killing strike if it had been aimed at him. It thumped into the shutter by his head and all but struck him as the wooden panel flew inwards, banging against the casement jamb, reverberating loudly upon his ears. Footsteps were heard below as someone ran up the wooden stairs, crying out in alarm.

Jamie closed the shutters quickly and put one of the metal candle sconces upon the floor, dropping a bench down gently onto its side and cursing out loud all the while, just as the door was flung open to reveal a servant at the door with William Fisher behind him.

"What ails you, man?" Fisher asked, exasperated in the now dim light illuminated by only one further candle.

"I tripped over the cursed bench and dropped the

sconce, burning my fingers on hot wax, the cursed plague upon this whoreson candle," Jamie swore.

Fisher grinned and the servant nodded and closed the door. Relieved, Jamie breathed a sigh of relief then cursed again under his breath. "Damn that heathen Italian for a crock-legged donkey. He nearly skewered me." He burst out laughing at his companion in arms once more, glad that he no longer felt alone and isolated.

He relit the candle and went to the shutter, where by twisting and turning and with the aid of his dagger he managed to extract the bolt. He felt the parchment around the shaft, and breaking the seal unfolded it. The parchment was crumpled by the impact, yet still legible in most parts when it was laid flat upon the table. He read it and re-read again, clenching his fist in glee. *So retribution is swift, and vengeance shall be mine upon this night of the Epiphany. Sir John, your life and those of others shall be forfeit,* he promised himself.

Chapter Forty-Eight

William Fisher's House, London: 9th January

"What news of Eltham, Master Fisher? Do we succeed, and has the king been taken or put to the sword?" Oldcastle called out as a messenger was heard galloping into the courtyard and sliding to a halt.

At the sound of his voice Fisher turned, his face grave. "I fear not, my lord. The mummers are taken, the king is free and now he resides in the Palace and is alert to our plans, I'm bound."

Oldcastle's face creased in rage. "By God, I'll not believe it!" He turned, smashing his meaty fist into the palm of his other hand, his mind at once racing. Experienced soldier that he was, he began thinking of strategies that would offer him freedom and allow him to gain the upper hand. "Then we must make haste to the Wrasteleyre on the Hope, for there we can unify with our army from the shires and still defeat the king.

"Master Fisher, stay here with Sir Roger Acton and

assemble the men from London. Pass through Aldredesgate, Crepelgate and St Stephen's Gate. Thereafter we shall assemble at Smythefeld and then to St Giles-in-the-Fields, where we shall do battle with the king. Come, let us bustle." When he saw Jamie arrive, he added, "Ah, Sir James, your advent here is timely. We move to the Hope, there to command our forces. Arm yourself, for the time is nigh."

Oldcastle called for his squire to bring his harness and arm him. Jamie, his mind racing, did the same, beckoning a servant whom he had asked to aid him in the past to check his harness was complete and in good order. He had discovered that two leather straps on the right hand vambrace and left cuisse had frayed and needed replacing, but Sir John's armourer had repaired the pieces and now all was laid out shining in readiness. He stripped off his jupon, and pulling on his arming doublet he began the long process of arming, aided by the servant, who struggled at times with the unfamiliar buckles and straps.

All had to be properly fitted so that the weight was evenly distributed and fell from the torso attached to the strips of leather from the doublet. It took some thirty minutes in all, and as usual he had on his specially made sabatons, ridged for fighting on foot and square toed, without the long trailing tips that he found cumbersome. They were fully articulated, and he walked with ease, a testament to the Milanese armourer who had made them to his specification.

He tried the movement of each his limbs, asked for one of the new straps to be loosened around the cuisse, and then made two deep squats and lunges to test the give and feel of the harness. Satisfied, he buckled on his sword belt holding his two weapons in place. Picking up the shield bearing his coat of arms that showed a stylised form of his horse, Richard, he checked again the enarmes straps that secured the shield to his arm. He made one adjustment and pronounced himself ready. He would not normally need a shield with the quality of full Milanese plate armour, yet this day he wished to be identified. His padded arming coif was tied in place, but he left the mailed coif down and carried the bascinet helmet by its strap to hang upon the cantle of the borrowed horse that he was to ride.

He moved forward, the familiar feel of the weight of maille and harness coming back to him like a warm blanket. It was reassuring and gave him a feeling of invincibility. More knights were now in the courtyard preparing to mount, and he saw among them Sir Thomas Chaworth and Sir Richard Compton, with whom he had crossed swords upon their initial meeting. With no further need for secrecy, the party, led by Oldcastle, moved out to a clatter of hooves and armour as they headed north along St Martin's Lane to Aldredesgate and out to the fields and Smythefeld beyond.

It was late in the day and the gates were shortly to be closed, yet Sir John stopped to speak with a captain of the guard with whom he seemed on friendly terms, and was saluted in his turn.

Jamie took all this in, praying that Whittington's plans were now in place, for Oldcastle seemed to have control of the whole town, and with it the future of the realm. They reached the inn just as dusk was falling, a latent feeling of tension and expectancy in the air. The party of some fifteen men dismounted, among them knights, squires and servants, and entered the large inn from the rear courtyard.

The inn was already crowded with soldiers in various forms of maille and armour, all expectant, the atmosphere of upcoming combat almost palpable. Ale and wine were brought for the party and Oldcastle began the final preparations. "Now we shall bring a righteous order to this land with a new beginning and an orthodoxy to put down, to free our souls. A new reign shall begin this night and the old tyranny shall be banished as God is my witness. So let us salute each other, brothers in arms. Praise God and pray for victory this night. We wait upon the strike of Compline, and then let us sally forth."

A rousing cheer went up from the assembled company as goblets were raised in a toast. Jamie for his part joined in heartily, keen to not be thought of as a dissenter.

Westminster Palace

"Majesty, is it wise that a whole company of dukes should accompany you this night to make battle in the dark? Should we not wait until the morning, or first light at least, and then take them as the sun rises?" asked the Earl of Warwick, ever loyal to the new king. Having risen in status and friendship upon Henry's ascension to the throne, he was now, as Captain of Calais, more than ever one of his close confidants and battle commanders.

"Sir Richard, we are as ever mindful of your concern at our welfare. Yet this night will be the first battle of our reign, and we mean to be in at the kill. No whoreson blasphemers shall cause us to shirk our devoir, and this night we take all, showing England to be a united and strong land. Our father, God rest his soul, did not shrink from battle, and neither shall we.

"My liege men, let us mount and ride to the fields, for Compline is about to strike and we would capture our prey there in the net of their own deceit."

A captain of the guard arrived, bowing to the company.

"Pray speak, sir, is all in order? Are the gates taken?" the king demanded.

"Yes, sire, all three gates to the north are taken and in our control. Other guards have been sent to ensure that the gates to the east and west are also contained, so that any attempt to use them would be futile."

"And what of resistance? Were the rebels standing fast?"

"We met strong resistance at Newgate, Aldredesgate and St Stephen, Majesty, where we encountered strong forces of men-at-arms in Oldcastle's employ. We lost ten men to fighting, but we have killed many of the rebels, sire, and taken many others prisoner. The gates are now barred against any leaving the town without your permission, with archers ready and oil to repel all comers."

"'Twas well done, and we thank you for your service. And what of the wrestlers led by Mark of Cornwall?"

"They await your orders at Newgate, sire, to meet with

your forces leading us to an unsuspecting assault upon the Wrasteleyre on the Hope."

"Then my lords, let us make haste and not daddle, for battle awaits. Sir Richard," he said, addressing the Earl of Warwick, "you will take the Hope using Mark and his loyal wrestlers to gain access as friends to the Lollards who are there. Strike upon the bells of Compline, and we shall be in readiness at St Giles-in-the-Fields to attack the main force. Our brother, Prince John, you will attack the home of Master Fisher. Take all prisoners that you can, for we would wish to have as many as we can interrogated and put to trial. To horse my lords, battle awaits!"

The king waved a hand forward, as one the armoured knights and squires strode from the Great Hall to the waiting horses that were held by grooms in the courtyard before the doors. Mounted archers and men-at-arms waited patiently in the cold, and now caught up their reins for the short journey of less than a league to circumnavigate London from the west and arrive to the north at St Giles-in-the-Fields.

The great host soon came to Newgate, where the Earl of Warwick met with Mark and other men-at-arms, all mounted. They split from the main host, who entered the town at the king's command to bypass Smythefeld. They rattled through the near empty night-time streets as those abroad ran for their lives to the sides, pulling into doorways and alleys as the mighty army cantered over the cobbles.

They soon arrived at Crepelgate, and here, King Henry split his force again.

"Brother Prince Thomas, we ask that you take your men

and move through the gate of St Stephen upon the sounding of Compline, then take full force and charge the enemy ranks. We shall approach from the west, surrounding their company and letting none escape. Quarter shall be given upon surrender, and all must submit or die, without restraint. Go to brother, we shall look for you upon the field of battle."

Prince Thomas saluted his brother with a nod and a bow, and called his host forward to canter along the road parallel to the northern wall some six hundred yards to the next gate of St Stephen de Colemannestrate. They reached the gate, where they were joined by companies of men-at-arms, some of whom were already bloodied from the battles against those Londoners who had tried and failed to leave the town. Bodies lay about the streets in clumsy piles of twisted limbs and gapping wounds. Some were still moaning and heaving their last.

Even now, men who were shouting out were being put to the sword in case they alerted the Lollards from the shires who were assembling outside the walls. It was brutal work with no mercy shown and the snow was soon stained afresh with a red hue as blood seeped from the corpses to run in rivulets of spidery veins before it froze in the ice. Many thousands had begun to assemble, yet upon meeting with a concerted, well-armed force and a shower of arrows, the apprentices, guildsmen and clerks who had earlier so proudly proclaimed their faith and strength and loyalty to Oldcastle had either died or fled from the fight in fear of their lives.

A few sturdy men-at-arms, squires and knights had made a futile stand. They had gone down to a wall of steel in a clash of arms, to be killed or captured for ransom or trial. It had been a rout by the well-armed and disciplined forces of the king. Yet as all knew, if they had been allowed to assemble as one body under good leadership, and fight as a cohesive single force, it could easily have gone in their favour. Such were the fortunes of war.

Chapter Forty-Nine

The Wrasteleyre on the Hope Inn, Smythfeld

The company was being fuelled to a frenzy of action. Oldcastle had finished speaking, and knights and squires were giving a final look to their harnesses and arms. This moment before battle was the hardest, Jamie knew. It was a time when mistakes were made and tempers were hot with excitement. Bile rose in the mouths of many, and the blood coursed thick with anticipation as hands trembled, waiting impatiently for movement and action.

Jamie had taken a seat by the window casement and was looking out to the night where the green of Smythefeld lay, now cloaked in darkness and almost black in the night despite a fine layer of snow. Oldcastle moved now, reaching for the stairs to get a better view of the street outside as they heard a group of horsemen approaching. Sir John called up to Sir Thomas Chaworth, who had taken to the first floor along with others, to ease the crowding of the ground floor of the inn.

With all attention drawn away from him at Sir John's question, Jamie pulled up his mail coif as he mounted the stairs to look from that vantage point. He slipped on his helmet, buckled up the chin strap and drew on his metal gauntlets, flexing the articulated fingers, picking up his shield as he strode to the stairs. Some noticed him, yet said nothing as he climbed the wooden steps, turning at the dogleg to ascend the last flight of six steps. Jamie reached the first floor just as the bells for Compline sounded from the nearby Chapel of the Holy Cross, and drew his sword.

Oldcastle span around at the sound of the bells and made to return down the stairs. Then he saw Jamie advancing, his sword drawn. He was no callow youth and had fought in many battles through his time, and acted accordingly, snapping down his visor with a cry of "Traitor!" drawing his sword.

Full plate armour rendered a sword's edge nearly useless, and only the point would do real damage. Jamie knew this full well, and charged the last three feet to clash with Oldcastle, driving up and around with the edge of his shield to catch the pig snout of Sir John's bascinet helmet, striking with all his might and putting his full weight behind the blow. Oldcastle's head snapped sideways under the impact, which sent him crashing to the floor. Jamie made to stab with his sword at any vantage point that he could find in his oppressor's armour. Seeking the groin, he made to thrust the point home, all other thoughts driven from his mind, wanting only vengeance in his anger. It was a mistake. As his right arm started the flash of movement, a blade smashed into his chest. Jamie felt no pain as the plate of his armour was almost immune to any edged weapon. Yet the impact, brought double handed, was enough to drive him off balance, causing him to stab off target and catch Oldcastle's mailled leg, causing him to cry out in pain as the point snicked home into the meaty flesh of his thigh.

Jamie raised the shield to see not one, but two knights now launch an attack at him. One had his visor down, yet he saw by the distinctive arms upon his tabard of blazon gules and argent bars, bearing three black martlets that he was Sir Thomas Chaworth, his hated enemy. The other, protected only by a mail coif was Sir Richard Compton. The crossing slash of the Chaworth's sword was returned as he rotated it at the wrist to bring it up aimed at Jamie's shoulder. This time Jamie was prepared, and raised his shield to absorb the blow, driving the weapon away and extending his arm to push at Chaworth. In so doing he was exposed to the thrust of Compton's sword that skidded up the breast plate to hit the stop rib, before the point reached the gorget. Jamie did not hesitate, slashing across Compton's exposed face with the edge of his sword, sending Compton away blinded in a flash of steel, his face a bloody mess.

Stepping forward, Chaworth went now with a side guard away from Jamie's shield. Jamie held a middle guard and rotated to the right, sweeping around and down, aiming for the back of Chaworth's knee where he saw an opening. He struck the flared fan plate with such force that the knee collapsed forwards at the impact, unbalancing Chaworth, whose blade was too slow to parry the blow as it changed direction. Jamie drove up with the point of his sword, seeking the exposed area between the shoulder pauldron and the breast plate. This time he was successful, driving the point home through the mail to draw blood and a cry of anguish from Chaworth, who dropped his sword from a useless arm and cried, "Mercy! I yield, I yield!" He fell to the floor on his knees and held his hands up in supplication.

Jamie, furious at his surrender, stamped into his chest, driving him backwards out of anger and distrust that he may renege and stab him as he continued to fight others in the upper chamber. In his backward fall, Chaworth took with him a table, and with it a candle that fell to the floor amid the bone-dry rushes. Jamie had no time to hesitate, as a man-at-arms turned from the casement, his crossbow cocked, letting fly with a bolt as he turned thudding into Jamie's shield. Jamie ran forward, killing two men with angry slashes, the battle madness upon him brought on by all the pent up anger and frustration of the past months. The crossbowman put up an arm to surrender and lost it in a spray of blood.

A sword crashed into Jamie's helm from behind, rocking his head forward. He fell with the blow into a forward roll and rose into a standing position. His shield was lost, but he had gained the space and distance that he needed. Even as he rose he heard the sounds of battle below as the inn was being attacked by the king's forces.

The squire before him came on, heartened by his blow yet advancing with care, holding his blade for half-swording, as did Jamie. The blades crossed, and Jamie's slid up through the slit of the sallet visor, killing his opponent instantly. He withdrew the blade, which was covered in blood and gore, with a scraping of metal. Jamie recovered, for there were no more men to fight as they sank to their knees while the flames from the candle began to lick and take hold of the rushes and the tinder dry floor. He went to stamp them out, aided by the other frightened man-at-arms. When he raised his visor to breathe better as he stamped, he looked to where the recumbent figure of Oldcastle lay. He had gone!

Jamie searched around, cursing like a whore. He looked up and down the long chamber, seeing no way out other than small dormer rooms off the main hall. In one corner he saw a small back staircase that would lead to the main inn or courtyard. *That must be his escape route,* he realised.

He was about to run to the top of the stairs and give chase when he heard the sound of heavy footsteps on the main staircase behind him and turned to see whether it was friend or foe. Most of the sounds of fighting had quietened from down below and Jamie realised that he knew not who had won the day and he could be facing more danger. Stooping, he retrieved his shield, still with the crossbow bolt embedded in it, and realised that it had dented his vambrace, bruising the arm beneath where it had pierced the shield and punched through with the force of the strike. Only now did he begin to feel the pain in his arm. He manged to insert his arm beneath the bolt head. The angle was uncomfortable, but it would still work as a defence – and more importantly as a means by which to identify himself as an ally to the king. He knew that if the Lollards had won the day, this would be his last stand, and he took a deep breath and prepared himself to sell his life dearly.

The first figure to run up the stairs was Sir Richard Beauchamp, Earl of Warwick, easily identifiable by the tabard bearing the quartering of his arms and complicated marks of cadency. Jamie was unsure of his status and took a stance of the middle guard, his shield forward.

"Hold, Sir James, put up your arms. 'Tis I, Warwick." At this he pushed up his visor to be recognised, adding, "and we call you blanchemain this day and no longer traitor, for the king wishes you saved above all others and praised."

Jamie relaxed and put down his sword to rest the tip upon the floor, feeling the energy seep from him as his muscles relaxed and became leaden in the manner of all men after battle.

"You are well met, Sir Richard, yet I fear praise is not due, for the traitor Oldcastle escaped by the stair yonder, unless he was caught in your net below?"

"Nay, I fear not. The whoreson has more lives than a cat. We shall send out patrols to find him, fear not, as all his forces will by now be vanquished and the revolt put down."

"Praise God for that. And of Fisher? Is he too caught?"

"For certes yes, for good men were sent to arrest him under charge of Prince John, and they will not fail."

Jamie nodded and saw behind the earl the hulking figure of Mark, mailled and with his sallet helmet in place, carrying his prized poleaxe, the blade and spike of which were red with blood. It was a fearsome weapon in his hands, and he wielded it with the same ease as most men would a light battle axe.

"Mark, why 'tis good to see you, brother, and well met."

"Indeed, yet I see you needed no army to help you for you have done the work of ten men here," Mark mused dryly, looking around at the bodies and wounded strewn across the floor.

Jamie gave a wry laugh at Mark's jest. "Ah, yes, and upon that note I have a present in especial to be taken good care of, for here is Sir Thomas Chaworth, late of the king's court and now supporter in chief of the Lollards, God rot his black soul."

Earl Warwick called two men-at-arms to take the knight prisoner for trial in due course.

"How does Alice and my father? Is all well there?" Jamie asked, fearing the worst and not asking the direct question of his unborn child.

"All is well, fear not, mother and child thrive and will have companions in arms soon, for Emma too is with child and increases by the day."

"Then I congratulate you, and we shall celebrate together in due course, yet I worry for poor Emma, bearing a giant like you about her!" he joked, to relieve the tension.

Warwick too offered Mark his felicitations, for despite their differences in rank, he respected the huge wrestler and the way he had fought, taking on all comers in a flurry of blows and aiding him considerably in the battle below stairs in the inn.

"And what of my father?" Jamie probed.

"He comes about, as does John," Mark assured him. "Yet they have Cristoforo to thank for their lives, for he is a most deadly protector and took the day, by the rood he did. He has stayed this day and night with your father and family in case revenge should be taken and another attempt made to seize him, as John is weak and recovering from his wounds."

"Amen to that," Jamie said. "Then by your leave, my Lord of Warwick, I will return to my wife and see that she is well, and thank you for arriving as you did this hour, for it was most welcome."

"Go to, Sir James, and we shall talk more of this day and celebrate our victory at a more propitious hour."

The two men smiled and bowed in mutual respect. They might not be fast friends, but their lives were intertwined now on the same side in arms.

Chapter Fifty

Le Straunde, London

Mark had ridden with Jamie back through the gates into the city, and they had parted ways at Newgate, Mark heading to the east and Jamie riding on down to Fletestrete and across to his home in Le Straunde. He was weary, aching and dirty, and the horse he rode was recalcitrant and wanted continually to turn around and head for home, dragging its feet at every opportunity and resenting the heavy load it carried, as Jamie was still in full harness.

The horse had clipped along outside the town walls so that Jamie was not troubled by the Watch riding along La Ballie. He arrived at his new home exhausted and banged upon the front door demanding entrance, as the rear yard was barred for the night. A mournful howl and a series of loud barks began from within, and a casement was opened from above as an unidentified voice demanded to know who was calling at this late hour. Upon identifying himself, the casement was slammed shut and footsteps were heard from within. The low growling barks increased in their mournful song and as soon as the door was unbarred Jamie was greeted by a flash of grey and silver as the giant wolfhound launched herself through the door to stand up on her hind legs, her paws upon her master's shoulders as she licked at his exposed face.

Jamie laughed at her despite all he had been through, finally calling her off. "Down girl, down. Let me be, for it is my wife I should like to kiss, not you," he said, ruffling Forest's shaggy fur. She finally relented as a vison of white appeared in the doorway, decorous in white linen with a gold curtain of honeyed locks falling to her shoulders, her cornflower eyes wide with mixture fear and joy.

"My heart!" she called, embracing Jamie as closely as she could over the swelling of her stomach, shivering at the cold touch of his armour. "My love, let us get you out of harness, for you reek of battle," she cried. Jamie was lost for words, still not fully comprehending that he was free and back with his wife again. "Have hot water drawn and a bathtub filled," she ordered over her shoulder as servants appeared to attend to Jamie. A groom appeared, his eyes half closed with sleep, to take care of the horse and remove it to the rear courtyard.

With the horse taken from him, Jamie moved inwards, and the door was barred to the night. He stood as servants attempted to remove and unbuckle all the plate before aiding him to lift off the heavy maille coat and finally the arming doublet. Now wearing just a linen shift and hose he was led by his wife to the bathtub on the first floor. He sank into the hot water, feeling the tension ease from him as he answered a multitude of questions thrown at him by his wife.

Replete with wine and food, he sank into the feather mattress and fell into a troubled sleep in his wife's embrace. All that came to him were dreams of combat, and he twitched in the night, half-conscious as unbidden thoughts played upon his mind, reliving the days of exile and the battle of that night. He woke the next morning to find himself in a strange unfamiliar world of warmth and tranquillity, as for the first time in six months he was in his own home, safe and secure. Yet Jamie felt unrested after a troubled night's sleep that had been plagued with nightmares of blood and death.

The bells rang for Tierce as full daylight came, and a knock was heard upon the door below. A messenger was there in royal livery carrying a missive for Jamie, bearing the king's seal.

Jamie broke the seal and read the brief note that had been signed by the king in person.

Lady Alice looked on concerned: "What does it impart?" she asked.

"I am summoned this day to court at the hour of Sext, to attend upon the king; first in a private audience, and then at a meeting of the Royal Council," he replied, staring into the middle distance.

"That is surely a great honour, and it shows that he welcomes you back with open arms, my love. Do not repulse this olive branch, for as John said the ways of kings and the court are at times unfathomable, and you must embrace them where you can.

"My father, although a baron, must still bow to the rule of his king. So let us play their game. Smile and see what fortune you have brought to our door this day."

"You as ever have the right of it, my love, yet it still sits ill upon my shoulders of how poorly I was used." Jamie sighed, kissing his wife and making to rise from the bed.

※ ♛ ※ —

The king's private chamber, Palace of Westminster

A number of King Henry's intimates were gathered, including his brothers, Archbishop Arundel, the Lord Chief Justice and the Earls of Warwick and Arundel, together with other senior lords. None seemed to bear any scars of battle, for Jamie had learned that it had been a rout. The gathering at St Giles-in-the-Fields lacked a leader, and with Oldcastle missing, his army was a rudderless ship cast adrift among the terrible forces of the king and his brother. Many had been killed in the press and many others had fled, leaving the field of victory to the king. The uprising had been put down, and prisoners, all of whom were leading lights of the Lollard faction, taken to be put to trial.

Jamie stood before King Henry, taking in the measure of the man before him, noting how his hair made him look more mature yet more severe, shaved as it was almost like a monk to the sides of his head. This made the scar upon his cheek more prominent and drew attention to the disfigurement. Yet as a warrior king he cared little for such niceties, although it was said that he had become pious with his ascendency to the throne and now prayed fervently each day. His manner too had changed, and while he could still freeze a man's blood with his stare when roused to anger, he wished now to unite and reinforce the kingdom he had inherited. He now balanced ruthlessness and enforcing the law to the hilt, balanced with clemency and magnanimity.

Jamie was unsure of what to expect as the king came forward and placed his hands upon his shoulders.

"Sir James," he began, his smile bearing all the force it could upon Jamie. Many a man had succumbed to his charm and Jamie, despite his instincts, was no exception. "Once more you, our most trusted servant and household knight, have shone forth, never once deviating from your path of loyalty to our court and realm.

"For here, as well as in Scotland and in France, you have served us right well, and have proved again your unswerving devotion, despite hardships and accusations of disworship that were placed against your fair name. To wit, many could claim in small exoneration that all is still not well, so we wish to honour you in a singular manner, so that all may see the bond between us and perceive you as do we, as a loyal household knight. You are to be raised to the Order of the Garter in recognition of your service to our country."

Jamie would not have been more stunned had he been struck by a mace. The world span and he barely managed to bow. Yet the king had not finished. "One of the rebels captured had lands in Worcestershire and a manor there under lease. This shall now be decreed to you and your heirs in perpetuity.

"Well, Sir James, what say you?" the king asked, a wry

smile upon his face, releasing the young knight from his grasp.

"I say that your majesty is most generous, and I dearly thank you for your generosity and recognition. I shall remain, as ever, your most faithful and devoted servant," Jamie managed.

"Very good. Now go to, and later this day we shall announce this at a formal Council meeting, after which arrangements shall be made for the ceremony to invest you as a Knight of the Garter."

Jamie thanked the king and made to depart: "By your leave, Majesty," he said as he bowed three times and backed from the chamber. As the door was closed behind him he reeled in shock, yet his thoughts were disturbed by Alfred, Sir Richard Whittington's clerk, who was waiting for him outside the king's private chambers.

"Sir James, my Lord Whittington wouldst beg an audience with you ere you leave the Palace."

Jamie hesitated, well aware that it was Whittington who had sent him down this course, putting not just his life in danger but that of his family. He sighed in resignation, recalling his wife's words, and agreed to accompany the clerk.

Whittington's chambers were at once familiar to him, and as always well heated with a fire in the outer room and a blazing hearth within. Whittington himself looked a little more careworn and lined than when Jamie had seen him last, but despite this the statesman rose in a spritely manner as Jamie was announced, coming around his large desk to welcome him.

"James, by all that's Holy 'tis good to see you well," he

began, yet realised almost upon the instant that Jamie had put up an almost imperceptible barrier between them, a wall of defiance that at this moment Whittington would be compelled to breach if he were to reach the man beyond. "Come to the fire and warm yourself, for 'tis as frosty a day as ever there was and the cold does pierce me greatly," he said. "Though whether to my bones or my heart I know not. For I do perceive that the icy stare which exudes from you would chill Hell's own fires to naught."

"And you dost expect some other welcome from me? You staked me out as a goat before a wolf, with scant regard for my honour or the safety of my family. My father – your good friend, or so I thought – has been most badly used and his life nearly forfeited upon the altar of your motives for the realm and its safety. I and others close to me, even my wife who now is with child, were merely pawns in your courtly game of chess, and you would have happily sacrificed them as the extinguishing of a candle." Jamie snapped his fingers in exasperation in Whittington's face.

"You are right to be wroth. Yet consider, is this any different to being killed upon the field of battle, as would be your devoir to your liege lord the king as it is to die upon a fiat in his name as you have just accomplished? I think not, and would beg your indulgence in that cause. James, you serve well and right loyally, and all the while we cared for you and made every improvement to your station. You came through as I knew that you would, and the alternative? Why, 'twould be to have the scullion Oldcastle now in the Palace as Regent, and a terror as you saw in Paris wreaking havoc upon the thoroughfares of London, when you could and did save the day. And you have been well recognised in your turn, a Garter Knight no less? My Lord but you rise, James, and upon no one's tail but through your own good abilities. Now forgive an old man his wiles and let us be friends, for we have much to accomplish still, and you are nobler than this, to grutch me so!" Whittington charmed his way in, playing to Jamie's better nature.

"Bah," Jamie spat, "I say this now as an equal, despite your senior years. You are a cautelous rogue who would manipulate the Devil to turn loose all his souls and renounce evil."

Whittington remained stone-faced for a few seconds, then burst out laughing. "Aye, mayhap you have the right of it, Sir James, Knight of the Garter," he said, clapping Jamie upon the shoulder and calling Alfred to procure refreshment. "Then let us drink to the future of the kingdom and to our unholy alliance, for do you not think that would be most apposite?"

Historical Notes, 1413

Scotland and Richard II

There was indeed a false Richard, who some say escaped from the castle at Pontefract and fled to Scotland. The Scots certainly claimed the story was true, and used it as a threat to the English crown in the way I describe. The English sent spies to find out the facts, some of whom never came back. The French too were unhappy due to Richard's widow marrying Charles, Duke of Orleans, and sent a party of friars to Edinburgh to confirm the situation.

They eventually found out the name of the pretender, one Thomas Ward of Trumpington, who was found on the Hebrides and bore a striking resemblance to Richard. Despite debunking the ruse, rumours continually flew about that the old king was still alive, although these rumours were weaker now and he was no longer considered a threat.

The side drawbridge where Jamie escapes from Edinburgh Castle existed then, and gave access to the town and down to the port. These were extraordinary times in which truth was stranger than fiction.

Henry's death

The deathbed scene and the words used are all exact, and have been taken from original documents, so if the language sounds a little stilted and the punctuation looks a little strange it is because it was of its time, and I have kept faithfully to that. The same is true of the court scenes and many of Henry's speeches. The rest is my own imagination.

Paris and the Cabochiens

Everything I describe occurred, and the terror and bloody events involved put the later Revolution to shame. It was a terrible time for normal citizens to be caught up in the trouble, while the king was held and duped into signing away his rights to Caboche and the Assembly. The palace was divided into three parts, although little of it stands today and the street names were changed either after the revolution or the Second World War. Meanwhile, the bridges to the Île de la Cité were all in different places and had different names, so it took a great deal of research to find how everything fitted into place. If I have made any errors that might be spotted by eagle-eyed historians, I can only apologise.

Jamie and Cristoforo's escape by river was the only way out at that time, and the Seine was and perhaps still is a very treacherous watercourse with substantial differences in depth between high and low tides. Paris was in chaos, and only later when the Armagnacs managed to free the city and the king, all returned to normal. I would very much have liked to kill off both Burgundy and Caboche, but unfortunately history would not permit me to do so, and they fled to the Low Countries when their rebellion was finally quashed.

The residence of the Armagnacs, the Hôtel-de-Ville, fronted down onto the Seine, and was also used as the main home of the French government. The Armagnacs were warned of the rebellion by unknown sources, although an abbot and a spy based in Paris did alert the English as I allude to here, and the French crown eventually managed to hold out against the terror. So why not put Jamie into play to aid them? He is, as ever, in the thick of things.

England

King Henry V wanted to unite the English kingdom, and became more pious and God-fearing at the start of his reign as I have shown. The Lollard uprising was also a historical reality; the plotting was devious, and it nearly succeeded. All the timelines and events are factual – other than Jamie's involvement, of course – and Fisher, de Burgh and Kempford were all genuine people. The speeches at the trial of Sir John Oldcastle, Lord Cobham, are the actual words he used, as are the responses to them. I have shortened them, but the essence remains.

The wrestling match organised by Oldcastle took place and may have been part of the plot to take the king, but the king had been forewarned. By whom, I wonder? The old inns, the Axe and the Wrasteleyre on the Hope were also true, as was the story of Oldcastle's final escape.

But perhaps most remarkable of all was Oldcastle's escape from the Tower. This really took place, but no one knows quite how it was achieved. I used another authentic escape from earlier in history to foreshadow the use of chimneys, and this escape and the methods it involved are accurate. I acknowledge history once again here, for if it had not happened it would have been hard to make up. Fisher was involved, but that is all we know for certain, apart from the fact that Oldcastle escaped across the rooftops. At first he went to Cooling Castle, but he later moved to Fisher's house, where he stayed until early January. He succeeded in organising a group of fake mummers to try to kill the king and de Burgh and Kempford lost their nerve and turned traitor as I describe, foiling that aspect of the Lollard plot.

Sir Thomas Burton was the king's spy – or at least one of them – and was paid 100 shillings for his work against the Lollards. Burton's 100 shillings, for those who remember pre-decimal currency, equated to £5, but any attempt to put this into perspective is difficult, and no direct comparison works well here. We cannot say for example that £5 in those days would be worth £50,000 today. Monetary values are almost impossible to compare as things were priced and valued differently. However, to give an idea, Jamie's Milanese plate armour, which was not just bought but fitted and made properly, was incredibly rare, and very hard to get hold of in England. Such a suit would have set Jamie back £8 and 6 shillings, which perhaps illustrates that Burton's fee was a small fortune, perhaps the equivalent of being given a Ferrari, but as I say, some things are hard to compare...

Again, I would have loved nothing more than to have Jamie put Oldcastle and Chaworth – who really did side with the Lollards – to the sword, but it was not to be.

Historical Notes, 1413

Chaworth was taken and tried, but more of his fate will be revealed in the next volume, set in 1414.

The final rout and the taking of the gates took place on a cold winter's night in January 1414, as did the battle and the thwarting of the Scots and the Lollards of the Shires. The events took me slightly over into the first few days of the new year, but history is fickle that way, and I needed the events to come to a climax in this book rather than leave the reader hanging on a cliff-edge until next time!

Jamie and his friends will be back in 1414 for more adventures, and I hope that you enjoyed reading their story as much as I enjoyed writing and researching it.

On the armour and fight scenes, below are two fascinating links that show just how mobile knights in armour were and how quickly they could move. I think you will be surprised – I certainly was.

https://www.youtube.com/watch?v=RrNLcfwV30c (Minutes 11 to 12.30)

https://www.youtube.com/watch?v=5hlIUrd7d1Qn (the full video)

My thanks to the Exiles again for their helpful videos, which are always a great aid to planning my fight scenes.

I would as always love to hear your views so please do write to me at: simonfairfaxauthor@gmail.com

Until next time...

Simon Fairfax

Other books by Simon

If you have not read book 1 in the series click here to start reading instantly.

A Knight and a Spy 1410
Subterfuge or sword, which save the kingdom?

Sir James de Grispere, squire in training, is thrown into a world of treachery, the Hundred Years' War, revolts, battles, the wool trade, piracy and pivotal events. Medieval history is brought to life in this story of fifteenth century England and the fight for the crown.

Click here to read

Please do write to me with any questions or comments as I do like to hear from my readers:

simon@simonfairfaxauthor.com

To obtain two free short stories of the backgrounds to Jamie- A Squire in Training & Contessa Alessandria- Florence 1401 go to my website www.simonfairfax.com

And sign up to my mailing list for news, competitions and new releases.

A message from Simon

I know that you have a million choices of books to read and I can't tell you how much it means to me that you chose time to read one of my books. I really hope that you enjoyed it and found it entertaining.

If you did I would appreciate a few more minutes of your time, if I may humbly ask you to leave a review for other readers who may be trying to select their next reading material.

If for any reason you were not satisfied with this book please do let me know by emailing me at simon@simonfairfaxauthor.com

The satisfaction of my readers and feedback are important to me.

About the Author

Simon Fairfax writes in two different genres: International financial thrillers and medieval fiction.

He is a former Chartered Surveyor, Editor of an online polo magazine (having played polo for a number of years) and has practiced martial arts, fencing and shooting. He now restores old classic sports cars for fun.

As a lover of crime thrillers and espionage, Simon turned what is seen by others as a dull 9 – 5 job into something that is exciting, and as close to real life as possible, with Rupert Brett, his unwilling hero.

His latest medieval series now has three books released in a proposed 6 book series. The first, A Knight and a Spy 1410, is set in a tumultuous time at the English court. It tells the story of Jamie de Grispere, squire in training and his two companions as they fight the French to save Calais, Welsh treason and Scottish revolts. The fourth in the series, A Knight and a Spy 1413 will be published on the 31st August 2022.

Details of all his books can be found at www.simonfairfax.com or email him at simonfairfaxauthor@gmail.com

A Knight and a Spy 1410

A Knight and a Spy 1410

Sir James de Grispere, squire in training, is thrown into a world of treachery, the Hundred Years' War, revolts, battles, the wool trade, piracy and pivotal events. Medieval history is brought to life in this story of fifteenth century England and the fight for the crown.

Click here to read

A Deadly Deal

A Deadly Deal

The trading floor should be counted in deals not bodies, yet they are mounting in number. Can a dealer trade on his wits and manage to stay alive?

Set in the 80s flowing from London to Italy it features Rupert Brett, a new kind of hero, an ordinary man thrown into extraordinary situations.

Buy A *Deadly Deal* today to see if Rupert can leverage his only commodity and survive the brutal game of winner takes all?

Click to read

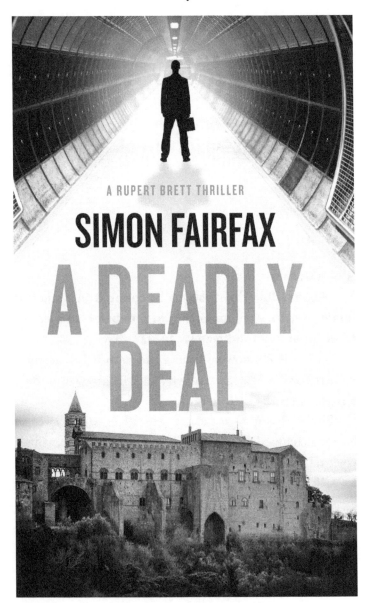

Acknowledgments

First of all my great thanks to my editor Perry Iles who helped so much in making my book come alive, my proof reader Charlotte Gledson BETA readers, Deb, Patricia and Sarah.

As always research has been the key to my work and it always surprises me how much went on in a single year in terms of pivotal events.

To this end I was aided by a fabulous book by Andy Johnson: Sir John Oldcastle of Herefordshire in an effort to fully understand the events surrounding the Lollardy revolt and why it all happened. I hope that I have done it justice. Other books that came into play here were Henry V's Medieval Navy by Ina Friel. With King Henry IV dying I now sadly leave Chris Given-Wilson's excellent book *HENRY IV* and Ian Mortimer's *THE FEARS OF HENRY IV.* Both give a brilliant insight to the events of the period. I would also recommend Ian Mortimer's *The time traveller's guide to medieval England* and I apologise if I have made any factual errors as a result. I now rely more on Christopher Allmand's *HENRY V* which gave me such a fascinating view into this extraordinary King's life, events and personality and Teresa Cole Henry V.

I have studied martial arts for most of my life from

teenage years onwards, including, Wing Chun, fencing and judo, all of which came into play for this novel as many of the throws and holds from judo are very similar to Cornish wrestling. Yet to add veracity, I attended the Armoured Combat Gloucester 'knight school' to wield a broad sword for real and see if everything I had written worked!

On battle scenes and fighting I am as ever in debt to the excellent videos produced by HEMA especially Mark Berryman of The Exiles branch and Mark Fuller of Norwich HEMA; and Modern History TV and Tod's Workshop.

Finally, my thanks to all the horses and particularly polo ponies- including Richard- who taught me so much.

Join me on Facebook

Printed in France by Amazon
Brétigny-sur-Orge, FR